"A passionate read! James Goll's perspectives are compelling."

—**Ché Ahn**, senior pastor, Harvest Rock Church,
Pasadena; founder and president,
Harvest International Ministry

"Must reading for those who want to understand and be part of one of the great end-time events in history—the restoration of Israel and the Jewish people. James Goll is a true prophet of God with a divine message that must be heard and heeded."

—**Jonathan Bernis**, Messianic rabbi; president,
Jewish Voice Ministries International

"Many people talk about loving the Jewish people. James Goll puts feet to his talk. God's heart and purpose for Israel are very important subjects for this hour."

—**Mike Bickle**, director, International House of Prayer,
Kansas City, MO

"A simple yet penetrating presentation of God's heart for Israel, this book is written with great prophetic integrity from one who has a proven ministry at the cutting edge of God's purposes in the earth today. Our response will determine future history."

—**Colin W. Dye**, pastor, Kensington Temple,
London City Church, London

"I rejoice over the prayer initiative presented in this book! May God give it wings. Israel gave birth to the Church in the first century; it is the calling of the Church to give birth to Israel in the last days."

—**Lars Enarson**, president, The Watchman International, Israel

"Here we see God's heart and intentions for the restoration and redemption of Israel and the Jewish people. James Goll issues a clarion call to the Church to participate in God's plan through repentance, intercession and God-directed deeds of righteousness."

—**Don Finto**, author, *Your People Shall Be My People*; director,
The Caleb Company; pastor emeritus, Belmont Church, Nashville

"Wisdom is calling to the Body of Christ to boldly identify with the nation of Israel, the origin of God's promises. *The Coming Israel Awakening* will stir you to embrace the place of our spiritual history and ultimate future. Highly recommended!"

—**Kingsley A. Fletcher**, senior pastor, Life Community Church, Research Triangle Park, NC

"*The Coming Israel Awakening* is a needed commentary on the past, present and future state of the Jewish people. This book uniquely reveals the vital role the Church plays in working to see God's will accomplished in Israel."

—**Francis Frangipane**, senior pastor, River of Life Ministries

"With extensive historical information, deep prophetic insight and the passionate heart of an intercessor, James Goll has sounded the shofar, calling forth a people possessed by G-d. In his plea that we seek the heart of the Father concerning the Jewish people and their destiny, Goll warns us not to forget what G-d remembers and challenges us to love the things that He loves—specifically, His covenant people, the Jews."

—**Marty Goetz**, Messianic Jewish recording artist

"As the Church, we have a mandate from God to bless Israel (see Genesis 12:3). The problem that leadership faces is how to motivate, instruct and inspire their people to do it. With this book, James Goll will put the words in our mouths and an urgency in our hearts."

—**Ken Gott**, Metro Church, Tyne and Wear, England

"There may be no more important ministry assignment to the Church of the new millennium. Superficial good feelings about Israel and excitement over prophetic events are no substitute for ignited, discerning intercession. Leaders and congregations—let us pray!"

—**Jack W. Hayford**, president, The International Church of the Foursquare Gospel; founding pastor, The Church On The Way; chancellor, The King's College and Seminary, Van Nuys, California

"One of the timeliest prophetic books I have ever read. If a book like this had been written prior to the Holocaust, history would look a lot different today. Every believer needs to read this book."

—**Cindy Jacobs**, co-founder, Generals of Intercession

"A challenge to the Church to participate in prayerful intercession and practical support for Israel as God's purposes unfold in these historic times. James Goll sounds a clear and passionate call to all believers to understand the times so that history can be written in the power and anointing of God."

—**Freda Lindsay**, co-founder, Christ to the Nations

"James Goll shows us how to pray in the events that will signal a release of the Spirit of God in the earthly realm like we have never seen before. His call to the Church opens the door for Christians to understand and accept their role in the final destiny of Israel and the Jewish people. May the burden of the Lord rest on you in a new way as you read this book."

—**Chuck D. Pierce**, president, Glory of Zion International

"If you don't read this book, you could miss the prophetic purpose of God for this last generation. With a keen understanding of the strategic importance of the Jew in God's plan, James Goll locates and places missing pieces of the prophetic puzzle. Important reading for this final hour!"

—**Sid Roth**, president, Messianic Vision; host, *It's Supernatural!* TV

"An enlightenment to the Church regarding the severe and appalling persecution of Jews by Christians through the ages. James Goll calls for heartfelt repentance and intercessory prayer accompanied by active deeds of love. This call to awaken is especially urgent and may close forever unless God's people respond."

—**John Sandford**, co-founder, Elijah House International

"James Goll walks us through the miraculous fulfillment of God's promises for a second great exodus. This is an exciting challenge to believers everywhere to take a radical stand on the side of God's chosen people."

—**Dutch Sheets**, author, *Intercessory Prayer*; senior pastor, Freedom Church, Colorado Springs

"James Goll writes with passion, clarity and purpose as he unfolds God's desire for the Church to stand in the gap for the Jewish people. This book stirred and challenged me. Please read this powerful, timely book today!"

—**Alice Smith**, executive director, U.S. Prayer Center

"Do you want to be close to the heart of God? Then get close to the things that are next to God's heart. Few can blow the trumpet of intercession like James Goll. *The Coming Israel Awakening* directs you into the purpose of God for Israel and the Jewish people. Read it and act!"

—**Tommy Tenney**, author, *The God Chasers* and *God's Dream Team*

"Critical reading for this prophetic hour. It not only imparts God's passion for the Jewish people, but it unveils key historical perspectives and strategic direction for the Church's role in this future, last-days awakening. Thank God He has spoken to us through James Goll."

—**Sandra Teplinsky**, Light of Zion Ministries, www.lightofzion.org; author, *Why Care About Israel?* and *Israel's Anointing*

"A prophetic call to intercession for the Jewish people at this strategic moment in time. James Goll does a marvelous job of tracing anti-Semitism and the plight of the Jewish people down through the ages. May the history books record the breaking of an anti-Semitic spirit by a Church that demonstrates the life of the Messiah!"

—**Barbara Wentroble**, author, *You Are Anointed*

The Coming
Israel Awakening

The Coming Israel Awakening

Gazing into the Future of the
Jewish People and the Church

James W. Goll

Chosen

a division of Baker Publishing Group
Grand Rapids, Michigan

© 2001, 2009 by James W. Goll

Published by Chosen Books
A division of Baker Publishing Group
P.O. Box 6287, Grand Rapids, MI 49516-6287
www.chosenbooks.com

Previously published by Regal in 2001 under the title *Exodus Cry*

Printed in the United States of America

Library of Congress Cataloging-in-Publication Data
Goll, James W.
    The coming Israel awakening : gazing into the future of the Jewish people and the church / James W. Goll.
        p.   cm.
    Includes bibliographical references and index.
    ISBN 978-0-8007-9440-8 (pbk.)
    1. Messianic Judaism. 2. Jewish Christians. 3. Jews—Conversion to Christianity. 4. Israel—Forecasting. 5. Judaism—Forecasting. I. Title.
BR158.G65 2008
231.7'6—dc22   2008042410

With a heart of gratefulness, I dedicate this book to all the forerunners of the prayer and prophetic movements throughout Church history who have prepared the way for us today. Israel is a reality, and both the Church and Israel shall fulfill their greater place of destiny in these last days. Yes, there shall be an awakening of both the Jewish people worldwide and the Body of the Messiah across the globe.

I am especially indebted to the late international teacher Derek Prince, whom the Lord used mightily to release the Father's imprint upon my heart and soul for both Israel and the Church. I also wish to acknowledge and thank the Lord for the life and ministry of Dr. Don Finto of the Caleb Company in Nashville, Tennessee. Papa Don secretes the anointing of Israel, and in recent years I have had the honor of drinking deeply from his well. Thank You, Lord, for these and other pioneers!

With a passion for prayer,
James W. Goll
Cofounder, Encounters Network
International Director, Prayer Storm

Contents

Part 4 A Prophetic Proclamation: Gazing into the Future

Foreword

Sid Roth

Have you noticed the excitement about Israel that is aflame in Christianity? In 35 years of frontline Jewish ministry, I have never seen such a move.

But things are shifting rapidly. We are at the time of the "fullness of the Gentiles." According to Romans 11:25, the blinders will come off the eyes of Jewish people at the fullness of the Gentile age. I have never witnessed such openness to the Gospel among Jewish people! Israel is on the brink of the greatest revival in history.

I have interviewed James Goll on my TV broadcast, *It's Supernatural!* concerning the visitation he describes in the pages of this book. I wholeheartedly agree with him: Israel and the Church will both be awakened from out of a long slumber to fulfill their destiny in these last days.

This book will prepare you for the prophetic purpose of God for this last generation. With keen understanding of the strategic importance of the Jewish people in God's plan, James Goll locates and puts into place missing pieces of the prophetic puzzle. *The Coming Israel Awakening* will equip you for this final and great hour.

Sid Roth
Host, *It's Supernatural!* TV

Acknowledgments

This manuscript you hold in your hands has been a work in progress over several years and involved an entire team of researchers, consultants, editors, intercessors, writers and spiritual advisors. I therefore have many dear people I wish to acknowledge.

Special thanks goes to Kathy Deering, Larry Walker, Steve Nance, Avner Boskey, Sid Roth, Kerry and Sandy Teplinsky, Don Finto, Richard Riss, Jane Campbell and the entire servanthood and leadership team at Baker-Chosen Books.

I also wish to acknowledge my family. This book was composed during one of the most difficult times in our lives, as my wife and I both had been battling cancer. As most of you know, Michal Ann graduated to heaven on September 18, 2008—always to be missed, but never forgotten.

Thanks, guys, for hanging in there with good ol' Dad while we have weathered some severe storms. You are troupers, and I thank you for your sacrifice.

Finally, I wish to acknowledge the gracious staff with which I have the honor of serving at Encounters Network and our body of prayer warriors around the globe. You lift up my hands constantly, and for this I am so very grateful. Blessings to all of you!

With thanksgiving,
James W. Goll

Introduction

The message of this book has been growing in my understanding and burning in my bones for many years. It is an invitation to take a journey and to participate in making history. As in the times of Queen Esther, this is a prophetic call to prayer before the throne of God and a daring challenge to be an answer to some of those prayers.

The Coming Israel Awakening is an exhortation to Gentile Christians to receive God's heart for the Jewish people. For Jewish people, both those who have accepted Christ as their Messiah and those who have yet to consider Him, this is a wake-up call to the times we are about to face.

Written with multiple sets of lenses, this manuscript weaves together:

- an appreciation of history,
- an overview of the unique relationship between the Church and Israel,
- the interplay of the prophetic and prayer,
- a glowing promise,
- a solemn warning
- and a call to take action.

Written from a prophetic and historical perspective, this journal traces God's footprints as He has faithfully fulfilled His promises to the people of Israel. As you walk along this trail with me, you will catch a glimpse of God's willingness to go to any length to see His Word become reality!

While ministering in England in 1999, my dear wife, Michal Ann, had a dream that has become a guiding light, supplying the spark and the vision for this book. In this vivid dream Michal Ann was shown a puzzle of the sky. It was called "The Horizon of Time." The interlocking pieces were mixed up, waiting to be properly assembled. As she peered at the sky, she had a strong sense of the lifelong call of God that rested upon our lives to help put together the pieces of a puzzle that would show God's purposes among the Jewish people. The puzzle in Michal Ann's vision included pieces from the past, present and future. I have followed the same basic outline in this book; I am following her dream.

Part 1, "The Coming Great Awakening," lays out the details of the parallel awakening that is taking place in the worldwide Church and among the Jewish people, who often are identified simply as "Israel." Part 2, "A Look at the Past: Historical Perspective," sets this information in a historical framework and in the context of God's purposes, from the first great Exodus to the present. Part 3, "A Radical and Sudden Change: A Contemporary Miracle," describes the dramatic events that occurred in the late 1980s and throughout the 1990s—events that literally reshaped the face of the world. Part 4 is called "A Prophetic Proclamation: Gazing into the Future." In this section we take out our telescopes and set our sights on the horizon. We focus on God's yet-to-be-revealed purposes. We ponder how He will put together the final pieces of the puzzle.

At the back of this book I have included a wealth of resources. The appendices include a special contribution by Don Finto, an overview of the history of Israel, the dates of Purim for the Esther fast, Scriptures for praying for Israel, a

18

reference list of Israel-related ministries, a glossary of terms and a recommended reading list.

Why read *The Coming Israel Awakening*? Because it contains a contagious prophetic spirit that will overtake you! It will stir you to step forward to do exploits for Jesus Christ! You will be touched by the fire of God and prompted to take your place as an intercessor "for such a time as this." After reading *The Coming Israel Awakening*, you will long to be at the core of His prophetic promises and appointments for our day. You will be ready to take a stand, to release intervention and to cut off the enemy's plans through the power of crisis intercession.

Come, walk in the shoes of many pioneers of the faith and forerunners in the Holy Spirit. We will honor our veterans and call forth new recruits. Yes, this is a new season of bringing apostolic application to prophetic revelation. Grab hold of the prophetic baton, and lift your voice on behalf of God's chosen ones: the people of Israel and the Body of the Messiah.

Together we can pray and exercise our faith for the completion of the return to the Land of Jewish people worldwide. We can participate in the promised last days great awakening— greater than the world has ever seen—and eventually welcome home the coming King: the Lord Jesus Christ. Blessings on you as you read!

Part 1

THE COMING
GREAT AWAKENING

1

The Winds Are Coming!

> And of the angels He says, "Who makes His angels
> winds, and His ministers a flame of fire."
> Are they not all ministering spirits, sent out to
> render service for the sake of those who will
> inherit salvation?
>
> Hebrews 1:7, 14

In early December 2006, I was supposed to fly to Long Island, New York, to be the first speaker at the Open Heavens Conference with revivalist Matt Sorger. But God had other plans. Prior to my flight I suddenly came down with a flu-type sickness. The conference planners quickly reshuffled the order of the invited speakers, while I took the day to rest and recover at my home in Franklin, Tennessee.

As I lay there in bed that day the Holy Spirit kept telling me, *The winds are coming! The winds are coming!* I did not understand what He meant, and I could not get any more information than that. All day long as I rested, I heard the same declaration: *The winds are coming!*

The next day I felt well enough to fly. As the first leg of my flight headed from Nashville to Baltimore, we encountered unusually strong winds. The plane was bouncing around like crazy. The pilot came on the loudspeaker to say that we were hitting winds of 160 knots and that these were the fiercest winds he had ever encountered in flight. When we finally landed safely in Baltimore—in winds that were still blowing forty to sixty knots on the ground—the plane was shuddering and shaking. I wondered how I would make my connecting flight, but I soon discovered that it did not matter. Nobody was going anywhere. As it turned out, the entire East Coast was affected by this weather pattern, and all the airports in New England were closed down. That meant I would have to layover in Baltimore for a day. I began to wonder if I would ever make it to this conference at all.

That night, lying awake in my hotel bed, I heard the same words once again: *The winds are coming.* What? More winds?

By morning the winds had died down enough for us to fly, and I finally made it to Long Island in time to address the closing session of the conference. As I sought the Lord beforehand, I felt that He wanted to give me words of knowledge for people at the beginning of the service (which is not my typical modus operandi), and again I heard, *The winds are coming.*

The winds are still coming? I thought they had already come and gone.

During the worship portion of the service, I was worshiping our awesome God, enjoying His presence and minding His business with my eyes closed. Suddenly I felt a wind blow across my face. I opened my eyes to see if I could find the air vents. I could not see any vents, so I went back to worshiping. Again I felt a wind blow. In an instant, the atmosphere shifted, and I began to scribble down words of knowledge as fast as the Holy Spirit gave them to me—people's names, cities and diseases. The air was permeated with the spirit of revelation.

Then a third time I felt the wind. This time when I opened my eyes—*whoosh*—an angel suddenly appeared in front of me, hovering and looking right at me. The angel was carrying a shofar and wearing a glowing white robe with a gold sash that went from the left shoulder to the waist. On the sash I could read the words "Israel Awakening." The angel blew the shofar right in my face and then vanished.

Israel Awakening

I have experienced angelic encounters before, but never before have I been given the name of the angel. Was "Israel Awakening" the name of this angel? Though I did not ask, I believe it was. But whether that was the angel's actual name or not, I do know that the angel had come from the throne of the Ancient of Days to convey a message to His people.

The angel, Israel Awakening, had come like a wind in our day to blow a trumpet and to awaken the Body of Christ in a new way. This particular messenger from heaven had been released to this generation to blow the shofar and to keep blowing it. The winds had come. The winds would continue to come. The atmosphere had shifted. The time for change had come.

The time had come for Israel to be awakened, for the Jewish people worldwide to wake up to the fullness of their identity in the Lord their Maker. A new spirit of adoption seemed to have become available from the Lord Jesus Himself to help prepare the Body of the Messiah to fulfill her call in these last days.

Church Awakening

Simultaneously, the time had come for the Gentile Church to awaken to her intercessory mission of compassion, to say yes

25

to her calling to stand in the gap for God's purposes in Israel and wherever the Jewish people reside on the globe. I believe the angel named Israel Awakening was the head of a legion of angels that had been released to bring a spiritual awakening to both the Jewish people (regarding God's purposes within Israel) and to the Body of the Messiah, the Church of Jesus Christ (concerning her role of supporting Israel in the end times, when the dispersed of Israel shall be gathered into the Kingdom of God). Centuries ago, the prophet Isaiah said, "The Lord GOD, who gathers the dispersed of Israel, declares, 'Yet others I will gather to them, to those already gathered'" (Isaiah 56:8).

First, God had sent the winds in the natural realm, and then He sent them in the spiritual. Why had the Spirit made such a point of telling me, *The winds are coming*? Because the angels are winds. "Of the angels He says, 'Who makes His angels winds, and His ministers a flame of fire'" (Hebrews 1:7). Why had they come? Because they are "ministering spirits, sent out to render service for the sake of those who will inherit salvation" (Hebrews 1:14). The Word of God will interpret the revelation sent from God.

God Confirmed His Word

After writing down the revelations God had given me and my encounter with the angel, I pulled out my sheet of paper with the various names and words written on it and began to minister to the people at the conference. Sure enough, present in the meeting were a man named Daniel and twelve women named Elizabeth, just as the Holy Spirit had indicated to me. I prayed for these people, and then I started to recount the angelic encounter. My host, revivalist Matt Sorger, was ecstatic because he, too, had written on a piece of paper that an angel had entered the meeting with me that night and that the angel's name was Israel Awakening. The Lord had confirmed His word.

The Great Awakening

But the word God gave me that night was not only for the people at that conference. Neither was it a word meant only for people who already have a heart for Israel. It is a word for you, whether you identify yourself as a Gentile or as a Jewish person, whether you believe that Yeshua (the Jewish name for Jesus) is the Messiah or not. Every one of us is going to be awakened to a new degree.

To be awakened implies that we are currently asleep, and to some degree all of us are indeed slumbering. Individually and corporately our eyes are shut, and we are sleeping. God is giving us a heads-up. The alarm clock is going off even as dawn is breaking on a new day. It is time to wake up to God's prophetic purposes in our generation.

The Church will be awakened. The Gentile (non-Jewish) Church, otherwise known as the Body of Christ, will be awakened by the supernatural activity of God. She will be awakened to her strategic and sovereign role in the last days. The sleeping Bride of Christ needs to wake up and assume her rightful place of intercession and cooperation with the Son of God. Her awakening concerns the priority of Israel in the last days and the Gospel of the Kingdom being preached and demonstrated to the ends of the earth, preparing the way for the Messiah's return. She will awaken to the place of the Jewish people in the Word of God, in the heart of God and in the move of God. She will awaken to her responsibility to watch on the walls for Jerusalem's sake:

> On your walls, O Jerusalem, I have appointed
>   watchmen;
>   All day and all night they will never keep silent.
>   You who remind the LORD, take no rest for
>   yourselves;
>   And give Him no rest until He establishes
>   And makes Jerusalem a praise in the earth.
>
> Isaiah 62:6–7

Not only will the Body of the Messiah be awakened to her important role, but Israel also will awake out of her long slumber and embrace her destiny at last. Yes, Israel will be awakened. The blinders will come off Israel's eyes (as a nation and as individuals), so that she can behold the goodness of the Lord even in the midst of a time of great trouble. Israel will rise to her prophetic destiny and role in the Middle East as descendants of Abraham. God will apprehend the Jewish people, and they will know their one true God!

In part, the Gentiles have been able to take off their blinders for the past two thousand years, embracing Jesus as their Savior and thereby becoming God's primary instrument for the establishment of His Kingdom on earth, while Israel has remained blind to her Messiah. This situation, however, is not meant to be a permanent one (see Romans 11 and the next chapter). Israel is not out of the picture. She has not disqualified herself from God's redemptive plan. God has not given up on using His chosen ones to establish His Kingdom on earth. Remember: God remains faithful when we are unfaithful. (Great is His faithfulness!) In fact, He plans to raise up and fully restore His original covenant people:

> Therefore say to the house of Israel, "Thus says the Lord God, ... 'I will vindicate the holiness of My great name which has been profaned among the nations, which you have profaned in their midst. Then the nations will know that I am the Lord,' declares the Lord God, 'when I prove Myself holy among you in their sight. For I will take you from the nations, gather you from all the lands and bring you into your own land. Then I will sprinkle clean water on you, and you will be clean; I will cleanse you from all your filthiness and from all your idols. Moreover, I will give you a new heart and put a new spirit within you; and I will remove the heart of stone from your flesh and give you a heart of flesh. I will put My Spirit within you and cause you to walk in My statutes, and you will be careful to observe My ordinances. You will live in the land

that I gave to your forefathers; so you will be My people, and I will be your God.'"

Ezekiel 36:22–28

An awakening of unprecedented proportions will occur, hand-in-hand with unprecedented troubles that will make God-fearing Jewish people in the land of Israel cry out to the one true God. Their prayers will rise alongside those of compassionate Gentile believers across the world.

Yes, the sleeping Bride of Christ will be awakened so that she assumes her rightful role, and yes, the land of Israel will experience a corresponding awakening. But in addition to all this, a fresh move of God will blow across the nations of the earth, wherever Jewish people reside, and Jewish people worldwide will be awakened.

During the Jesus People movement, which began in 1967, hundreds of Jewish people came to faith in Jesus as their Messiah. Signs and wonders accompanied this new outpouring of grace. More than a generation has gone by since then. Far from having dwindled into a historical anomaly, this move of God has become a steadily growing tide. And something new is still happening. As angels such as Israel Awakening are released across the earth, fresh oil is still being poured out.

The scope of what God is doing takes my breath away. The more I find out about it, the more meaning I find in the daily news and the more specific prayers I pray. A great move of God is in the making! In the chapters that follow, I will take a closer look at the well-orchestrated details of the past, present and future for God's people. An awakening is coming—indeed it has already begun!

Yes, Israel will be awakened for such a time as this!

2

The Gradual Awakening

Daughters of Jerusalem, I charge you
by the gazelles and by the does of the field:
Do not arouse or awaken love
until it so desires.

Song of Solomon 3:5, NIV

God has never taken His eye off His goal of restoring His Bride
to her rightful place. He has always planned to awaken her,
and He always intended to do it gradually and effectively.

This gradual awakening began a long time ago, and it has
happened by stages and degrees. We can see this as we examine how Scripture applies to the sweep of history, as well
as to the present day. The scriptural evidence proves that He
has been awakening Israel more and more, just as effectively
as He has been awakening the Gentiles for generations. The
awakening is past, present and future. Naturally, if we ourselves are waking up, then we want to be alert and watchful

for both the present and future, pronounced and gradual awakenings as they arise on the scene of time.

Paul's letter to the Romans contains the ABCs of God's plan. Paul calls God's yet-to-be-completed plan for Israel a "mystery" because it has been so hidden and so easily misunderstood:

> For I do not want you, brethren, to be uninformed of this mystery—so that you will not be wise in your own estimation—that a partial hardening has happened to Israel until the fullness of the Gentiles has come in; and so all Israel will be saved; just as it is written,
>
> > "The Deliverer will come from Zion,
> > He will remove ungodliness from Jacob."
> > "This is my covenant with them,
> > When I take away their sins."
>
> From the standpoint of the Gospel they are enemies for your sake, but from the standpoint of God's choice they are beloved for the sake of the fathers; for the gifts and the calling of God are irrevocable. For just as you once were disobedient to God, but now have been shown mercy because of their disobedience, so these also now have been disobedient, that because of the mercy shown to you they also may now be shown mercy. For God has shut up all in disobedience so that He may show mercy to all.
>
> Romans 11:25–32

Earlier in the same chapter, Paul also writes:

> Now if their transgression is riches for the world and their failure is riches for the Gentiles, how much more will their fulfillment be! But I am speaking to you who are Gentiles. Inasmuch then as I am an apostle of Gentiles, I magnify my ministry, if somehow I might move to jealousy my fellow countrymen and save some of them. For if their rejection is

the reconciliation of the world, what will their acceptance be but life from the dead? . . .

But if some of the branches were broken off, and you, being a wild olive, were grafted in among them and became partaker with them of the rich root of the olive tree, do not be arrogant toward the branches; but if you are arrogant, remember that it is not you who supports the root, but the root supports you. . . .

And they also, if they do not continue in their unbelief, will be grafted in, for God is able to graft them in again. For if you were cut off from what is by nature a wild olive tree, and were grafted contrary to nature into a cultivated olive tree, how much more will these who are the natural branches be grafted into their own olive tree?

Romans 11:12–15; 17–18; 23–24

In as many ways as he can express it, Paul is trying to say in this chapter that Israel will not be cast away. God's plan is to save the Jewish people as well as the non-Jewish people (the Gentiles) through a revelation of the Lordship of Jesus Christ—God's only Son and way for salvation. Israel is the original vine; the Gentiles are the grafted-in branches. If Israel's transgression and failure have meant that the Gentiles could come to God (be grafted in), how much more can we count on God's mercy to be shown to the Jewish people? In fact, it will be easier to graft them back in than it was to graft in the Gentiles because they are part of the rootstock. Israel has been in a "temporary stupor" while the Gentiles have become awakened (grafted) into life, but the stupor is only temporary. Israel will be awakened as well!

Gentle, Rude and Great Awakenings

In the book *The Call of the Elijah Revolution*, which I co-authored with Lou Engle, I speak of three stages and types of the overall awakening. We can see these three awakenings—the gentle, the rude and the great—in world events and Church history, as well as in the Bible.

Gentle Awakening

If you have been a Christian for any length of time, then you know that the past twenty years or so have been marked with a growing awareness of God's desire for intimacy with His people. God's awakening process has taken the form of outpourings of His Spirit designed to help people fall in love with Him. These outpourings have been called "The River," "The Father's Blessing," "renewal," "outpourings" or even "revival." People across the earth have experienced God's presence firsthand and have grown in their freedom to love, laugh and enjoy the goodness of the Lord.

Three primary aspects have characterized these outpourings of the Holy Spirit's presence. First, an intercessory prayer movement of unprecedented proportions has arisen—one that shows no signs of waning. It has taken many forms, from multiple prayer-oriented ministries such as 24/7 "harp and bowl" worship and intercession to the Global Day of Prayer to simple, faithful, individual prayer and fasting. (Our ministry hosts an Internet-based global Prayer Storm where people around the world enter into "The Hour That Changes the World." See www.prayerstorm.com for more information on how to become part of this.) Christians—especially those in the evangelical/Pentecostal/charismatic/third-wave segment of the Church—have been awakened by their loving Father and now are devoted to "keeping watch" night and day.

Second, we have seen an amazing upsurge of interest in prophetic words from God, not to mention a corresponding increase in the technological means of transmitting what He says. No longer does the word *prophetic* bring to mind odd predictions of distant future events uttered by strange wilderness prophets. As God speaks through a variety of people, His word is welcomed by those with open hearts.

33

Finally, this prophetic restoration has come on the heels of the restoration of evangelism as an important task of the Church. Each of these—prayer, prophecy and evangelism—is an aspect of God's gentle awakening.

Alongside signs of revival in the Church, we have seen many developments among the Jewish people and the nation of Israel. Messianic Jewish congregations are multiplying, even within the nation of Israel, and unprecedented waves of immigration from all over the world have swelled the population of that country.

Historically the Jewish people have experienced waves of revival in terms of coming to faith in Jesus as the Messiah. The first waves, of course, were captured in the first chapters of the book of Acts. In more recent history (the 1880s through 1900, prior to World War I), a new wave hit Europe; some say that as many as 100,000 Jewish people came to faith.[1] Between 1967 and 1975 (at the same time that Jerusalem was being reestablished under Jewish control), the charismatic renewal, which gave rise to many of the developments I mentioned above, was burgeoning all over the world. This charismatic "Jesus Revolution" scooped up many Jewish people across America. That is when Jews for Jesus and other similar organizations were born, proclaiming, "Yeshua is alive!" The news certainly was met with skepticism, but a number of people, especially young people, became His disciples. Messianic leaders—"fathers," if you will—rose up in fulfillment of Malachi 4:5–6 (NKJV):

> Behold, I will send you Elijah the prophet
> Before the coming of the great and dreadful day of
>   the LORD.
> And he will turn
> The hearts of the fathers to the children,
> And the hearts of the children to their fathers,
> Lest I come and strike the earth with a curse.

Not only did the "fathers" rise up, but the "children" took hold of the covenant God had made with Abraham, Isaac and Jacob as they learned how to honor the patriarchs.

In the early 1980s, the nation of Israel experienced a minor revival, which was major for those days. Perhaps fifty to eighty Jewish people became believers in Yeshua as the Messiah. Subsequently, in the early 1990s significant parts of the former Soviet Union (Russia, Ukraine and Belarus) experienced stirrings and awakenings. Thousands of people from northern lands immigrated to Israel (more about this later in this book). Waves of the Jewish people have come (to faith and/or to the Land), and they keep coming. While the exact meaning remains a mystery, Revelation 7:4 gives a specific number: 144,000 from the twelve tribes of Israel who will be "sealed." The fruit of that sealing is portrayed in subsequent verses:

> Behold, a great multitude which no one could count, from every nation and all tribes and peoples and tongues, standing before the throne and before the Lamb, clothed in white robes, and palm branches were in their hands; and they cry out with a loud voice, saying, "Salvation to our God who sits on the throne, and to the Lamb."
>
> Revelation 7:9–10

The plan is under way. Gradually and gently the Jewish people have begun to wake up. Gentile believers have been awakening, too, becoming aware of their responsibilities toward their Jewish brethren as they become yoked with God's agenda. They have learned that praying for Israel means tapping into God's purposes for the nations of the earth. World revival is coming, and so is the Lord Himself—and all of it is connected to the Jewish people. Each of us has a role to play. We have to wake up to the global realities even as we act locally in obedience to the Holy Spirit.

These developments are part of what I call the "gentle awakening," in which God woos His people. In His kindness and mercy God wants to restore people to righteousness and true life. When they do not respond to His repeated, gentler overtures, He—still because of His kindness and mercy—resorts to what I call a "rude awakening."

Rude Awakening

When people turn their faces to the wall and refuse to wake up to the Lord's gentler awakenings, they set themselves up to be shaken awake—rudely. God wants to wake up as many people as possible in time for the global great awakening that lies in the near future. Time is growing too short for a merciful God to wait for everybody to respond to His gentle awakenings.

Central to the Lord's awakenings is holiness. The prophet Amos described how He drops His plumb line to see how the obedience of His people measures up.

Thus He showed me, and behold, the Lord was standing by a vertical wall with a plumb line in His hand. The LORD said to me, "What do you see, Amos?" And I said, "A plumb line." Then the Lord said,

> "Behold I am about to put a plumb line
> In the midst of My people Israel.
> I will spare them no longer.
> The high places of Isaac will be desolated
> And the sanctuaries of Israel laid waste.
> Then I will rise up against the house of Jeroboam
>   with the sword."

Amos 7:7–9

When God's plumb line, which is His absolutely perfect standard of righteousness, shows how sinful people are, He begins to set off alarms to get their attention. This can entail much shaking and quaking, often quite literally. Natural disasters fall into the category of rude awakenings, as do terrorist attacks and wars.

Rude awakenings often are not pleasant. In fact, they can seem like one disaster after another. And yet they can be effective. Rude awakenings drive people to their knees in surrender to their sovereign Lord. People repent, which is another way of saying they begin to line up with that divine plumb line. (God will get His way one way or another!)

Today we are on the verge of what could be called the "perfect storm." At this hour of time and history multiple forces are colliding and converging, coming together at one time—economics, political ideologues, unusual weather patterns, new diseases and widespread viruses, wars and rumors of wars. The rude awakening has begun.

Where Israel is concerned, the rude awakening can be used to drive people back to their ancestral land. It can give them a new heart, a "heart of flesh," to replace the old, stony heart of blind disbelief. The prophet Ezekiel portrayed this transformation:

> Therefore say, "Thus says the Lord GOD, 'Though I had removed them far away among the nations and though I had scattered them among the countries, yet I was a sanctuary for them a little while in the countries where they had gone.'"
>
> Therefore say, "Thus says the Lord GOD, 'I will gather you from the peoples and assemble you out of the countries among which you have been scattered, and I will give you the land of Israel.'"
>
> When they come there, they will remove all its detestable things and all its abominations from it. And I will give them one heart, and put a new spirit within them. And I will take the heart of stone out of their flesh and give them a heart of flesh, that they may walk in My statutes and keep My ordinances and do them. Then they will be My people, and I shall be their God.
>
> Ezekiel 11:16–20

This is truly "life from the dead" for the Jewish people and for the world (Romans 11:15). It will precede the greatest awakening of all time and the final return of Jesus Christ, the Messiah.

The whole world is gripped in a war. Some, speaking prophetically of the days in which we live, term it "World War III." It is a war of terror and jihad in which radical Islam is out to destroy the West, including Israel. Threats are credible. Violent death occurs daily. And yet most Westerners are quite comfortable, relatively unaware of the situation and for the most part unaffected by it. They ignore the defiant threats of Iranian President Mahmoud Ahmadinejad and Osama bin Laden while they concern themselves with personal matters.

This world war touches every continent. It features human rights abuses, genocide, corruption and overt hatred, which are more often than not clothed in religious terminology. It is a spiritual war with physical manifestations. And it is going to get worse.

The right response is not fatalism or denial; it is prayer—and lots of it. It is time for the Prayer Storm to strike the nations! Pray for protection and relief, and do not forget to focus sharply on the real goal: awakening. Nobody should sleep through such a rude awakening. It is time to wake up! Why? Because God also declares it is going to get better! The dark will get darker, and then light will shine forth and penetrate this temporary present darkness!

Global Great Awakening

On the other side of the gentle and rude awakenings lies the greatest awakening of all time! This awakening will affect all people, because it is the prelude to the climax of the ages: the return of Jesus/Yeshua, Christ and Messiah, and the ushering in of His millennial reign.

No one knows fully what this awakening will look like, but we do know how to prepare for it. What should our prepara-

38

tions look like? For starters, they should include a response to the voice of God, whether His voice is an inaudible whisper or a shout through our pain (to paraphrase C. S. Lewis). As I wrote in *The Call of the Elijah Revolution*, God never speaks just to hear His own voice. Whenever God speaks—and He is speaking all the time—He speaks with purpose. Whenever God purposes to do something in the world, He speaks to His people, calling them to prepare the way. "Surely the Lord GOD does nothing unless He reveals His secret counsel to His servants the prophets" (Amos 3:7). When God was ready to establish a nation through whom a Savior would come, He spoke to Abram and gave him a son in his old age. When God was ready to deliver that nation from slavery in Egypt, He spoke to Moses. When God was ready to call His people back from sin and idolatry, He spoke to Elijah, Isaiah, Jeremiah and the other prophets. When God was ready to send His Son into the world, He spoke to Mary and Joseph.

Today God is moving mightily in the world, and He is calling His people to join Him in what He is doing. He is calling forth the "Annas" of the Temple and the "John the Baptists" to prepare the way. He is the Lord of history, and He is looking for prophets who will declare His word and for intercessors who will birth that word through prevailing prayer and bring it to fruition.[2]

Having gotten their attention, God is calling to action a large number of believers around the earth. These Christians are radical. They have heard His call to become modern-day Nazarites. They are single-minded and single-hearted, sold out to the task of reclaiming a lost world for the Kingdom of God. These are the latter-day "Esthers," "Elijahs," "Elishas" and "Jehus." Disregarding the high personal price, they have banded together and are willing to live sacrificially and to pray and fast and take a stand for righteousness and revival.

The goal of their prayers is the ultimate awakening of Israel. "All Israel will be saved; just as it is written, 'The Deliverer will come from Zion, He will remove ungodliness from Jacob'"

39

(Romans 11:26). The second part of that passage is quoted from the prophet Isaiah, who wrote, "'A Redeemer will come to Zion, and to those who turn from transgression in Jacob,' declares the LORD" (Isaiah 59:20).

The prophets pointed to this. Jeremiah wrote: "'They will all know Me, from the least of them to the greatest of them,' declares the LORD, 'for I will forgive their iniquity, and their sin I will remember no more'" (Jeremiah 31:34). Zechariah added,

> And I will bring the third part through the fire, refine them as silver is refined, and test them as gold is tested. They will call on My name, and I will answer them; I will say, "They are My people," and they will say, "The LORD is my God."
>
> Zechariah 13:9

This is a final awakening, a wonderful closing to the story of God's chosen people, the Jewish people. The last days are upon us. Whether you are a Gentile or a Jew, wake up. Do not miss the day of His manifested presence and His soon coming!

Means of Awakening

Paul—by birth and upbringing a Pharisee and by rebirth an apostle to the Gentiles—further expressed the "ways and means" of the awakening process by writing to the church in Corinth:

> Indeed Jews ask for signs and Greeks search for wisdom; but we preach Christ crucified, to Jews a stumbling block and to Gentiles foolishness, but to those who are the called, both Jews and Greeks, Christ the power of God and the wisdom of God.
>
> 1 Corinthians 1:22–24

Christ crucified. The cross and all it entails—all its seeming nonsense and all its offensiveness—provide a dramatic means of awakening. This awakening will not come easily. A fire of purification comes along with it (see Ezekiel 20:33–38; Zechariah 13:8–9).

The first stirrings of awakening entail the outright preaching of the Gospel of the Kingdom. "I am not ashamed of the gospel," Paul said, "for it is the power of God for salvation to everyone who believes, to the Jew first and also to the Greek" (Romans 1:16). But the Gospel must be incarnated as well; it must be clothed in human form.

Isaiah 60:5–16 portrays the Gentiles incarnating the Gospel by serving the Jewish people as they help them return to the land of Israel. And as Isaiah 49:6 and other prophetic passages indicate, without Israel the salvation of the rest of the Gentiles cannot occur. So this serving business is not one way. As my friend Avner Boskey puts it, "It is as if we are going to get stuck in the doorway. 'You first, please.' 'No, you first, please.'" The bottleneck in the doorway happens only if we incarnate the Gospel that we preach. We must become the Word of God! Unless we incarnate the Gospel, there is no serving, no power, no wisdom and no fulfillment of the promise.

Awakening for a Purpose

What is the point of all this Israel awakening? Why does God make so many promises to Israel? He has not given such promises to other nations.

I see Israel as the eldest son in God's family. If you know anything about families, you know what that means. It means that the Jewish people will have both the extra measure (a double portion, if you will) of blessing and also the added responsibilities of the eldest son in a family. The Israelites have been called to do something with what they have been given. They are called to serve. They are called to speak out like the nation of prophets that they are, proclaiming the news of God's coming to the world and telling them what He is like.

As Paul explained in the middle of Romans 11, "The gifts and the calling of God are irrevocable" (Romans 11:29). That verse is not just about spiritual gifts and calling in general. It is embedded in the middle of a chapter about the Jewish people! God selected them thousands of years ago, and He has not changed His mind. The existence of the Gentile Church does not alter the plan; it enhances it. The Gentiles are supposed to pray for the Jewish people to answer this calling. They are supposed to usher in the Messianic Jews who are the remnant of Israel. Then that Jewish remnant, spurred on by their Gentile brethren, is called to be a light and a servant to the nations, as we can see:

> Paul and Barnabas spoke out boldly and said, ". . . Behold, we are turning to the Gentiles. For so the Lord has commanded us, 'I have placed you as a light for the Gentiles, that you may bring salvation to the end of the earth.' "
>
> Acts 13:46–47

> He says, "It is too small a thing that You should be My Servant
>   To raise up the tribes of Jacob and to restore the preserved
>   ones of Israel;
>   I will also make You a light of the nations
>   So that My salvation may reach to the end of the earth."
>
> Isaiah 49:6

All these shakings and awakenings are for a purpose. God is restoring a prophetic people for Himself. He wants to raise up a mighty army under the banner of His name. He wants the Jewish people to be on fire with His love for the world. "The world" includes all Gentile nations—First, Second and Third World; secular and religious; people of all colors and persuasions (yes, including the Muslim world)—until the fullness comes to the Gentiles and they receive life from the dead (see Romans 11:12, 15).

Apparently God wants to do the impossible: He wants to raise up an army out of a valley of dry bones (see Ezekiel 37). The story is a familiar one, and it can be applied on many levels of our lives. But have you ever thought about the fact that those bones are Jewish? It says so, right in that chapter of Ezekiel:

> Then He said to me, "Son of man, these bones are the whole house of Israel; behold, they say, 'Our bones are dried up and our hope has perished. We are completely cut off.' Therefore prophesy and say to them, 'Thus says the Lord GOD, "Behold, I will open your graves and cause you to come up out of your graves, My people; and I will bring you into the land of Israel. Then you will know that I am the LORD, when I have opened your graves and caused you to come up out of your graves, My people. I will put My Spirit within you and you will come to life, and I will place you on your own land. Then you will know that I, the LORD, have spoken and done it," declares the LORD.'"
>
> Ezekiel 37:11–14

The restored army is headed into the land of Israel. They have a task. Their objective is to secure the territory for the coming King:

> [They know] the time, that it is already the hour . . . to awaken from sleep; for now salvation is nearer to us than when we believed. The night is almost gone, and the day is near. Therefore let us lay aside the deeds of darkness and put on the armor of light.
>
> Romans 13:11–12

It is time to wake up, so that as further shakings come we will be able to stand with our conquering King, ready to reach out to the trembling, fearful ones who will be coming to Him in fulfillment of His word through the prophets. Let us seize the moment and see a compassionate army of healing ambassadors flood the global scene. This gradual awakening will result in salvation for the Jewish people, which will help to usher in world revival that includes transformation of society and ultimately the Second Coming of Jesus. It all is connected with Israel. It all is connected to His Word. It all is connected to the Son of God receiving the rewards of His suffering. See how vital it is for Israel to awaken!

Yes, the time has come! Just as the angel blew the shofar in my face, it is time for shock waves of His presence and demonstrations of His power to awaken Israel from her slumber and the Church from her sleep.

3

The Parallel Awakening

It is already the hour for you to awaken from sleep;
for now salvation is nearer to us than when we
believed.

Romans 13:11

God is at work, and He will complete what He has started.
By rousing both the Church and Israel from their slumber,
He will enable them—together—to be ready to receive Him
as Lord when He returns. This awakening process is a parallel one; it involves both Israel and the Church, as is evident
throughout biblical prophecy, history and current events.

There are three kinds of awakening to consider, three
realms in which awakening has occurred and will occur:

1. the awakening of the message and the raising up of the
   messengers of the Lord;

2. the matching up of time and destiny; the awakened promise of God coming to fruition in *kairos* time; and
3. true "Israel awakening" in the Body of Christ—one in which the Church awakens to her role for Israel and Jewish people awaken to their Messiah.

In this chapter I will explore each of these kinds of awakening. But first we need to skim our history books, paying particular attention to some little-known facts.

Early History

Most of us do not realize that a twin awakening of the Church and Israel has been underway for centuries. It has been hardly noticeable for most of that time and has become more obvious only in the past three-quarters of a century.[1]

Where the history of the Church is concerned, we must start at square one: the birthday of the Church on Pentecost in A.D. 30—which actually marks the establishment of the first Messianic congregation. That first "Upper Room" church was composed of Jewish people, many of whom had walked with Yeshua and who had become convinced that He was the Messiah. At first, Gentiles were not part of the picture.

Jewish or Gentile?

But within only a couple of decades, a new and burning issue had arisen. The big question was: *Do Gentiles need to become Jews in order to be Christians?* As we know, the question was answered in the negative. No, God's salvation is available to anyone who believes that Jesus was the Son of God and that He died on the cross and rose from the dead. With that, evangelism took off across the non-Jewish Roman Empire. Whole churches were planted in regions without a single Jewish person in residence. Then came the destruction of the Temple in Jerusalem in A.D.

46

70 and the subsequent dispersion of the Messianic community of believers. Most of them fled to what is now Jordan.

In A.D. 85, leading Jewish rabbis decided to expel from their synagogues all believers in Yeshua. At the same time, the Gentile believers resolved that they no longer wanted their churches to reflect Jewish values or traditions. In A.D. 135, the nation of Israel ceased to exist. The Messianic Jewish community ended up in a kind of a no-man's-land, and this situation only became worse after A.D. 370, when Christianity became the official state religion of the far-flung Roman Empire. A few Messianic believers persisted in gathering near Jerusalem until the fifth century, meeting under difficult circumstances. After that time, Messianic congregations disappeared, although individual Jewish believers have always persisted underground, most often as members of the Gentile Church, stripped of their Jewishness. The Second Council of Nicea in A.D. 787 decreed that to continue as a practicing Jew was strictly forbidden within the Christian Church.

For centuries every branch of Christianity resolved that the Jewish component of the Church would be extinguished and repudiated. Prophetic promises were interpreted to apply to the Church in broad, spiritual terms. Although the future of the Jewish people was prophesied in Scripture, it was rarely taken literally.

A Future and a Hope

By the end of the Middle Ages, however, a shift began to occur. Following are some excerpts from an excellent historical sourcebook called *The Puritan Hope* by Iain Murray, which is still in print:[2]

> Neither Luther [1483–1546] nor Calvin [1509–1564] saw a future general conversion of the Jews promised in Scripture; some of their contemporaries, however, notably Martin Bucer and Peter Martyr, who taught at Cambridge and Oxford re-

47

spectively in the reign of Edward VI, did understand the Bible to teach a future calling of the Jews. In this view they were followed by Theodore Beza, Calvin's successor at Geneva. . . .

The first volume in English to expound this conviction at some length was the translation of Peter Martyr's Commentary upon Romans, published in London in 1568. The probability is strong that Martyr's careful exposition of the eleventh chapter [of Romans] prepared the way for a general adoption amongst the English Puritans of a belief in the future conversion of the Jews. . . .

Hugh Broughton (1549–1612) . . . had the distinction of being the first Englishman to propose going as a missionary to the Jews in the Near East, and also the first to propose the idea of translating the New Testament into Hebrew for the sake of the Jews. . . . Though given no preferment in the English Church he was so well known in the East on account of his learning that the Chief Rabbi of Constantinople wrote to him in 1599 and subsequently invited him to become a public teacher there. . . .

[In 1577] William Perkins [of Christ's College, Cambridge] . . . speaks plainly of a future conversion of the Jews: "The Lord saith, 'All the nations shall be blessed in Abraham': Hence I gather that the nation of the Jews shall be called, and converted to the participation of this blessing: when, and how, God knows: but that it shall be done before the end of the world we know."[3]

. . . In his famous book, *The Bruised Reed*, . . . [Richard] Sibbes writes: "The Jews are not yet come in under Christ's banner; but God, that hath persuaded Japhet to come into the tents of Shem, will persuade Shem to come into the tents of Japhet (Genesis 9:27). The 'fullness of the Gentiles is not yet come in' (Romans 11:25), but Christ, that hath the 'utmost parts of the earth given him for his possession' (Psalm 2:8), will gather all the sheep his Father hath given him into one fold, that there may be one sheepfold and one shepherd (John 10:16). The faithful Jews rejoiced to think of the calling of the Gentiles; and why should not we joy to think of the calling of the Jews?"[4]

. . . Peter Martyr and William Perkins . . . had placed that event [the future conversion of Israel] very close to the end

48

of time. Martyr interpreted the word "fullness" in Paul's statement "Blindness in part is happened to Israel, until the fullness of the Gentiles be come in" (Romans 11:25) to mean that Christ's Kingdom among the Gentiles will have reached its fullest development, indeed its consummation, by the time that Israel is called.

Zinzendorf and the Moravians

In 1727, Count Nicolas Ludwig von Zinzendorf (1700–1760) established a vibrant community of Moravian believers on his estate in Herrnhut, Germany. To this day many of us know about their wide-ranging missionary endeavors, which were supported by 24/7 prayer—a prayer meeting that went on for more than a hundred years. One important but hidden aspect of their life together concerned the unity of the brotherhood. As they understood it, full restoration of the Body of Christ cannot occur until the unity between the Jewish people and the Gentile Church is fully restored. The Moravians sent Samuel Lieberkuhn to the Jewish ghetto in Amsterdam, and he set up a prototype Messianic community there among the Sephardic Jews (those who had been forced out of Spain) within the Great Synagogue of Amsterdam. Lieberkuhn's associates at Zinzendorf's Hernnhut community also set up a secret Messianic congregation, complete with celebrations of Shabbat, the Jewish feasts and Jewish weddings. They communicated with like-minded believers in the underground Messianic Jewish community from London to Constantinople by encoded documents. These Messianic believers conducted themselves outwardly as ordinary orthodox Jews.

Changing Ideas about Replacement Theology

Gradually over the next 150 years, the Messianic movement grew in size and strength until it began to go public in the

1830s. Some leaders in the Gentile Church started to realize that "replacement theology," the idea that the Church has replaced Israel completely in God's plans and purposes, was flawed. They changed their minds about what should happen when a Jewish person becomes a disciple of Jesus; rather than insisting that all new believers repudiate their Jewishness and join a Gentile church, they began to approve the idea of forming Hebrew Christian congregations. The Anglican Church was particularly supportive of the idea of an authentic Jewish expression of Christianity, even setting up a center in Jerusalem for Hebrew Christians. Throughout the nineteenth century, the Hebrew-Christian movement spread quickly. It was a gradual, stage-by-stage awakening that started to accelerate. A variety of congregations appeared in England, Germany, Austria, Hungary, Poland, France and elsewhere.

In chapter 5 you can read about a rabbi-scholar named Joseph ben David Rabinowitz in Russia, who in 1884 established one of the world's first legal modern-day Messianic congregations. The First Assembly of the Israelites of the New Covenant began with forty families who converted, or as we have come to say, "became completed Jews." The congregation grew greatly, but most of its members were lost to war and the Holocaust.[5]

In the Holocaust (1933–45), the Nazi "final solution" to the so-called problem of the existence of Jews, at least six million Jewish men, women and children were murdered. The horrors of this mass destruction provided unexpected impetus to the Messianic movement. One important factor, of course, was the establishment of the State of Israel in 1948. Such a thing had never happened before—a people who had retained their national identity for centuries of dispersion having their geographical homeland restored to them. Now many of the ancient prophetic words began to make sense in a more literal way.

Then came the 1960s. With the Second Vatican Council (1962–65), the Catholic Church acknowledged both the irrevocable covenant of Israel and the call of Israel in end-time history, declaring that history would not be fulfilled until Israel found and followed the Messiah. In the 1967 (Six-Day) War, Israel regained Jerusalem as the capital city—and this happened to parallel the explosion of the charismatic Jesus movement in the Western world. Now developments began to accelerate even faster. Jewish believers in Yeshua, their ranks swelled by young men and women, began to focus on establishing corporate expressions of Messianic faith that were separate from traditional Christian churches. Hebrew-Christian alliances began to change their names to reflect this shift. (For example, in 1975 the American Hebrew Christian Alliance was renamed the Messianic Jewish Alliance of America.) Since the 1960s, the Messianic movement has grown nearly 5 percent per year.

Don Finto, a Christian pastor who has become a statesman on behalf of Jewish believers and Israel, summed up these developments in a quote from *Your People Shall Be My People*:

> It was during that era [the Jesus movement that started in 1967] that a great majority of today's leaders in the messianic Jewish movement came to faith in Yeshua. Joseph Shulam, a native Israeli Messianic leader in Jerusalem, says, "In the early 1960s, it was difficult to find even two dozen Jews in Jerusalem who believed in Yeshua the Messiah. Those who were around lived under a terrible fear of being exposed and totally ostracized by the Jewish community. Now, fifty years later, there are hundreds, if not thousands, of Jews in Jerusalem who believe that Yeshua is the Messiah and participate in one of the nine Hebrew-speaking congregations which meet in Jerusalem. If the L-rd would grant us in the next fifty years the same kind of growth in the Body of the Messiah as we had in the last fifty years, we will have a Messianic Jew as the president of the State of Israel!"[6]

It is still happening. History is being made every day. We are living in the middle of exciting times!

The Message and Its Messengers

The shofar of the angel named Israel Awakening is meant to awaken not only a slumbering Gentile Church but also the Jewish people worldwide, scattered by the diaspora. It is meant to awaken both groups to their purpose and destiny in this generation. In our lifetimes, one of the first blasts of the shofar took place a little over forty years ago when the message of the Jesus movement came forth. In the context of the proclamation of the message of the Gospel, large numbers of messengers were raised up, then trained and established in positions of authority and respect. I quote from many of them in this book.

I was in a secular college in 1973, and I remember being glued to the news reports. I had read the book called *The Late, Great Planet Earth* by Hal Lindsey, and now the Yom Kippur War was unfolding in Israel. It seemed that prophecy was being fulfilled. Blood was being shed in Israel, and at the same time the Jesus people were rising up.

More blood has been shed in Israel again in recent years. Perhaps we are in a rebirthing (awakening) moment. Perhaps it is an apostolic awakening, an apostolic reformation. I am talking about authentic, unbridled Christianity being restored across the globe. I am talking about people who are willing to lay down their lives for the Gospel of the Kingdom, people who are willing to plant and reap, people who are sold out to Jesus and to the true apostolic Gospel message of Romans 1:16—to the Jew first and also to the Greek.

At present, this awakening and restoration may seem insignificant. It may seem that only a tiny percentage of a remnant is waking up. But the whole sleeping giant is about to be awakened. We cannot feel the shifts because we are in a huge ship, but the ship is beginning to turn. The Lord is gathering and regathering. He is releasing authentic apostolic faith with power to make Kingdom impact in times of trouble. It could be that we are starting to live in the book of James:

> James, a bond-servant of God and of the Lord Jesus Christ, to the twelve tribes who are dispersed abroad: Greetings. Consider it all joy, my brethren, when you encounter various trials, knowing that the testing of your faith produces endurance. . . . Every good thing given and every perfect gift is from above, coming down from the Father of lights, with whom there is no variation or shifting shadow. In the exercise of His will He brought us forth by the word of truth, so that we would be a kind of first fruits among His creatures.
>
> James 1:1–3, 17–18

Time and Destiny

The Lord is gathering and releasing apostolic faith to people who have heard the shofar. They are awake. Just as Esther was ready at a critical time in Jewish history (see Esther 4:14), they, too, are poised "for such a time as this." The promise of God and the time of God are coming together. Time is ripe. Destiny is knocking.

It is as if Israel is God's timepiece, and we need to set our watches by what we see Him doing with His people. It is as if God's time begins and ends in the capital city of David, from which we can expect to see the Son of David reigning forever.

"Pray for the peace of Jerusalem: they shall prosper that love thee" (Psalm 122:6, KJV). That psalm does not read, "Pray for the peace of Boston" or "London" or "Toronto." It does not even say, "Pray for the peace of Damascus" or "Cairo" or "Baghdad." If our lives are going to be in focus, we must have our focus where God's is: on Jerusalem. As I have stated in my book *Praying for Israel's Destiny*, there is only one city in the entire Bible for which we all are commanded to pray by name: Jerusalem! The time has never been more right to pray for the peace of Jerusalem.

We must wake up and redeem the time. "Therefore be careful how you walk, not as unwise men but as wise, making the most of your time, because the days are evil" (Ephesians 5:15–16). Look again at Romans 13:11, which I quoted at the beginning of this chapter, quoted here in the Amplified version:

> You know what [a critical] hour this is, how it is high time now for you to wake up out of your sleep (rouse to reality). For salvation (final deliverance) is nearer to us now than when we first believed (adhered to, trusted in, and relied on Christ, the Messiah).
>
> Romans 13:11, AMP

It is time to be like the sons of Issachar who—as we are fond of quoting—"knew the times" and possessed notable wisdom. What did the sons of Issachar have knowledge about? Here is the entire line: "the sons of Issachar, men who understood the times, *with knowledge of what Israel should do*" (1 Chronicles 12:32, emphasis mine). This is the time and the season to awaken and to receive the same revelation of heart that was upon the sons of Issachar. This is the hour for the remnant (which includes you and me) to discern the time, to know what Israel should do.

Statistical evidence alone proves that we are indeed in the midst of an extraordinary time in which Israel's physical and spiritual homecoming corresponds with burgeoning world revival. Take a look at some of it:[7]

- At the birth of Zionism (the movement based on the idea that Israel's destiny lies in having a homeland) in the late 1800s, the ratio of believers to unbelievers was 1 to 27. A little over 100 years later, that number is 1 to 5.

54

- Seventy percent of all those who have ever come to faith in Jesus/Yeshua have come to faith since the first Zionist conference in 1897.
- In 1897, 3 percent of Africans considered themselves Christians. Today the number stands at 50 percent.
- In 1897, the population of South Korea was 1 percent Christian. Today it is close to 40 percent, and the world's largest church, in Seoul (Yiodo Full Gospel Church), has more than 700,000 members.
- Seventy percent of the people who have become believers since 1897—and more than 50 percent of those who have come to faith since the time of Jesus—have become believers since 1948, the year the State of Israel was established.
- India has 103 million believers and counting, with new churches being planted among the Hindus at a rate of one every seven minutes.
- The number of evangelical believers is growing 3.5 times faster than the population of the world.[8]
- More Muslims have come to faith in Jesus since 1980 than in a thousand years before then. Worldwide, Islam is growing at a 3.2 percent rate annually, but worldwide faith in Jesus is growing at 6.9 percent annually.[9]
- As much as 20 percent of Indonesia's population is now Christian.
- Both the birth of Zionism and the birth of Pentecostalism occurred around the turn of the nineteenth century.
- In 1948, both the beginning of the Latter Rain Revival (a largely American healing revival) and the birth of the State of Israel occurred.
- The year 1967 marked both the beginning of the Jesus movement (as a result of which many Jewish young people became believers) and the Six-Day War in Israel

55

The Coming Great Awakening

(as a result of which Jerusalem was restored as the capital city).

True "Israel Awakening"

All of this evidence points to the fact that we are in the midst of a *kairos* season, a strategic time when a true Israel awakening is occurring within two groups at the same time and in two ways at the same time. An Israel awakening is happening in the Body of Christ (which is awakening to both the importance of Israel and the urgency of participation in God's plan) and in the Jewish people and Israel (who are waking up to the reality of the Messiah).

So we are in a time of mutual awakening and a time of mutual activation. It is time to take a stand, and it is time to move out and win new territory. Tasks lie before us. Whether we are Jewish or Gentile, it is time to pray and proclaim, to give and receive. For some of us, it is time to take radical action.

Some of us will be used in direct, one-on-one power and compassion evangelism. Some of us will donate funds, take trips, even pack up our families and move. Many of us will be affected by social and economic shakings, and we will have our commitments tested. God has brought revival to the Gentiles in order to position and equip the Church to help Israel, and He is preparing Israel to usher in His coming. Through everything, we must pray without ceasing.

It is a great and perilous day, and it is time to align our hearts with God's. I had a dream in which a watch was given to me. On the face of it was a Star of David, and it was the eleventh hour. In the dream, I could hear the clock ticking. I knew I needed to pray for Israel and the Church to awaken, and to stay awake and obedient.

If we remain obedient to God's voice, then we can reverse the decrees of the past. The Toward Jerusalem Council II has made this their stated purpose. Here is how they introduce their goals:

> Toward Jerusalem Council II is an initiative of repentance and reconciliation between the Jewish and Gentile segments of the Church. Our vision is that one day there will be a second Council of Jerusalem that will be, in an important respect, the inverse of the first Council described in Acts 15. Whereas the first Council was made up of Jewish believers in Yeshua (Jesus), who decided not to impose on the Gentiles the requirements of the Jewish Law, so the second Council would be made up of Gentile Church leaders who would recognize and welcome Jewish believers in Yeshua back into the Body of Messiah without requiring them to abandon their Jewish identity and practice. The Toward indicates that we do not have the authority to call such a Council, but we can work and pray for those who can. The ultimate purpose in unifying the Body and restoring Jewish believers to their rightful place is in preparation for the coming of the Lord Yeshua (Jesus) in glory and the full accomplishment of His work of redemption in the Kingdom of God.[10]

God is using political and economic shaking. He is using terrorism and war. He is using oil and blockades. He is waking people up to the realities of the immediate future, and He is calling His people to action. In light of the crucial time in which we find ourselves, consider the message of Romans 15:26–27. The bracketed notes are mine:

> For Macedonia and Achaia [the Gentiles] have been pleased to make a contribution for the poor among the saints in Jerusalem. Yes, they were pleased to do so, and they are indebted to them [to the Jews, for being the rootstock]. For if the Gentiles have shared in their spiritual things, they are indebted to minister to them also in material things.
>
> Romans 15:26–27

Divine Intervention

We are living in a time of obvious divine intervention. As Israel continues to come back to the Land, the Lord is going to continue to open her eyes. That is what is happening. Reliable sources tally up more than 400,000 Jewish people who believe that Yeshua is the Messiah.[11] The worldwide count has not been this high since the book of Acts was written. The prophets tell us that Israel's return to the Land signals a time of spiritual awakening. We are living in the intersection of God's promises and their fulfillment.

Jewish people are making *aliyah* (literally, "going up") in record numbers. Some of them are returning to Israel as faithful believers. Most are not. Either way, this is a fulfillment of prophecies such as the one in Deuteronomy 30 and the story of the valley of dry bones in Ezekiel 37, where we see the rebirth of a dead people. In 1882, the Jewish population of what was then called Palestine was only 24,000 people. In 1948, the Jewish population was not even a million. Today, only sixty years later, the population of Israel is five million and counting. The people have come from more than 140 other nations, and they represent nearly a hundred different language groups.[12]

And what about the others who claim the Land? How should we view this contentious situation? We can find a clue in Ezekiel 36, the chapter right before the one about the dry bones. The Lord God speaks to Ezekiel:

> And you, son of man, prophesy to the mountains of Israel and say, "O mountains of Israel, hear the word of the LORD. Thus says the Lord GOD, 'Because the enemy has spoken against you, "Aha!" and, "The everlasting heights have become our possession."'"
>
> Ezekiel 36:1–2

What are the "mountains of Israel"? The mountains are in Judea and Samaria, going up into Galilee, in what is called the West Bank today. The enemy is the radical Islam spirit (not the Arabs themselves), and God goes on to promise the Israelites help:

> "I will vindicate the holiness of My great name which has been profaned among the nations, which you have profaned in their midst. Then the nations will know that I am the LORD," declares the Lord GOD, "when I prove Myself holy among you in their sight. For I will take you from the nations, gather you from all the lands and bring you into your own land. Then I will sprinkle clean water on you, and you will be clean; I will cleanse you from all your filthiness and from all your idols. Moreover, I will give you a new heart and put a new spirit within you; and I will remove the heart of stone from your flesh and give you a heart of flesh."
>
> Ezekiel 36:23–26

God promises help, prosperity and provision to those who formerly set themselves against His name and His people. Of course, for everyone a choice is involved. Everybody can choose to accept the offer or not. Those who accept will have a front-row seat as the final drama unfolds.

Testimonies of God's Faithfulness

With the new "heart of flesh" that God promises to provide, the choice becomes easier, even in unlikely places. I think of a well-educated Jewish man who had become an atheist during the course of his education. He took a trip to Central America. One day in Guatemala, he saw a bunch of people who were entering an unusual-looking house, and he followed them. After a while the people started moving to the front of the room, so he went along. A man was dipping something like a cracker in something that he could not identify, and putting it on people's tongues. He accepted one and went back to his seat, thinking that it was an odd thing to be doing. Suddenly the power of God fell on him and he shook for half an hour. He did not know what to make of it. Soon after, a couple of Guatemalan women were talking to him about Jesus, and he could understand them perfectly even though he did not know much Spanish. His heart began to soften. He began to recognize the possibility that God was alive and active. He started wondering, *Is God real?* At that instant an earthquake shook the building and everyone ran outside. He was convinced. Today this man partners with others, both Jewish and non-Jewish, to bring as many people as possible to the One who reached down and saved him. His story is one of divine intervention.

Frequently we hear stories about Muslims or others who are closed to the Gospel being visited in dreams by Jesus. In 2007, *Israel Today* reported the following story about an ultraorthodox rabbi:

> Monday, April 30, 2007—A few months before he died, one of the nation's most prominent rabbis, Yitzhak Kaduri, supposedly wrote the name of the Messiah on a small note which he requested would remain sealed until now. When the note was unsealed, it revealed what many have known for centuries: Yehoshua, or Yeshua (Jesus), is the Messiah. . . . With one of Israel's most prominent rabbis indicating the name of the Messiah is Yeshua, it is understandable why his last wish was to wait one year after his death before revealing what he wrote. . . .
>
> A few months before Kaduri died at the age of 108, he surprised his followers when he told them that he met the Messiah. Kaduri gave a message in his synagogue on Yom Kippur, the Day of Atonement, teaching how to recognize the Messiah. . . . Kaduri's grandson, Rabbi Yosef Kaduri, said his grandfather spoke many times during the last days about the coming of the Messiah and redemption through the Messiah. . . .
>
> Rabbi Yitzhak Kaduri was known for his photographic memory and his memorization of the Bible, the Talmud, Rashi and other Jewish writings. He knew Jewish sages and celebrities of the last century and rabbis who lived in the Holy Land and kept the faith alive before the State of Israel was born.
>
> Kaduri was not only highly esteemed because of his age of 108. He was charismatic and wise, and chief rabbis looked up to

him as a *Tsadik*, a righteous man or saint. He would give advice and blessings to everyone who asked. Thousands visited him to ask for counsel or healing. His followers speak of many miracles, and his students say he predicted many disasters....

In an interview with *Israel Today*, Rabbi David Kaduri, the 80-year-old son of the late Rabbi Yitzhak Kaduri, denied that his father left a note with the name Yeshua just before he died. ... David Kaduri confirmed, however, that in his last year, his father had talked and dreamed almost exclusively about the Messiah and His coming. "My father has met the Messiah in a vision," he said, "and told us that he would come soon."

Israel Today was given access to many of the rabbi's manuscripts, written in his own hand for the exclusive use of his students. Most striking were the cross-like symbols painted by Kaduri all over the pages. In the Jewish tradition, one does not use crosses. In fact, even the use of a plus sign is discouraged because it might be mistaken for a cross.

But there they were, scribbled in the rabbi's own hand. When we asked what those symbols meant, Rabbi David Kaduri said they were "signs of the angel." Pressed further about the meaning of "signs of the angel," he said he had no idea. Rabbi David Kaduri went on to explain only that his father had had a spiritual relationship with God and had met the Messiah in his dreams.[13]

While this account is hotly disputed within Israel, it shows the continuing potential for such occurrences, and it builds faith in the saving power of Yeshua. Something is stirring. The promise and timing of God are intersecting—and the intersection is in the shape of a cross!

God is always faithful, and He is particularly faithful when we are faithless. His incredible mercy and grace reach into the darkest places. He reaches hearts, although not without a battle. Here we are, in a time of the maturation of wickedness, which is also a time of the maturation of righteousness. God is a covenant-keeping God. He is true to His Word. When the Church was not yet in existence, He had Isaiah prophesy these now-familiar words:

For Zion's sake I will not keep silent,
   And for Jerusalem's sake I will not keep quiet,
   Until her righteousness goes forth like brightness,
   And her salvation like a torch that is burning.
The nations will see your righteousness,
   And all kings your glory;
   And you will be called by a new name
   Which the mouth of the LORD will designate.
You will also be a crown of beauty in the hand of the
      LORD,
   And a royal diadem in the hand of your God.
It will no longer be said to you, "Forsaken,"
   Nor to your land will it any longer be said,
      "Desolate";
   But you will be called, "My delight is in her,"
   And your land, "Married";
   For the LORD delights in you,
   And to Him your land will be married.
For as a young man marries a virgin,
   So your sons will marry you;
   And as the bridegroom rejoices over the bride,
   So your God will rejoice over you.
On your walls, O Jerusalem, I have appointed
      watchmen;
   All day and all night they will never keep silent
   You who remind the LORD, take no rest for
      yourselves;
   And give Him no rest until He establishes
   And makes Jerusalem a praise in the earth.
                                        Isaiah 62:1–7

Have all kings come to her glory? Not yet. Have all nations streamed to that light? Not yet. With the awakening of Israel, the "not yet" will change. Right now we live in the "until" clause. We do not need to understand all the details to believe it. There is a great end-time awakening in God's heart, and we are seeing the evidence in a parallel movement as both Israel and the Church are awakened to their prophetic destiny.

Part 2

A LOOK AT THE PAST

Historical Perspective

4

The Hunters Are Coming

I will say to the north, "Give them up!"
And to the south, "Do not hold them back."
Bring My sons from afar
And My daughters from the ends of the earth.

Isaiah 43:6

"In eighteen months, 'the hunters' will begin to be released."

The audible voice of the Lord awakened me with these words early on Easter Sunday morning, April 4, 1999. The bedroom in our home, then located in a residential area called Hunters Run in Antioch, Tennessee, was filled with the tangible, manifested presence of God.[1]

More understanding came as I continued to listen that morning. The Holy Spirit began to speak again, telling me that our family would move from our urban residence in Hunters Run to a "place of seclusion." The relocation would affect our family personally, of course, but it would also be a

prophetic act, releasing a statement to many. God was calling for His people to draw closer to Him, to make Him their
secret hiding place and to help others find places of safety in
a time of potential persecution when various people of God
could be "hunted down."

Our geographical move from Hunters Run would serve as
a spiritual barometer of sorts, providing a reading of future
events concerning the Church and the Jewish people. This
Easter morning message was a wake-up call to pray effective,
fervent prayers for a second great exodus of the people of
Israel—before and after "the hunters" would be released.

In the first Jewish Exodus Moses led the people out of
captivity in Egypt, out of slavery, through fierce trials and
sharp losses and eventually to the Promised Land. This second exodus, which had been predicted for centuries by the
prophets, would involve all the ancient players, this time in
modern disguises.

Have We Forgotten What God Remembers?

Twenty-first-century people have forgotten what God remembers. God made a promise to the Jewish people in ancient times, and He intends to keep it:

> "Therefore behold, the days are coming," declares the LORD,
> "when they will no longer say, 'As the LORD lives, who brought
> up the sons of Israel from the land of Egypt,' but, 'As the
> LORD lives, who brought up and led back the descendants
> of the household of Israel *from the north land and from all
> the countries where I had driven them.'* Then they will live on
> their own soil."
>
> Jeremiah 23:7–8, emphasis mine

Many well-meaning Christians have concluded that the
Jewish people and the modern state of Israel play no role
in the fulfillment of biblical prophecy, while others set their

66

end-time prophecy clocks by what happens in Israel. Many of these opinions are based upon how the Jewish people themselves view and react to Jesus the Messiah. It is true that no one can be saved apart from repentance and faith in Him, but we quickly forget that each of us was lost before the Lord pursued and found us in His mercy.

God's dealings with the children of Israel involve His faithfulness more than their faithfulness. We should examine carefully God's promises and predictions concerning the Jewish people on the basis of who made those promises, not on whether or not the recipients of the promises deserve them. No one deserves the mercy and grace of God, but He extends them to all of us anyway. God remembers His promises, and He keeps them to the thousandth generation (see Deuteronomy 7:9 and Psalm 105:8), and He made some promises about the Jewish people that have yet to come to pass. As you will see, we are right in the middle of their fulfillment today.

We are living in a "hinge" period of time. At the moment a door of destiny is open for the Jewish people. That door may soon close forever unless God's people pray. Whether by a gentle wooing or a rude shaking, God wants to gather Jerusalem under His wings (see Luke 13:34).

Two Great Regatherings

God's promise in Jeremiah 23 (above) echoes an earlier passage by the prophet:

> "Therefore behold, days are coming," declares the LORD, "when it will no longer be said, 'As the LORD lives, who brought up the sons of Israel out of the land of Egypt,' but, 'As the LORD lives, who brought up the sons of Israel *from the land of the north and from all the countries where He had banished them.*' For I will restore them to *their own land which I gave to their fathers.*"
>
> Jeremiah 16:14–15, emphasis mine

These Scriptures speak of two great regatherings of the Jewish people from dispersion back to Israel. One took place in Moses' day and is described in the book of Exodus. The other must happen after the arrival of the Messiah and before His return.

Throughout the centuries, God has delivered or restored small remnants of Jewish people from places of captivity to Jerusalem for specific purposes. We see this, for example, in the life and ministry of Nehemiah, the prophet, when God opened the way for him to return from Babylonian captivity with a remnant to rebuild the walls of Jerusalem. Yet none of these restorations meets the criteria for the great ingathering of which Jeremiah spoke, the one in which the Jewish people come "from the land of the north and from all the countries where He had banished them."

The late Bible teacher Derek Prince defined "the land of the north" in his book, *The Last Word on the Middle East*:

> Yet a day is coming, declares Jeremiah, when this great Passover deliverance will pale into insignificance by comparison with the second ingathering of the Jewish people from all lands—particularly from the land of the north, which includes Germany, Poland and Russia.[2]

A glance at a map confirms that Eastern Europe is part of the land of the north. Moscow, the capital of Russia and the former seat of Communism, lies 1,660 miles north and just two degrees longitude east of Jerusalem.

More about the Coming Exodus

I believe that this last-day ingathering, this second great exodus of the Jewish people from the land of the north, will eclipse the first great Exodus from Egypt in both magnitude and scope, and that we will see even greater miraculous signs and wonders. More than one million Jewish people have already immigrated to Israel from the land of the north since the reestablishment of the nation of Israel sixty years ago. That means, however, that only about one-third of the Jewish people living in the northern regions of the world have made *aliyah* (literally, "going up") to their ancient homeland in Israel. Meanwhile, the door of opportunity is beginning to close in the republics of the former Soviet Union. The "bear" is on the rise once again.

God's people have a biblical and moral responsibility to pray. We must act upon His will for the descendants of Abraham, Isaac and Jacob. As the recipients of the benefits of His love through us, many Jewish people will come to know and receive Jesus Christ as the Messiah of promise.

The Lord always uses the hearts and hands of man to accomplish His will in the earth. After all, Paul, the beloved apostle of our Lord and Savior, called us co-workers with Christ Jesus. God spelled out in advance what He would do and how He would accomplish it. This passage can be found in the second part of Jeremiah's prophecy about the Jewish remnant:

> "Behold, I am going to send for many *fishermen*," declares the LORD, "and *they will fish for them*; and afterwards I will send for many *hunters*, and *they will hunt them* from every mountain and every hill and from the clefts of the rocks."
>
> Jeremiah 16:16, emphasis mine

Fishermen Lure; Hunters Drive

Some people who are otherwise well versed in the Bible raise their eyebrows in surprise when the subject of "fishers and hunters" comes up. What is Jeremiah talking about? Fishermen use bait to lure and entice something to a desired place. Hunters drive and chase down their quarry, and the ultimate goal is destruction.

God extends mercy before He releases judgment. He has called the descendants of Abraham, Isaac and Jacob to return to their homeland. First He has sent benevolent fishermen to encourage, woo and entice the Jewish people to obey God's call. These fishermen are benevolent because they wish only good for the Jewish people. Their mission is to extend mercy and deliverance toward a divine destiny and away from impending danger. The fishermen are part of the "gentle awakening" that I described in the second chapter of this book who act as prophetic forerunners in the Holy Spirit.

And the hunters? Historically they appear to be the violent ones. They come after the fishermen have tried to lure the people to safety. We will cover this in greater detail in the following chapters. God will use the hunters to drive out the Jewish people, to reverse their dispersion to faraway lands, to bring them back home. This involves strife and real threats, even destruction and death.

The Jewish people in Europe received advance warning about Hitler and the Nazi party from many fishermen. Only a few heeded the warning. The day came in 1938 when Hitler released his Gestapo and SS hunters to hunt down and round up every Jewish person they could find. Their goal was the absolute annihilation of the Jewish people. Hitler, among others who hate the Jewish people, was one of a long line of hunters. Without a doubt, such hunters are part of the rude awakening that has to follow the warning of the fishermen.

The Second Great Exodus

As a Christian, what is my role in this second great exodus? What is yours? I believe that in this new millennium a revolution is underway in the Church. A crucial component of this revolution involves a remnant of the Church that will capture the Father's passion for the Jewish people, His ancient covenant people. I believe God will breathe life upon this ancient prophecy of Zechariah:

I will pour out on the house of David and on the inhabitants of Jerusalem, the Spirit of grace and of supplication, so that they will look on *Me whom they have pierced; and they will mourn for Him, as one mourns for an only son, and they will weep bitterly over Him like the bitter weeping over a firstborn.*

Zechariah 12:10, emphasis mine

I realize that this passage has at least two theological interpretations, but in my view, this prophetic promise speaks both to the Church and to Israel in a parallel understanding. Jesus is the Son of David, and the Church makes up in part "the house of David" (see Acts 15:15–17). Gentile followers of Christ are "of the house and lineage of David" because they have been grafted into the Vine, Jesus Christ.

Many Christian leaders stop here, but in the Bible the prophet goes on to say, "and the inhabitants of Jerusalem." We could make a serious mistake by ignoring the literal meaning and application of this prophetic passage, especially when we are living in the middle of its fulfillment. You flat out cannot interpret the city of "Jerusalem" as the "Church"; it is not proper biblical interpretation.

Ancient Foes in Disguise

From the earliest times our enemy, Satan, has tried to hunt down the Jewish people and obliterate them. He hates Israel, the covenant people of God, and all that they stand for. He wants to erase all traces of Israel. In subsequent chapters I will lay out much of this history for you, inglorious but necessary.

As a people, Israel has suffered one conquest after another. Families have been torn apart, and faith in the God of Abraham, Isaac and Jacob has almost succumbed under the crusades and pogroms and absorption into foreign cultures. Within our living memory, we have had the Holocaust in Europe as well as catastrophic warfare in the Middle East. Within biblical memory, we know about enslavement and

71

exile, apostasy and attempted genocide. An alliance of hatred has perpetrated these demonic horrors.

Alliance of Hatred

Today there is a renewed alliance of hatred. You will recognize the names of some of these evil allies. They have been allied in the past in their hatred of God's people.

Consider the following prophetic psalm, which many Bible teachers agree has yet to be fulfilled. Nowhere in this passage do we see "Egypt," which would make us think of the first Exodus, or even "the land of the north," which could apply to persecution and emigration in more recent times. Look at this particular alliance of hatred against Israel:

> O God, do not remain quiet;
>> Do not be silent and, O God, do not be still.
> For behold, Your enemies make an uproar,
>> And those who hate You have exalted themselves.
> They make shrewd plans against Your people,
>> And conspire together against Your treasured
>> ones.
> They have said, "Come, and let us wipe them out as a
>> nation,
>> That the name of Israel be remembered no more."
> For they have conspired together with one mind;
>> Against You they make a covenant:
> The tents of Edom and the Ishmaelites,
>> Moab and the Hagrites;
> Gebal and Ammon and Amalek,
>> Philistia with the inhabitants of Tyre;
> Assyria also has joined with them;
>> They have become a help to the children of Lot. . . .
>> Pursue them with Your tempest
>> And terrify them with Your storm.
> Fill their faces with dishonor,
>> That they may seek Your name, O LORD.

Let them be ashamed and dismayed forever,
And let them be humiliated and perish,
That they may know that You alone, whose name is
the LORD,
Are the Most High over all the earth.

Psalm 83:1–8, 15–18

In her book *Why Care About Israel?* Sandra Teplinsky explains this psalm in more detail:

Verses 5–8 tell how every nation in the neighborhood (except Egypt) unites against Israel: Edom and the Ishmaelites (southern Jordan and Saudi Arabia); Moab (central Jordan) and the Hagrites (Syria and Arabia); Gebal (southern Jordan); Ammon (central Jordan) and Amalek (Sinai desert); Philistia (Gaza Strip area); Tyre (southern Lebanon) and Assyria (Syria/Iraq). Verse 4 sounds their bellicose battle cry: "Come . . . Let us destroy them as a nation, that the name of Israel be remembered no more."[3]

Doesn't this line sound familiar? "Come, and let us wipe them out as a nation, that the name of Israel be remembered no more." Haven't we heard that quite often lately? It should make us think of statements from the likes of Mahmoud Ahmadinejad, who has been president of Iran (modern-day Persia) since August 2007, and from spokesmen for the anti-Semitic Hamas party, who won the majority of legislative seats in the governing council of the Palestinian Authority in January 2006, and whose charter calls for the destruction of the State of Israel in favor of a Palestinian Islamic state in Israel, the West Bank and the Gaza Strip.[4]

"Let us wipe them out as a nation" has been the rallying cry of the enemies of Zion from King Nebuchadnezzar to Emperor Hadrian to President Ahmadinejad. The members of the conspiracy have evolved over time, but the goals have remained the same: always, first and foremost, a conspiracy against God Himself (see verse 5).

73

The ancient place names have been replaced now with names such as Lebanon, Iraq, Syria and Saudi Arabia, countries that have supported the terrorist activities of Hezbollah (the political/paramilitary organization based in Lebanon) or Iran, financiers of al-Qaeda (the radical Islamic terrorist coalition responsible for the 9/11 attacks).

The ancient palace protocols and weaponry have been replaced with new ones, possibly even nuclear weapons. No "peace process" will deflect these. A leader of Hamas said at a rally in Gaza: "They have tried to pressure Hamas to abandon resistance and to abandon arms . . . but they failed. Hamas will not change its constant principles. Hamas will stay faithful to jihad, to resistance, to guns, to Palestine."[5]

Same Song, Second Verse

Psalm 83 echoes the rhetoric we hear multiple times a day over the wire services and the Internet. The same psalm also provides us with words to pray. In addition to praying for "the peace of Jerusalem" (Psalm 122:6), we can pray for God to act against her foes. We can invest ourselves in the battle, fasting and praying for God to defend His people, and to open their hearts to His Son:

> In that day the LORD will defend the inhabitants of Jerusalem, and the one who is feeble among them in that day will be like David, and the house of David will be like God, like the angel of the LORD before them. And in that day I will set about to destroy all the nations that come against Jerusalem. I will pour out on the house of David and on the inhabitants of Jerusalem, the Spirit of grace and of supplication, so that they will look on Me whom they have pierced; and they will mourn for Him, as one mourns for an only son, and they will weep bitterly over Him like the bitter weeping over a firstborn.
>
> Zechariah 12:8–10

74

It is all connected, as you will be able to see if you hang in here with me and reach the end of this book. All the centuries of strife and conflict, all the many key players, whether nations or individuals, and all the evil alliances are connected with each other. If we examine the evidence, even present-day news stories reveal new connections. Could it be, for example, that present-day Hamas can be connected to the "land of the north" in the ancient prophecies? After all, politically and militarily, Hamas is backed by Syria, which is backed by Iran, which is in turn backed by Russia—in the north. Do the dots connect or not? Time will tell for sure.

All of Abraham's Descendants

By the way, when we are talking about the fulfillment of prophecy and about prayer, we should always remember the other people groups who have descended from Abraham. Abraham had more children after Ishmael and Isaac. After Sarah died when her son, Isaac, was forty years old, Abraham married Keturah, who bore him many children. Here is how I explained it in my book *Praying for Israel's Destiny*:

> Before Abraham died he gave gifts to the sons of Keturah and sent them far away from his son Isaac, to the land of the east (see Genesis 25:6). One of the sons of Keturah was Midian, the father of the Midianites. Some of the descendants of Keturah went to what was called Persia. Others were, apparently, scattered into Assyria.[6]

Abraham sent a blessing with all of his sons. Isaiah prophesied about some of them:

> A multitude of camels will cover you [Israel],
> The young camels of Midian and Ephah;
> All those from Sheba will come;

75

They will bring gold and frankincense,
And will bear good news of the praises of the
LORD.

Isaiah 60:6

Could it be that the wise men who brought gold, frankincense and myrrh to the infant Jesus were descendants of Keturah? No one can say for sure, but that line from Isaiah seems to make a connection. At the least, the descendants of Abraham and Keturah have a prophetic destiny. And if we consider another one of Isaiah's prophecies, we can see all of Abraham's children being regathered:

> In that day there will be an altar to the LORD in the midst of the land of Egypt, and a pillar to the LORD near its border. [Hagar was an Egyptian, and she found Ishmael an Egyptian wife.] It will become a sign and a witness to the LORD of hosts in the land of Egypt; for they will cry to the LORD because of oppressors, and He will send them a Savior and a Champion, and He will deliver them. . . .
>
> In that day there will be a highway from Egypt to Assyria, and the Assyrians will come into Egypt and the Egyptians into Assyria, and the Egyptians will worship with the Assyrians.
>
> In that day Israel will be the third party with Egypt and Assyria, a blessing in the midst of the earth, whom the LORD of hosts has blessed, saying, "Blessed is Egypt My people, and Assyria the work of My hands, and Israel My inheritance."

Isaiah 19:19–20, 23–25

I also said in *Praying for Israel's Destiny*:

> There will be, according to Isaiah, a highway from Egypt to Assyria, and people will go freely back and forth—probably right through the middle of Israel—worshiping God together. . . . After much pressure, and the probability of an all-out war in the Middle East, God will make Himself known to the Arabic peoples and they will turn to Him. Isaiah described the length

to which they will go: "They will even worship with sacrifice and offering, and will make a vow to the LORD and perform it" (Isaiah 19:21). . . .

Notice that this move of God will also impact Assyria: Turkey, Iraq, Iran and other Middle Eastern territories. . . .

Imagine: The very area of Asia Minor where the early Church of Jesus Christ once flourished will rise again out of the ashes into genuine, vibrant worship. Lands that appear to be held captive to the devil through Islam will be delivered and cleansed of their impurity. After thousands of years of broken promises, hatred and enmity between Arabs and Jews, this will truly be a glorious day—a day in history when the curse is reversed and the blessing of the Lord emerges.[7]

The Spirit of Haman

This brings us to another fascinating connection that we would be well advised to make. In ways too numerous to count, it is as if the genocidal, specifically anti-Semitic spirit of Haman has stepped from the book of Esther into new death-dealing entities, not the least of which is Hamas. The similar-sounding names are no accident.

I write this about Haman on my Prayer Storm website:

Haman's lineage is significant. . . . He was a descendant of Agag, who was a king of the Amalekites in the days of Saul and Samuel. Saul defeated Agag but disobeyed the Lord by allowing him to live. . . . Being an Amalekite, Agag was part of the group of people who were long-term enemies of Israel. Because of their treatment of the children of Israel in the days of Moses, God declared war on Amalek "from generation to generation" (Exodus 17:16). In Jewish teaching, Amalek is seen as the epitome of anti-Semitism.

Haman therefore had a heritage of enmity toward the Jewish people. As the book of Esther unfolds, we see how Haman was used to exhibit this generational hatred toward God's chosen people.

77

The problem is that this ancient, malevolent spirit has plagued our planet throughout the generations. It has no regard for human reason, logic, good intentions or mere religious pursuits. This dark spirit of anti-Semitism—or what may be called "the spirit of Haman"—is on the loose once again.[8]

Haman himself is long gone, hanged on the gallows he had built for Mordecai. But it is as if his brother Hamas has risen up in his place. Hamas has its origins in the Moslem Brotherhood, which was founded to protect the purity of the Islamic faith. But by 1987, after the Islamic revolution in Iran, it had developed into a militant political organization. And once again, as in Haman's day in the court of the Persian King Ahasueras (Xerxes), it is a Persian "king," the president of Iran, Mahmoud Ahmadinejad, who allows Hamas free rein.

What is the goal of Hamas? To destroy the State of Israel and to reclaim the land as Islamic territory. Their tactics? Suicide bombings and other means of calculated, fear-inducing violence, largely against civilians. Infiltrated by a powerful Hamas, the peace of Jerusalem has become fragile indeed.

It is as if somebody pushed a "replay" button, except for one thing: Where is Mordecai? Where is Esther? Where are the God-inspired strategies that can pull down the spirit of Haman?

If God is to prevail in the Middle East, He must first prevail in the hearts of Gentile Christians and their Messianic Jewish counterparts, inspiring concerted prayer, fasting and strategic action. The hunters are already active, and more hunters are right behind them. An edict has gone forth. Will Mordecai step forward to inform and to summon the people? Will the Church (the Bride, therefore Esther) beautify herself and covenant to fast and pray? Who will be bold enough to volunteer?

The Eighteen Months

In 2000, when Ehud Barak was the prime minister of Israel, opposition leader Ariel Sharon paid a visit to the mosque of the Temple Mount in Jerusalem's Old City. Ostensibly, the purpose of his visit was to reaffirm that the holy site would remain under Israeli control, and it was not meant as a provocation. The Palestinians, however, certainly took it as a provocation, and riots broke out. Within a few days it became clear that the peace process had broken down.

Arabs point to Sharon's visit as the beginning of the second *intifada,* or concerted, armed uprising of the Palestinians against Israel. What followed was an unending stream of suicide bombings and other "incidents." Ariel Sharon was elected prime minister in 2001, and he served until he was felled by a stroke in April of 2006 and was replaced by his deputy, Ehud Olmert. This second intifada rages on to this day.

Sharon's visit to the Temple Mount took place on September 28, 2000. Interestingly enough, this is almost exactly eighteen months after I heard the words with which I began this chapter: "In eighteen months 'the hunters' will begin to be released."

What "hunters" were released at this time? As it turned out, many of these modern-day hunters are allied with Hamas, which assumed new power in early 2006.

The anti-Semitic spirit of Haman the Agagite had been elevated once again to a false seat of honor and authority (see Esther 3:1).

The Next Moves

The only non-futile response to this development is the same response of Mordecai and Esther: Purim-style prayer and fasting led by God-inspired generals with heavenly strategies. It is all right for the Jewish people to celebrate Purim as a great victory, which they do. But we must realize that the same genocidal spirit has returned—with reinforcements.

It is time to cry out on behalf of the Jewish people. Again and again, disregarding the personal cost, we must join to-

79

gether to pray and undertake radical fasting so that the evil Haman spirit will not have his way. Please read more about existing efforts in chapters 8 and 11 and in appendix F, as well as on my website, www.israelprayercoalition.com.

Hunters in Parallel

Now, lest we forget about the connection between developments involving Israel and those involving the Church, let's take a broader look at what the hunters are doing elsewhere in the world.

About a year after Sharon's visit to the Temple Mount, I happened to be taking a morning shower at home when I heard the words, *The hunters have just been released*, followed by *Go turn on the TV.*

With a sense of foreboding, I pulled on my clothes and ran into our bedroom and turned on the television. Just as I clicked it on, I saw with my own eyes the Twin Towers fall. It was September 11, 2001.

Since that coordinated al-Qaeda suicide attack, which killed three thousand civilians (many of whom were not Americans), the so-called War on Terror has ensued. As with Hamas and Hezbollah and other fraternities of violence, the perpetrators are radical, anti-Semitic Muslims. Their targets, however, are not limited to Israel and its people. The targets of al-Qaeda are any non-Muslims who represent the face of the West, which includes the Church worldwide.

Osama bin Laden, Ayman al-Zawahiri and others issue statements via videotapes and *fatwas* (a *fatwa* is a legal ruling based on Islamic law). Islamic extremists use such statements to express their view that Islamic law allows them permission to undertake violent acts that might otherwise be illegal. They are hunters. We are the hunted.

In terms of a last-days perspective, what do these hunters do? By extreme means, they drive people to seek refuge.

But where can security be found? Not in the United States, and not even in the Pentagon. What is the best refuge? In the arms of God alone. Collected together within His embrace, fear dissipates. The people of God can hear His heartbeat. From that secure place, prayers arise and aid pours out to help others reach God's refuge before they are annihilated.

Hunters may be used to redemptively drive the Jewish people to return to Israel and/or to accept Yeshua as Messiah. Hunters may be used even to drive non-Jewish people to seek God and His Son and to offer assistance to others who are being hunted. Always remember: Mercy triumphs over judgment!

A New Generation

Previous generations of Christians, if they did not practice outright hostility to their Jewish brethren, lapsed into indifference. By default and passivity, they supported anti-Semitism wherever it appeared, and their failure during World War II will live on in particular infamy.

This new generation, of which you and I are a part, has a huge challenge before it. We must lay aside every preconceived idea, presumption and preference in our effort to involve ourselves in what God says He will do with the Jewish people. As fishermen, we have been sent to warn and lure men and women to places of safety. Because of the hunters, though, we have also been sent to receive and provide for the hunted ones, introducing them to the One who always welcomes His own.

Speaking of places of safety, it did happen personally for us. The Goll family did indeed move from Hunters Run, with the supernatural help of the Lord, to a secluded location near Nashville. (In many ways Nashville is becoming a city of spiritual refuge and material support for those who are friends of Israel.)

We may not have our Hunters Run address anymore, but our time here has not been a retreat from the battle. In fact, we have been confronted by health-related "bombs" and challenges of a demonic nature. But our Lord has also provided for our family a sanctuary from which we can reach out to help provide refuge and strength for both the Church and Israel. I want everyone to hear me loud and clear: "The Lord is victorious and He is good all the time!"

How about you and your family? You cannot afford to be indifferent. The hunters are coming. They are already here. We must find out what role He wants us to play. The future of the world literally hangs in the balance.

What will you do about it?

5

The Birth of a Nation

> Who has heard such a thing? Who has seen such
>   things?
> Can a land be born in one day?
> Can a nation be brought forth all at once?
> As soon as Zion travailed, she also brought forth
>   her sons.
>
> Isaiah 66:8

The well-being of the Jewish people has always hinged on the balance of the level of their obedience to God, His faithful promises to their forefathers and His eternal purpose and love for them. In general terms, when God's people obey Him, they prosper. When they do not, judgment falls upon them.

This principle comes from Deuteronomy 28 and has been repeatedly seen in action in the history of Israel (see Judges 2:6–23). This biblical law of "sowing and reaping" still applies, even under the grace of God received through the finished work of Jesus Christ.

The Jewish History of Suffering

Over the millennia, Jacob's descendants have suffered greatly and have been greatly blessed as well. British Bible teacher Lance Lambert says of them:

> No other nation in the history of mankind has twice been uprooted from its land, scattered to the ends of the earth and then brought back again to that same territory. If the first exile and restoration was remarkable, then the second is miraculous. Israel has twice lost its statehood and its national sovereignty, twice had its capital and hub of religious life destroyed, its towns and cities razed to the ground, its people deported and dispersed, and then twice had it all restored again. Furthermore, no other nation or ethnic group has been scattered to the four corners of the earth, and yet survived as an easily identifiable and recognizable group.[1]

The first exile took place under Babylonian rule. As for the second great exile, Roman forces serving under the Roman commander Titus destroyed and dismantled Jerusalem in August, A.D. 70, exactly as Jesus prophesied 37 years earlier. The Romans killed 600,000 Jewish residents and deported 300,000 more to locations scattered around the Empire.[2]

Sixty-five years later Roman Emperor Hadrian's forces, led by Bar-Cochba, crushed the last Jewish uprising. Those forces hated and persecuted Jewish and Gentile followers of Christ. Some observers believe this might have helped plant early seeds of anti-Semitism in the fledgling Church.

Jerusalem Declared "Off Limits"

Hadrian's hatred for the Jews burned so bright that he changed Jerusalem's name to *Aelia Capitolina* (his given name was Aelius) and declared it "a Roman city forever which no Jew could enter under pain of death." He built a temple to Jupiter on the site of the former temple where sacrifices had been made to Jehovah.[3] Then he renamed the land *Syria Palaestina* (Latin for *Philistia*). Caesar overlooked one "minor" detail: Unlike the powerless gods of Rome, the God of Israel was and is alive and well.

The Jewish people in Jerusalem and Judea were recaptured, died violent deaths or were scattered to distant lands. This second dispersion following the death and resurrection of Jesus the Messiah lasted far longer than the first. It would not end after five hundred—or even a thousand—years.

The devastated city of Jerusalem became the most contested urban real estate on earth, as for two thousand years various nations, empires and religious factions battled for its possession. All the while, its builders and original residents, the Jewish people, were forced to seek refuge in Gentile cities and nations around the world but could call none of them "home." That all changed in one day (as we will learn toward the end of this chapter). Eighteen hundred and thirteen years after the destruction of Jerusalem under Hadrian, a new nation emerged from the birth pangs of World War II and the horrible Holocaust, just as Isaiah prophesied (see the Scripture passage quoted at the beginning of this chapter).

Before every birth must come birth pangs. The Scriptures clearly predicted the two great dispersions and the persecutions they represented. They also describe the regathering of the Jewish people and the rebirth of Israel.

The Rebirth Begins

In 1855, Hudson Taylor, a Christian physician and missionary to China, saw in the Spirit that a great end-time revival would occur in the land of the north. Taylor was full of the Holy Spirit and entirely surrendered to God. Known as a man of great self-denial, heartfelt compassion and powerful prayer, he interceded for the salvation of the Chinese every morning for forty years.

While on a ministry furlough in England, Taylor suddenly stopped in the middle of a sermon and for a few moments stood speechless with his eyes closed. Finally he explained to his audience:

> I have seen a vision. I saw in this vision a great war that will encompass the whole world. I saw this war recess and then start again, actually being two wars. After this, I saw much unrest and revolts that will affect many nations. I saw in some places spiritual awakenings. In Russia I saw there will come a general, all-encompassing, national, spiritual awakening, so great that there could never be another like it. From Russia I saw the awakening spread to many European countries, and then I saw an all-out awakening followed by the coming of Christ.[4]

Twenty-six years later, in 1881, Russia's tsar, Alexander II, was murdered, and his son, Alexander III, succeeded him. Alexander III hated the Jewish people, and that year a "pogrom" (an organized massacre or persecution of Jewish people) swept through Kishinev, the capital of Moldova, adjacent to Romania and Ukraine.

As life for the persecuted Jews became more difficult under the tsar, Zionist ideas about a Jewish homeland gained strength and followers. Some Jewish leaders began to search for a place of refuge, a homeland for the world's displaced Jewish population. The first *aliyah*, or immigration, to Israel took place in 1882. Jewish immigrants established a Jewish colony called *Rishon Lezion*. The term *anti-Semitism* entered the English language in 1882 as well, and it was defined as "hostility toward or discrimination against Jews as a religious, ethnic or racial group."

The First of the Fishermen

During this time of rebirth God sent prophetic voices of Christian and Jewish "fishermen" to His chosen people. These

86

divine messengers never used force; gently and persistently they warned the Jewish people and wooed them toward God's plan to deliver those who took heed. In virtually every case, His goal was to preserve a remnant and return them to their ancient Land of Promise.

In the same year that the first *aliyah* to Israel took place, a prominent Jewish leader named Joseph Rabinowitz journeyed from Kishinev to Palestine (as Israel was called at that time). He was an unofficial delegate representing some like-minded Jews who wanted to see if Palestine was the right place to establish a Jewish homeland.

Rabinowitz was a *Haskala*, or "Enlightenment," Jew who first searched for truth while studying the Talmud with a Chassidic rabbi and later sought understanding through extensive reading of more liberal writings by so-called enlightened Jewish teachers. He deeply loved his people, and disappointments he experienced and witnessed finally convinced him they would find safety among Gentile nations only as long as it was convenient for their unwilling hosts.

During his brief stay in Palestine, Rabinowitz went to the Wailing Wall in Jerusalem at the beginning of a Sabbath day. He watched in dismay as Jews who had gathered there for prayer struggled to worship and weep at the wall amid "the jibes and harassments of the Muslims."[5] (The Sultan of Turkey controlled Palestine at that time from his capital in Constantinople.) The level of desolation Rabinowitz witnessed in the Promised Land shocked him.

What he saw in Palestine, coupled with the situation of the Jewish people in Europe and around the world, greatly troubled him. Just before sunset one evening, Rabinowitz visited the Mount of Olives. He sat down on a slope near Gethsemane.

As he pondered the troubling scene, a passage from the Hebrew New Testament he had read fifteen years earlier flashed in his mind: "So if the Son makes you free, you will be free indeed" (John 8:36). In that moment, he began to realize that Jesus was the King and Messiah, the only One who could save Israel. Rabinowitz returned to his temporary residence, where he read John's gospel. He was struck by John 15:5: "Apart from Me you can do nothing."[6]

Rabinowitz Establishes the First Messianic Congregation

When Rabinowitz returned home he studied the Hebrew New Testament. He later played a key role in distributing Bibles to other Jewish people. In Kishinev he told his Jewish friends about his Mount of Olives experience. He did not claim to know if the land of Palestine was the hope of the Jewish people. Then, touching his chest, he would say, "This is the land, the land of the heart. It is what God wants us to obtain." He would sometimes add, "The key to the Holy Land lies in the hands of our brother, Jesus."[7]

In Kishinev, Rabinowitz and forty families established the world's first modern-day Hebrew-Christian, or Messianic, congregation, called Israelites of the New Covenant.[8] His ministry and writings had great impact in Russia and Europe and were known around the world.

In 1888 Rabinowitz said, "I have two subjects with which I am absorbed: the one, the Lord Jesus Christ, and the other, Israel."[9] A year later while visiting London he said: "Russia is like the ocean; the Jews there are like shipwrecked people; and since by God's mercy my feet are on the Rock (which is Jesus) . . . I am shouting and signaling to my shipwrecked people to flee to the Rock."[10]

The establishment of Rabinowitz's Messianic congregation in Kishinev marks the beginning of the time of fishermen sent to the Jewish people in Europe, and specifically in the land of the north. It was the start of a great paradigm shift!

Herzl Dreams of a Sovereign Jewish State

Fourteen years after Rabinowitz viewed the life-changing sunset in Jerusalem's Mount of Olives, Theodor Herzl, a Jewish attorney and writer, penned an essay titled *Der Judenstaat* ("The Jewish State"). That essay, published in 1896 and subtitled *An Attempt at a Modern Solution to the Jewish Question*, changed the course of Jewish history. Herzl dreamed of reestablishing a sovereign Jewish state on Jewish soil. Under the prophetic anointing of a true fisherman from God (God can speak prophetically through anyone He chooses), Herzl wrote:

> In the world as it is now, and for an indefinite period will probably remain, might precedes right. It is useless, therefore, for us to be loyal patriots, as were the Huguenots, who were forced to migrate. If we could only be left in peace . . . but I think we shall not be left in peace.[11]
>
> The idea [of a Jewish state] must radiate out until it reaches the last wretched nests of our people. They will awaken out of their dull brooding. Then a new meaning will come into the lives of all of us. . . .
>
> Therefore, I believe that a wondrous generation of Jews will spring into existence; the Maccabees will rise again . . . and we shall at last live as free men on our own soil, and die peacefully in our own homes.[12]

Zionist Congress Meets in Basel

In 1897, Herzl orchestrated the first worldwide gathering of Jews since A.D. 70. The delegates to this Zionist Congress, held in Basel, Switzerland, established the World Zionist Organization. Herzl became its first president. (Amazingly, I was in Basel in the fall of 1997, one hundred years to the day after the Zionist Congress first met. I spoke at a prophetic conference held within blocks of the site where Herzl and his Jewish friends gathered.)

In his inaugural address Herzl prophesied, "We are here to lay *the foundation stone* of the house which is to shelter the Jewish Nation."[13] In his diary entry for September 3, 1897, shortly after he returned from the Zionist Congress, Herzl went one step further and declared:

> Were I to sum up the Basel Congress in a few words—which I shall guard against pronouncing publicly—it would be this: "At Basel I founded the Jewish State." If I said this out loud today I would be answered by universal laughter. Perhaps in five years, and certainly in fifty, everyone will know it.[14]

Rabinowitz was right. In November 1947, fifty years later, the United Nations General Assembly decided to recognize the right of the Jewish people to have their own state.

God raised up and released fishermen to pursue and save the Jewish people in both the religious and secular realms. Both Rabinowitz and Herzl brought hope and direction to their people, but the work of Rabinowitz revealed the greater plan of the God of Abraham, Isaac and Israel.

Britain's Role in Israel's History

The shadows of World War I settled on the nations of the world even as God's fishermen began to draw His people back to their biblical homeland. Yet the borders and gates of Israel remained in the antagonistic grip of the Turks until God supernaturally intervened.

During the war, Britain ran out of acetone, which is a component used to gelatinize a highly explosive mixture of nitroglycerin, guncotton and a petroleum substance called cordite. Cordite was the primary element of explosives at that time.[15] Until war broke out, Britain had purchased all of its acetone from Germany, now its principal enemy. The acetone shortage literally put the entire nation at risk. In desperation, Winston Churchill, then the first lord of the admiralty, summoned a brilliant Jewish chemist named Chaim Weizmann to the British War Office. He asked him to develop a synthetic version of cordite that did not require acetone and placed every available government facility at his disposal.

While British forces under General Edmund Allenby battled Turkish troops for control of Palestine, Dr. Weizmann developed and produced 30,000 tons of an acetone-free synthetic cordite that was even more explosive than the original version. When Weizmann was asked what he wanted in return for his vital service to Great Britain, he said, *"If Britain wins the battle for Palestine,* I ask for a national home for my people in their ancient land."[16] Chaim Weizmann would later become the first president of the reborn nation of Israel.[17]

Weizmann received his answer on November 2, 1917, when British Foreign Minister Arthur James Balfour issued a statement on behalf of the British government, with the approval of the Cabinet:

> His Majesty's Government views with favour the establishment in Palestine of a national home for the Jewish people, and will use their best endeavors to facilitate the achievement of this object, it being clearly understood that nothing shall be done which may prejudice the civil and religious rights of existing non-Jewish communities in Palestine, or the rights and political status enjoyed by Jews in any other country.[18]

Through a miracle on December 11, 1917, General Allenby took possession of Jerusalem without firing a single shot. Before entering what is called the Old City, the general sent planes over Jerusalem during daylight hours to learn the size and deployment of the Turkish troops within its walls. He also had the planes drop leaflets calling for the Turks to surrender, and for some reason the Turkish forces fled the city during the night.

Author Ramon Bennett reported:

> The dropped leaflets, signed with the name of "Allenby," were taken by the Turkish Muslims to be a directive from "Allah"

for them to leave the city. No shots were fired in the capture of the Old City of Jerusalem. General Allenby, a devout Christian, would not ride his horse into the city. He dismounted, and cap in hand, led his horse and his troops into the City of the Great King.[19]

Britain finally forced Turkey to sign an armistice in October of 1918. The area the world called Palestine was in British hands.

At the end of the war Britain was given a mandate, or official authority, to administer most of the Middle East. After years of political maneuvering and high-level betrayals, more than 70 percent of the land promised to the Jewish people was placed in Arab hands and named "Trans-Jordan." Yet there was One who remembered His promises to the Jewish people. He was unmoved by riches, politics or the schemes of men and nations; and His promises would come to pass.

The British government imposed severe immigration quotas on Jewish immigrants who wanted to go to the Promised Land. Yet despite seemingly impossible obstacles, determined Zionist groups defied the quotas and established colonies in *Eretz Israel* ("the land of Israel").

The World's Birth Pangs

The nation of Israel's labor pangs grew stronger and more violent with each decade, signaling that birth was imminent. As always, the dragon of old waited and schemed to destroy the divine seed of God's will before its birth or immediately after delivery.

While the voices of many fishermen such as Herzl raised the alarm of danger to the Jewish people in Germany, Russia and the Balkans, only a fraction of those people heeded the warning. Meanwhile the world went through violent labor pangs of its own.

92

In Russia, the doctrines of Marx, Lenin and Trotsky ignited fires of violent change. In 1917 those fires plunged Russia into the darkness of atheistic Communism, producing an ungodly broth in opposition to both Christians and Jews.

Meanwhile Germany struggled with economic and social woes after its humiliating loss in World War I. A little-known man from Austria (born seven years after Rabinowitz had pondered the truth of the Messiah on the Mount of Olives) penned a journal of hate called *Mein Kampf.* He rapidly rose in Germany's political ranks on a wicked wave of anti-Semitism and his extremist nationalistic doctrine of Aryan supremacy. The man's name was Adolf Hitler, and he is one more in a long line of historical examples of a hunter who has been released. As his grip closed on the reins of the German government, nation after nation ignored Hitler and the Nazi phenomenon. Leader after leader overlooked the growing army of Brown Shirts that surrounded the Nazi kingpin.

But the One who never sleeps knew what was afoot. Once again He sent fishermen to warn His people before the coming trauma was fully released.

Jeb Zabotinsky was one such fisherman. An early Jewish pioneer in Israel, he traveled in 1933 throughout Europe—and Germany in particular—warning, "There is no future for you here. Come back to your land while the doors are still open."[20] Thousands heeded the admonitions of Zabotinsky and others to flee the north, but millions of Jewish people in Germany, Austria and the Balkan countries did not.

Nuremburg and Concentration Camps

Hitler came into power that same year and issued the Nuremburg Decrees, which denied Germany's Jews any legal or citizens' rights. In the years that followed he removed even more rights as he gained and consolidated power, first as Germany's chancellor, and then as *Fuhrer* (literally "the leader").

93

While the world observed, Hitler established five concentration camps for Jewish people within Germany's borders (they included two sites that would gain horrendous infamy: Buchenwald and Dachau).[21] He claimed that his actions were legal under international law, since the camps dealt with an internal problem that had nothing to do with the citizens of other nations. Most world leaders accepted this argument, reasoning that the Jewish people had no country or government per se.

By 1938, Hitler felt his power was strong enough to defy world opinion on a larger scale, so he suddenly "annexed" neighboring Austria into his Third Reich in what was called the *Anschluss*. The book *Operation Exodus II* aptly depicts the scene: "Overnight Hitler did in Austria what took him five years to do in Germany. He took away all the rights of the Jewish people, confiscating their businesses and instituting his atrocities immediately."[22]

The League of Nations, the toothless precursor to the United Nations, had neither the power nor the will to stand up against the bully ruling Germany. When the League of Nations failed to act, American President Franklin D. Roosevelt called a meeting of national leaders. He wanted them to discuss ways to rescue the Jewish people from Germany and Austria.

Fifteen weeks after the taking of Austria, representatives of 32 nations met in Evian-Les-Bains, France. On July 6, 1938, the conferees argued for hours over which delegate would chair the meeting. Moreover, after two days of halfhearted wrangling, no nation, not even Great Britain or the United States, was willing to take in more than a token number of Jewish immigrants. Hitler sent spies to monitor the opinions and determinations of the nations represented in Evian.

Nazis Begin the Holocaust

According to author Steve Lightle, Hitler's spies reported to the Fuhrer, "You can do anything you want to the Jews; the

94

whole world does not want them." Lightle said that one German newspaper, referring to a Nazi plan to sell Jewish lives to the nations at the meeting, declared in a headline, "Jews For Sale, Who Wants Them? No One."[23]

Once Hitler's spies confirmed that none of the nations whose representatives met at Evian were prepared to protect or offer sanctuary to more than a few Jewish people from Germany, Austria or Eastern Europe, Hitler knew that nothing stood in the way of the "Final Solution." Evidently the report also convinced Hitler that he was dealing with sheep, because less than two months later Germany's armies engulfed Poland in a *blitzkrieg*, or "lightning war," and catapulted the world into World War II. Barely one month later the Germans went on a rampage of their own called *Kristallnacht* ("Crystal Night"), during which they smashed the windows of synagogues, Jewish businesses and homes, marking the full-scale beginning of the Holocaust.

By 1942, Hitler was ready to expand his extermination of Jewish people beyond the borders of Germany and Austria to include all of Europe. At the Wannsee meeting in Berlin, he essentially authorized the total annihilation of the Jewish population in Europe, exactly as he envisioned in his demonically inspired book, *Mein Kampf*. The Nazi war machine brutally murdered six million defenseless European Jews before it was finally stopped in 1945. Pastor Ulf Ekman of Sweden wrote in his book *The Jews: People of the Future*:

> There are no words to describe the suffering it inflicted. It is impossible to depict the wretchedness and misery in its wake. That it was perpetrated at all is heinous. That it was committed by a nation that was considered the cultural elite of Europe is incomprehensible; and that it was done by Christians is a shame beyond words.[24]

First God sent Jewish and Gentile fishers to warn the Jewish people of their danger, but only an estimated 600,000 heeded the warning in time to flee. Once the hunters gained momentum, they exterminated two-thirds of the nine million remaining Jews. Not one nation represented at the Evian meetings had clean hands. Nor, as we shall see in the next chapter, was the Church guiltless in this unspeakable tragedy.

In spite of the hatred that led to the massacre of six million Jewish victims, God still had a plan to restore His ancient covenant people to their land. The world would learn firsthand that nothing and no one could stand in His way.

The nations of the world were shocked to see images of the atrocities carried out by Hitler's henchmen at German concentration camps in Buchenwald, Dachau, Bergen and Belsen. For a brief window of time after the end of World War II, people in most of the Allied countries softened their attitudes toward the Jewish people who survived the Holocaust.

Fighting the "Other War"

Throughout World War II the British had fought another war of sorts: a war to end Arab-Jewish conflict in the Holy Land. Still administering official authority in the Middle East, the British were caught in an age-old struggle. The Arabs rejected Jewish immigration by conducting a nonstop campaign of vandalism and terrorism against the settlers. To defend themselves against the Arabs, the settlers organized underground vigilante and defense groups such as the *Irgun*, the *Stern Gang* and the *Hagana*. At first most of these groups limited their activities to defense only, but as Arab atrocities increased, the Jewish groups kept pace (especially the violent Stern Gang). In an effort to appease the Arabs, the British limited Jewish immigration to the Promised Land. Despite Britain's best efforts to stop them by imposing severe quotas on Jewish immigrants, the Hagana worked tirelessly to help rescue desperate refugees from the Holocaust in Europe.

By 1947, the British occupation forces and the British people were so exhausted with the struggle that the Empire returned the "Palestine problem" to the United Nations. A U.N. committee was formed to investigate and eventually recommended to the General Assembly that the Promised Land be divided, or "partitioned," equally between the Jews and the Arabs.

What happened next could only be attributed to the intervention of God.

Russia, hungry for the petroleum reserves in the Middle East, desperately wanted to see Great Britain remove its military forces from the region. The best way to make that happen was to back Israel's desire for independence. In his book *The Miracle of Israel*, the late Gordon Lindsay, founder of Christ For The Nations, described what happened next:

> The Russians, witnessing Britain's dilemma, had secretly facilitated the migration of 100,000 refugees through Central Europe. Soviet officials helped them get on ships at Black Sea ports. Andrei Gromyko, Soviet foreign deputy of the U.S.S.R., pled their case before the U.N. saying:
>
>> It would be unjust if we deny the Jews the right to realize these aspirations to a state of their own. During the last war the Jewish people underwent indescribable suffering. Thousands are still behind barbed wire. The time has come to help these people not by words but deeds.
>
> Because the Russian bloc voted in favor of the Jews (vote 21–20), the Jews gained the right to plead their case before the U.N.[25]

A Day for Jewish People to Rejoice

That day in that subcommittee marked the first time in U.N. history that the U.S.S.R. and the United States jointly supported a major decision. Finally the Partition Plan came to a

97

vote in the General Assembly, where a two-thirds majority was needed for passage. Jewish people in Israel and around the world kept their ears glued to their radios. The U.N. resolution to partition the land and allow the Jewish people to reestablish the nation of Israel passed on November 29, 1947, and Jewish people around the world danced for joy.

Within three days more than 40 million Arabs pitted themselves against the 600,000 Jews already living in Israel. Declaring a holy war, or *jihad*, Arab leaders publicly vowed, "We are going to kill all Jews or drive them into the sea."[26] They were so confident that they warned all the Arabs who were living peacefully within the borders of the Jewish partition to move out of their homes for a few days until the Jewish people were wiped out. Ironically, this is the true origin of the Palestinian refugees.

The battle for survival went on for months during the time between the U.N. vote authorizing the partition of the Promised Land and the final withdrawal of Britain from the region. As it prepared to end its administration, the British government did little to stop the violence, but it was careful to continue deporting every Jewish immigrant who did not have a visa. Only the determination and organization of the Hagana defenders saved the Jewish people from annihilation in their own land.

Israel Becomes a Nation

In the U.N., opponents to the formation of a Jewish state worked feverishly to stop Israel from declaring independence, but they became entangled in red tape. At one minute past midnight on May 15, 1948, the British mandate ended and the nation of Israel was reborn.

While Israel's opponents continued to argue in the U.N., they were interrupted with the announcement that U.S. President Harry S. Truman officially recognized the new state of Israel and extended full diplomatic privileges. The U.S.S.R., eager to make sure the British never returned to the Middle East, shocked the world by quickly recognizing the nation of Israel as well![27]

Tiny Israel and its fledgling army of six thousand men desperately prepared to face the Arab armies. The same day that the nation of Israel was reborn, the Arab nations surrounding Israel—Egypt, Transjordan (present-day Jordan), Syria, Lebanon and Iraq—attacked. Israel survived her war for independence, but she did not gain full control of her capital city. The city of Jerusalem was subsequently divided in two, and Israel controlled only half (the Arabs controlling the other half) until the Six-Day War in 1967. [For a more detailed explanation of this period in Israel's history, see appendix B, "Overview of Israel's History."]

Gordon Lindsay wrote:

> On December 4, 1948, thousands gathered around the tomb of Herzl, raised their right hand and took the oath, "If I forget thee, O Jerusalem, let my right hand forget her cunning." Mr. David Ben-Gurion summed up the feelings of the people of Jerusalem and all Israel when he declared, "Israel's position on the question of Jerusalem found a clear and final expression in statements by the government and all parties of the Knesset [the Israeli equivalent of Congress or Parliament] on December 5. Jerusalem is an inseparable part of Israel, and her eternal capital."[28]

Yes, Jerusalem is in the center of God's heart and attention. It is the only city mentioned in the entire Bible for which all peoples in all generations are to pray by name. The existence of Jerusalem under Jewish rule is a modern-day miracle—an authentic fulfillment of the prophetic Word of the Lord. Indeed, the jealousy of God rests over the destiny of this great city. Prophecy is written about this walled ancient dwelling place. Our posture toward the reunification of the city of Jerusalem under Jewish rule is important to God. And what is important to God must become important to His people.

Yes, this is Israel, the only nation on earth to be born in a day through the supernatural intervention of God. He prepared the ancient home for His displaced covenant people; now He is once again sending out fishermen to forewarn the Jewish people dwelling in the land of the north of a growing danger lurking in the land.

The fishermen are calling, "Come forth now! Come forth from the land of the north! Come from the four corners of the earth!"

6

Touching the Apple of God's Eye

"Ho there! Flee from the land of the north," declares the LORD, "for I have dispersed you as the
four winds of the heavens," declares the LORD.
"Ho, Zion! Escape, you who are living with the
daughter of Babylon."
For thus says the LORD of hosts, "After glory He
has sent me against the nations which plunder
you, for he who touches you, touches the apple
of His eye."

Zechariah 2:6–8

Tom Hess, an international prayer leader and a modern-day
fisherman of God, remembers seeing an inscription on a wall
in the Nazi death camp at Auschwitz quoting the philosopher
Santayana: "He who does not learn from the lessons of history

is doomed to repeat them."[1] This statement could qualify as a prophecy for the Church.

Virtually everyone has heard about the Holocaust of World War II in which Adolf Hitler and the Third Reich murdered six million Jewish people in cold blood. Few people know that professed Christians, as has happened many times throughout history, helped birth and carry out that organized murder! In fact, Hitler modeled some of his most heinous anti-Semitic schemes on official policies drafted centuries earlier by Roman Catholic and Protestant leaders.[2] Even though most Christians in Europe did not pull a trigger, release poison gas or burn the crime evidence, nearly all of them looked the other way. A few believers aided the Jewish people, and some shared concentration camp cells and died alongside their Jewish brethren—but most did not.

Dr. Michael L. Brown, a theologian and Jewish disciple of the Messiah, quotes Eliezer Berkovits, a respected Jewish thinker, about the "moral and spiritual bankruptcy" of Christian religion and civilization:

> After nineteen centuries of Christianity, the extermination of six million Jews, among them one-and-a-half million children, carried out in cold blood in the very heart of Christian Europe, encouraged by the criminal silence of virtually all Christendom, including that of an infallible Holy Father in Rome, was the natural culmination of this bankruptcy. A straight line leads from the first act of oppression against the Jews and Judaism in the fourth century to the Holocaust in the twentieth.[3]

At the time of this writing, the beginning of the 21st century, survivors of the Holocaust still live among us. They give vivid testimony to the horrors of modern anti-Semitism gone mad in many of the world's most "enlightened" European nations.

To our shame, some of the greatest Church leaders helped pave the way to death camps in places such as Auschwitz and

Bergen. They did it through anti-Semitic writing and teaching. They underscored it by the sheer force of their influence from the pulpit. Everyone must join Jewish people today in remembering the Holocaust with the words "Never again!"

Church Edict against the Jewish People

When Berkovits mentioned the "first act of oppression" against the Jewish people by Christians in the fourth century, he was referring to an edict issued by the Roman Catholic Church in response to the doctrines of Saint John Chrysostom (347–407). This early Church father was the patriarch of Constantinople, yet he described the Jewish synagogue as "a place of meeting for the assassins of Christ . . . a den of thieves; a house of ill fame, a dwelling of iniquity, the refuge of devils, a gulf and abyss of perdition."[4]

Many scholars consider Chrysostom to be one of the greatest and most compassionate Church fathers. Yet the writings of this renowned saint reveal at least one dangerous flaw. He said, "As for me, I hate the synagogue . . . I hate the Jews."[5] Ironically, Chrysostom's name literally means "golden-mouthed." He used his gifts of persuasion to birth the Christian doctrine (popular even in this century) that anyone who persecuted the Jews was acting as an "instrument of Divine wrath."[6]

Anti-Semitic Rhetoric Spreads

A who's who of Church leaders and thinkers echoed Chrysostom's sentiments in an avalanche of anti-Semitic rhetoric. These leaders included Eusebius of Caesarea, Gregory of Nyssa, Augustine and Jerome.[7] During the dark years that followed, many Jewish people living under the shadow of the Christian Church of that day were forced to be baptized as Christians or face one of three dim choices: expulsion, torture or death.

In A.D. 327, the Church Council of Nicea declared that for the benefit of Christianity, Jewish people could exist only "in seclusion and humiliation." Fourteen years later Constantine II prohibited marriage between Christians and Jewish people.[8]

In 1095, Pope Urban II decided to help Emperor Alexius I of Byzantine recruit knights from the West to battle the Turkish Empire. While presiding over a church council at the Cathedral of Clermont in France (the nation of his birth) in 1095, Pope Urban preached a fiery sermon to crowds outside of the cathedral and, on November 27, launched the First Crusade. He urged his listeners to liberate the holy city of Jerusalem and offered them a spiritual reward: "Whoever for devotion alone, not to gain honour or money, goes to Jerusalem to liberate the Church of God, can substitute this journey for all penance."[9]

Historian Bernard Hamilton said that when the pope finished his sermon, "the crowd shouted, 'God wills it, God wills it!' and surged forward to take the cross." The pope appointed a former knight who had become a priest to lead the Crusade, but events quickly spiraled out of control.[10] Armed with the pope's promise of forgiveness of past sins and "sins recently committed," nobles, knights, soldiers, farmers and housewives rallied to march to Jerusalem.

The Crusades Begin

The first assault was called the Peasant's Crusade because it was made by an unauthorized and poorly equipped army of mostly untrained peasants, including women. They were quickly defeated, and most of its members were killed or enslaved.

The pope's promise, however, was a strong incentive. Even soldiers who had been excommunicated from the Church were welcomed back to the fold with open arms if they made a vow to purge Jerusalem and the Middle East of all infidels. They were also released from any debt they owed to Jewish people and had blanket permission from the pontiff to rob Jewish people on the journey to and from Jerusalem.[11]

Unfortunately, many of these crusaders decided to purge Europe of its own infidels by attacking any Jewish person they encountered on their journey to the Promised Land. Pastor John Hagee of Texas, who teaches extensively about the Church and Israel, writes:

> On the First Crusade [there were a total of fifteen of them over a period of about five hundred years] to the Holy Land, the crusading armies left a trail of Jewish blood across Europe. Within a three-month period, twelve thousand Jews were slaughtered in Germany as the crusaders screamed, "The Jews have killed our Savior. They must convert or be killed."[12]

According to Michael Brown, the leading slogan of the day throughout Europe was, "Kill a Jew and save your soul!"[13]

Pope Innocent III is considered one of the "saviors" of the Jewish people, and he did try to stop some of the killing in later years. Yet his writings clearly indicate that he also felt the Jewish people deserved to "wander over the face of the earth, without rights, except by gracious concession, without a home . . . as if they were beings of an inferior species."[14]

Jerusalem Captured

The First Crusade successfully captured Jerusalem in the summer of 1099, but the crusaders spent their first week in the holy city in an unholy slaughter of the Jewish and Muslim citizens of Jerusalem. One historian says the men who carried the cross into Jerusalem took Holy Communion and "heartily devoted the day to exterminating Jewish men, women and children—killing more than ten thousand."[15] Is it any wonder, therefore, that spiritual darkness blanketed

105

the Church in the medieval period and beyond when it presumed to murder anyone who was identified as a Jew in the name of Christ?

In 1182, France expelled Jewish people from its borders, and Austria did the same in 1421. After that they were expelled from the cities of Cologne (1424), Augsburg (1439) and Mainz (1473). Warsaw, Poland, expelled its Jewish population in 1439, followed by Sicily (1492–93). Lithuania expelled all Jewish people from its borders (1495), as did Portugal (1496–97) and Nuremburg (1499).[16]

These dates are important because they indicate that most of Europe was closed to Jewish people by the time the infamous Spanish Inquisition began in 1480. That means that Spain's Jewish refugees simply had no place to go.

Spain Targets Its Jewish Citizens

Until the savagery of the Third Reich in the twentieth century, the Spanish Inquisition was the unrivaled pinnacle of Christian anti-Semitism in human history. Spain's large population of Jewish people was the target of this unholy Inquisition.

Haman, the enemy of the Jewish population described in the book of Esther, seemed to take human form again in the person of Friar Tomas de Torquemada, the pope's personally appointed grand inquisitor. Torquemada, whom we will meet again later in this chapter, was also the confessor to Queen Isabella, and he used the full powers of the Church and the Spanish crown to hunt down and persecute any and all Jewish people. Ultimately, he wielded so much power in Spain that even the king and queen feared his disapproval.

History of Jews in Spain

The first Jewish people to visit Spain (called Tarshish in most instances) were presumably Israelite traders who negotiated

106

the purchase and shipment of gold and silver for the construction of Solomon's Temple. The region later became a safe haven for Jewish exiles following the invasion by Babylon and the destruction of Solomon's Temple.[17] Obadiah the prophet referred to these exiles and mentioned another name for Spain when he prophesied:

> And the exiles of this host of the sons of Israel,
>   Who are among the Canaanites as far as Zarephath,
>   And the exiles of Jerusalem who are in *Sepharad*
>   Will possess the cities of the Negev.
>
> Obadiah 1:20, emphasis mine

The *Doubleday Dictionary* identifies *Sepharad* with Spain and describes the *Sephardim* as "the Spanish and Portuguese Jews or their descendants."[18] Some historians believe these Sephardic Jews helped found the nation of Spain sometime before the birth of Christ. In any case, even more Jewish people fled to Sepharad after the destruction of Herod's Temple in A.D. 70.[19]

Jewish people throughout the Roman Empire suffered even more persecution than usual after Emperor Constantine converted to Christianity and named it the state religion. Persecution against Jewish people intensified when the increasingly influential Church fathers began to preach anti-Semitic themes in their sermons, teachings and letters.

Then, in A.D. 586, a king named Reccared converted from Arianism to Roman Catholicism, which was again declared the state religion.[20] Given the clearly anti-Semitic stance of the Church in that era, it was predictable that laws and decrees directed against the Jewish people would increase dramatically.

During a series of Church councils convened in Spain over the next 125 years, the Jewish religion was virtually outlawed. The Church required Jewish people to be baptized as Christians or be reduced to the status of slaves, suffer the confis-

107

cation of their property and see all their children above the age of seven be placed in Christian homes.[21]

Golden Age for the Jewish People of Spain

In A.D. 711, African Moors gained power in Spain's southern region and spread the influence of Islam. During this time, ironically, the community of Spanish or Sephardic Jews enjoyed a golden age of economic, artistic and scientific achievement. Jewish people rose to the highest ranks of government and were honored for achievements in business, literature, the arts, the sciences and philosophy. In fact, many Jewish people from other Arab nations moved to Spain.

Christians, who had maintained power in the north, drove the Moors out of Toledo in 1085. While the Moors (with Berber reinforcements) and Christians sparred in Spain for nearly a century, the Jewish people never regained their position of power.

Some of these Jewish people trickled across the border to France. But they found opposition there, too. In 1235, the Council of Arles required people identified as Jews to wear a yellow circular patch (does this sound familiar?), and the Jewish people began to stand out from the French population in an unavoidable and dangerously conspicuous way.

The Spanish Inquisition

Problems in Spain accelerated after Pope Clement IV authorized the Spanish Inquisition to investigate the lives of Jewish people, especially those who had chosen to join the Church. Late in the fourteenth century, Spanish Church leaders preached an increasing number of anti-Semitic messages, triggering such an epidemic of violence that in 1391, over a three-month period, fifty thousand Spanish Jews were killed in a total of seventy communities.[22]

When Queen Isabella of Castile and King Ferdinand of Aragon united their kingdoms through marriage in 1479, they were concerned about the unyielding "Jewishness" of Jewish individuals who converted to Christianity to avoid death or persecution during previous persecutions from the Church. They were called converses or *Marranos*, which means "pigs" in Spanish. They were equally hated by unconverted Jews and by the Church. At the request of Ferdinand and Isabella, Pope Sixtus IV in 1480 established the office of inquisitor general and appointed Friar Tomas de Torquemada to the post.[23]

Spain's surviving Jewish citizens were given just four months to decide whether they wanted to leave the country or remain and join the Roman Catholic Church. As many as four hundred thousand abandoned their homes and businesses to flee Spain, after paying exorbitant exit taxes to officials. For some reason, fifty thousand Jewish people decided to remain in Spain.[24] Many of them did not live long.

Michael Brown reports in *Our Hands Are Stained with Blood*:

It is estimated that thirty thousand Marranos were burned at the stake in Spanish Inquisitions from the fifteenth century until 1808. In addition to this, in 1492, all non-baptized Jews were expelled from the country.[25]

Jews Offer to Underwrite Columbus

According to Dr. Dell Sanchez, the pastor of a bilingual, multicultural church in San Antonio, Texas, there is historical evidence that on the night before Christopher Columbus set sail on his first voyage to the New World in 1492, Spain's King Ferdinand and Queen Isabella met privately with Minister of Finance Isaac Abranbanel and two wealthy nobles, Gabriel Rodriguez Sanchez and Santangel.[26] These three influential men were Sephardic Jews, and they offered to underwrite the voyage of Columbus. They knew the royal coffers did not contain enough money to pay for Columbus's venture, even though for many years the Jewish population had been taxed and their property largely confiscated by the Church and the Crown. In return for their investment, the three men begged the monarchs not to expel the Jewish people from Spain.

Just as the royal couple accepted the offer, the door burst open and the pope's grand inquisitor, Friar Tomas de Torquemada, ran into the room waving a crucifix and screaming that "the blood of all Jews" would now be on the hands of the king and queen. Ferdinand and Isabella took the money but reneged on their agreement. Instead of protecting their remaining Jewish people, they issued a decree ordering the expulsion of all unconverted Jews from Spain. This amounted to a death sentence, since virtually all of Europe had already expelled Jewish people from their borders. They were welcome nowhere.

To make matters worse, the Spanish monarchs successfully exported their Inquisition and persecution of the Jewish people to Portugal, spelling the doom of thousands who had fled there. This anti-Semitic spirit was even exported to the New World, where it would surface with deadly wickedness in Spanish territory in what is now Mexico, Texas and California.

Nothing matched the brutality and evil of the Spanish Inquisition—until Hitler and his Nazi henchmen. The Third Reich adopted and perfected the techniques and policies forged by Torquemada and the Church clerics of the medieval era.

Ulf Ekman quotes a question posed by a famous survivor of the Nazi death camps that expresses the way the victims of the Spanish Inquisition must have felt:

> The [late] renowned Nazi hunter, Simon Wiesenthal, has described how he was rescued from the bullets of a firing squad. While he stood there in a line awaiting execution and Jews died beside him, the soldiers suddenly stopped shooting. They

had heard church bells, and took a break from the killing while they went to vespers. How can a Jew who has gone through these things ever believe in a Christian again—especially since the Christian Church, Christian theologians and Christian countries have led the field in anti-Semitism?[27]

The Answer Lies in God's Word

The answer to this question cannot be found in a book of philosophy or in official public statements issued by churches or Christian groups. It is found in God's Word and in our active obedience to His commands concerning Jerusalem, Israel and the Jewish people. We begin with repentance, proceed with prayer and follow through with active deeds of intercession and love, following the example of our Savior.

It seems logical to assume that if Jesus wanted to convert mankind by force, He would not have gone through the agony of death on a cross. He could have simply commanded legions of angels to force every man, woman and child to bend their knees before Him. But our Savior does not resort to force. Instead He allows us to choose to follow Him.

The Church has not done well in following Jesus' example. As we have seen in this chapter, history is strewn with examples of times when Christians condoned violence to either convert or eliminate those who did not believe. One of the Church's primary targets through the years has been Jewish people, and Jewish people have noticed.

In his book *Our Hands Are Stained with Blood*, Michael Brown translated the words of an Israeli writer who expressed the Jewish view of the way the Christian Church has portrayed the Gospel of Christ to the Jew:

> Instead of bringing redemption to the Jews, the false Christian messiah has brought down on us base libels and expulsions, oppressive restrictions and burning of [our] holy books, devastations and destructions. Christianity, which professes to

111

infuse the sick world with love and compassion, has fixed a course directly opposed to this lofty rhetoric. The voice of the blood of millions of our brothers cries out to us from the ground: "No! Christianity is not a religion of love but a religion of unfathomable hate! All history, from ancient times to our own day, is one continuous proof of the total bankruptcy of this religion in all its segments."[28]

This is not the model Jesus demonstrated to His followers. Jesus does not save the lost through force, coercion or military action. The Prince of Peace builds His Kingdom with the weapons of love, grace and mercy. Religion at its worst forces its way through hatred, harshness and cruelty. Church leaders in nearly every century seem to miss this important point.

In the face of such diabolic evil, God's Word stands unchanged and eternally true. It does not matter how many current events and impending crises become human history. We should never forget God's ominous warning to every human being, every human institution and every nation among men that he who touches Zion touches the apple of His eye (see Zechariah 2:8).

Recovering from Spiritual Bankruptcy

In virtually every crisis leading to the persecution of the Jewish people, Christians have had an opportunity to step into the gap as fishermen, to warn, encourage and assist their escape to safety or help them return to Israel. During the Holocaust, Corrie ten Boom and a few other Christians risked or lost their lives helping Jewish citizens escape, but most Christians remained silent.

In the 1970s and 1980s, a faithful generation of godly Christian pioneers and forerunners brought a message of warning and encouragement to the Jewish people. This group included Sid Roth, Gordon Lindsay, David Chernoff, Joel Chernoff, Dan Juster, Derek Prince, George Otis, Jack Hayford, Moishe

Rosen (Jews for Jesus) and many others who found creative ways to touch the "apple of God's eye."

These men of God should be honored, and many continue to have influential and effective ministries. But a new generation must arise, put on the mantle and build upon the foundation that has been laid. The Church must face the issue of what God is doing among the Jewish people.

Our role as Christians is to pray and intercede for the Jewish people. We must do whatever God tells us to do, particularly to help them escape the land of the north and return to their biblical homeland. We are destined to blow a trumpet and declare God's fresh purposes to this generation—whether the message is popular or not.

As Santayana was quoted on that death camp wall, we can learn from the mistakes of the past and prevent history from repeating itself. The Church repeatedly failed to demonstrate the love of Christ Jesus toward the Jewish people in times past, which produced disastrous results. Never again!

Our faithful prayers and righteous deeds must provide proof that we have recovered from our spiritual bankruptcy and now have more than enough of God's love to extend helping hands to the Jewish people. Our godly lives and gracious ways must draw a new line straight from the heart of the Messiah to their hearts—even if they choose not to accept Christ as their Messiah once we have done these things.

We can no longer afford to look the other way. Our Master simply will not have it. Our sermons, conversations and influence must be used to preserve and protect God's ancient covenant people until they come to know their true Messiah. Our lives and conduct must model God's unconditional love for the Jewish people, not man's unreasoning hatred of those who seem "different."

The challenge is that these things can only come to pass in the crucible of prayer over the fire of obedience.

Part 3

A RADICAL AND SUDDEN CHANGE

A Contemporary Miracle

7

When the Walls Came Tumbling Down

> How great are His signs
> And how mighty are His wonders!
>
> Daniel 4:3

I will never forget watching television reports of East German youth tearing down the Berlin Wall. Nearly delirious with joy, they swung sledgehammers, iron bars, chisels and anything else they could find. Emotions flowed freely in a frenzied attempt to topple the twelve-foot walls that had separated Germany and imprisoned East Berlin for 28 years. It was a historic spectacle!

The dramatic scene unfolded on Thursday, November 9, 1989, barely a month after East Germany had celebrated its fortieth and final anniversary as a country. Major news organizations from around the world showed up after jubilant

Germans began to disassemble sections of the 103-mile-long Berlin Wall. The border guards merely watched without interfering.

Before the "wall came tumbling down" I participated in a prophetic gathering in Kansas City in which Paul Cain announced prophetically, "Communism is going to be communwasm." A few years before that I had been ministering with seer prophet Bob Jones, and I heard him share that the Russian Jews would come forth from the land of the north and then after that would come a time when there would be the need for "cities of refuge"! Sure enough, Cain's prophetic word was fulfilled, and the Wall was removed. I now possess a piece of the Berlin Wall that I acquired during one of my intercessory visits to Berlin. I keep it as a reminder that in God all things are subject to change.

The fall of the Berlin Wall signaled the inevitable collapse of the Communist regime that overshadowed Russia and its satellite states. Day by day, people around the world watched as the Soviet machine disintegrated.

Finally, approximately two years later, we learned that Soviet leader Mikhail Gorbachev would step aside, and the Soviet Union as we knew it was no more. Newly chosen president Boris Yeltsin and the Commonwealth of Independent States (CIS) took the lead, 75 years after the Communists seized power under the atheistic direction of Lenin.[1]

Another Wall That Fell

The Berlin Wall was not the first fortress around a city to tumble. Centuries ago another bulwark fell, sending shock waves throughout the nations. That event, too, signaled catastrophic and convulsive change in the affairs of mankind and in the balance of power over the world's most contested real estate.

> Now Jericho was tightly shut because of the sons of Israel [who surrounded it]; no one went out and no one came in.

118

The LORD said to Joshua, "See, I have given Jericho into your hand, with its king and the valiant warriors. You shall march around the city, all the men of war circling the city once. You shall do so for six days. Also seven priests shall carry seven trumpets of rams' horns before the ark; then on the seventh day you shall march around the city seven times, and the priests shall blow the trumpets. It shall be that when they make a long blast with the ram's horn, and when you hear the sound of the trumpet, all the people shall shout with a great shout; and the wall of the city will fall down flat, and the people will go up every man straight ahead."

Joshua 6:1–5

In a sense, the walls of Jericho were more formidable than the Berlin Wall. The Jericho rampart was wide enough for six chariots to run abreast. The walls were not designed to keep unarmed people in. They were designed to keep the strongest armies of men out. Yet they fell. Why? Was it the force of arms or the fierce attacks of skilled soldiers that brought them down? No, they collapsed upon themselves under the power of what I call prophetic acts of prayer. In other words, they disintegrated in obedience to God's direct command.

For seven days the people did not shout or utter a word in their time of battle. Just imagine: not even a word of criticism could be heard! They walked around in silence because God had told their leaders to do so. But then came a sound at the end of the seventh march on the seventh day. A shout of prophetic declaration arose from the people. The rest is history. Believers of the one true God obeyed His command in faith, and the impossible was made possible.

The East German army erected the mighty Berlin Wall in 1961. It went up because over a twelve-year period 2.7 million people had fled the nation into West Berlin.[2] At the end of World War II Berlin was divided, with West Germany controlling a portion. But the city lies completely within the borders of what was then East Germany. The Wall was built to keep the East Germans inside, not to protect them against dangers from the outside. This wall was fortified by armed soldiers, tanks, tank pits, machine guns, concertina wire and a whole slew of other devices. Yet not one bullet or tank shell was involved in its demise. What happened to bring it down? How could such a thing come to pass?

In actuality, the fall of the Wall was merely the final fruit of events that occurred beyond the realm or physical boundaries of the once-feared Iron Curtain, of which East Germany was a part. The Berlin Wall collapsed on itself because the demonic principalities and powers upholding the Iron Curtain were dislodged. Like the walls of Jericho, the Berlin Wall fell because God's power prevailed. The shout of praise preceded the walls of Jericho falling down, and a mighty movement of prayer preceded the Berlin Wall's collapse in our day. This resulted in a dramatic shift of power that triggered an unprecedented movement of people across national borders.

The Truth behind the Fall of the Iron Curtain

"God events" played a part in the fall of a modern superpower. Let's look back at a few of them.

A Christian Embassy Birthed in Israel

In a strategic public move, godly believers established the International Christian Embassy in Jerusalem with the goal of comforting God's people and summoning the Church to pray for Israel. On Passover 1980, the Embassy held its first of many Mordecai Outcry events to publicly expose the mistreatment and imprisonment of Jewish Russians.

God simultaneously launched an invasion in the spirit realm. While God has always loved the Russian people and the many other people groups within the U.S.S.R., He had no love for the antichrist spirit motivating and sustaining the Communist regime. That government's dismal track record of persecuting Christians and Jews within its borders finally reached the point of no return in the heavens.

God Dispatches Prayer Commandos
to Strategic Locations

God began to lead small groups of "prayer commandos" to strike from strategic places in the U.S.S.R. at the root of key historical events that had launched evil into the world. He also sent prayer teams into East and West Germany to battle in the spirit realm.

The prayer commandos entered these nations armed only with the name of Jesus Christ, the Word of God, the power of the Holy Spirit and a divine commission to release prophetic prayers in strategic places. It was a replay of the battle between little David and the monolithic Goliath, who, at the time, ruled the north.

International intercessory prayer movement leaders Kjell Sjöberg, Johannes Facius, Steve Lightle and Gustav Scheller, who carried a forerunner anointing upon their lives, assembled a prayer conference in Jerusalem. Participants prayed for Israel and the release of Soviet Jewry. During the gathering, the Holy Spirit set apart Lightle, Facius and two other intercessors for a prayer mission to the U.S.S.R.

One month after Soviet leader Mikhail Gorbachev took power, the four-person team arrived, commissioned with a mandate from Isaiah 62:10 to "go through the gates" of the U.S.S.R. and prepare the way for the Jewish Russians to return to their biblical homeland.

Commandos Pray in Russia

Team members also felt led to follow a strategy found in Zechariah 1:18–21. Dubbing themselves "the Four Smithskis" after the blacksmiths, or craftsmen, described in this passage, they set out in Jesus' name to "terrify the four horns of the nations that lifted up their hands against the land of Judah."

(In both the Old and New Testaments, the term "horn" is often used to refer to the leaders or the power of nations or empires on the earth.)

In many of the U.S.S.R.'s Jewish centers, the team circled giant statues of Lenin, then proclaimed the idols would fall. The intercessors sought key transportation locations along the "exodus route" to Israel and asked God to open up a highway of departure for the Jewish people who would leave the land of the north.

The team went to the Potemkin Staircase, the gate of Odessa, a port city in Ukraine, which at the time was part of the Soviet empire. This famous staircase features a broad series of massive steps leading from the city's opera house in the city square to the waters of the Black Sea at the port of Odessa.

Obeying the leading of the Lord, the four intercessors prayed in the Spirit as they walked up and down the staircase. The ever-present Communist secret police (KGB) followed them closely down the stairs, trying unsuccessfully to decipher their words. When the prayer team members reached the bottom of the staircase, they quickly turned around to retrace their steps. The red-faced secret agents were so close and surprised that they literally ran back up the stairs as fast as they could![3]

The Lord uses different people at different seasons. He always has His forerunners who go before and pave the way for others so that they, too, can take their turn carrying His baton in this prophetic relay race. Years later Scheller and others watched the first shipload of Russians leave for Israel from that very port. I, along with others, have stood on those same stairs in Odessa, at the edge of the Black Sea. As intercessory watchmen, we spoke forth that this port would remain open, and we lifted up a cry: "Let My people go!"

"Invasion Mission" Launched

From late December 1985 to early January 1986, Facius and Lightle returned to the Soviet Union along with twelve other intercessors from a number of nations. This would be their most important and historic prayer assignment behind the Iron Curtain. It could be called an "invasion mission." Their first assignment was to launch a "spiritual missile" at the office (specifically, the spiritual principality behind the office) of Soviet President Mikhail Gorbachev in the Kremlin.

On New Year's Eve 1985, during a bitterly cold afternoon, the fourteen praying men marched double file "just like a commando unit carrying a spiritual missile."[4] One of the intercessors had previously been to Gorbachev's office and was able to guide the others right to the target. Lightle later wrote about what happened:

> The sign to launch our missile was for me to take off my hat, although the wind was blowing and it was snowing. . . . I'll never forget what happened. It was wild, because we had to march like a commando unit, but God gave us tremendous joy. . . . As we were marching, we had big smiles on our faces. We turned the corner. . . .
>
> I had not seen so many police, KGB and army people before. No Russian person walks down that sidewalk, but there we were. The KGB came running across the street, about forty or forty-five of them. They were stunned as they walked along with us. They didn't know what we were planning to do, but it didn't affect us a bit. When we got right in front [of the door leading to Mr. Gorbachev's office] to where I could reach out and touch the door, I took off my hat.[5]

While the men smiled at their anxious and confused KGB "escort" squad, they also spoke into the spirit realm and released a deadly missile from God's Word. It was the same word that brought down another king who dared to reject God's commands. Thousands of years earlier, Samuel the prophet had delivered that fatal missile from heaven, dislodging King Saul, a Jewish ruler who had misused his authority:

> Because you have rejected the word of the LORD,
> He has also rejected you from being king. . . .

123

The Lord has torn the kingdom of Israel from you today and
has given it to your neighbor, who is better than you.

1 Samuel 15:23, 28

With the divine payload delivered to its target, the fourteen
men abruptly turned around and walked away from Gorbachev's office. Going back the way they had come, they left
their bewildered and unsuspecting KGB escorts scratching
their heads.

Six years later to the week, on Christmas Day 1991, Scheller
and his wife were watching television in Odessa, Ukraine.
Gorbachev came on the air and announced, "I hereby dis-
continue my activities at the post of president of the Union
of Soviet Socialist Republics." Scheller summed it up: "With
him disappeared the Soviet Union."[6]

Team Attacks the Spirit of Death

During the same trip the prayer team also had invaded
Lenin's tomb in Moscow. It is reported that many Russians
had called the tomb "holy" even though they did not believe
in God.

Through divine intervention, the intercessors found themselves alone in what amounted to one of the Soviet Union's
most "holy" shrines to the spirit of death. For decades, line
after line of schoolchildren were brought to that tomb to
honor the spirit of death hovering over the remains of the
father of the Communist revolution. On this day, God dis-
patched a commando team of prophetic intercessors to destroy the demonic power behind this idol.

The Lord miraculously arranged for the guards in the tomb
to be distracted. Responding to a problem outside of the
shrine, they rushed away, leaving the team alone to drop their
"bomb" in the Spirit. As team members encircled the decaying
body of Lenin encased in glass, they broke the power of the
spirit of death in that place in the name of Jesus Christ.[7]

124

Focus on Russia's Jewish People

In the 1980s, Tom Hess led a 24-hour Prayer Watch in Washington, D.C. In those days I often joined Hess in his Supreme Court Prayer Watch in the nation's capital and called for God's intervention through prayer and fasting. Hess later took an assignment to lead the Jerusalem House of Prayer for All Nations on the Mount of Olives, and Dick Simmons, of Men for Nations, one of my early mentors, has now led prayer and intercession for our nation for several years on the same site.

In 1985, Hess led a team to Egypt and Israel. While praying on Mount Sinai for the Jewish people, the Holy Spirit told Hess he was to go to America and Russia to help prepare for the future exodus.

In late 1986, Hess felt he was to take a team of 38 Jewish and Gentile believers on a prayer journey to Russia. They were greeted at the Leningrad airport by the KGB, but later they managed to meet with and encourage Russian Jewish dissidents called *refuseniks* (see chapter 9 for further information on refuseniks). The team traveled to Moscow and completed a prophetic Jericho March around the Kremlin. While at Red Square, they prayed for the release of the Jewish people living within the borders of the Soviet Union.

On Yom Kippur the team visited a Jewish synagogue in Moscow, where they provided clothing and Bibles to many Russians. Members also serenaded their KGB escorts with "O Come Let Us Adore Him," something neither group will ever forget.

This strategic visit took place simultaneously with the summit meeting in Iceland between U.S. President Ronald Reagan and President Gorbachev. When Hess's group finally reached Jerusalem they stood on the Mount of Olives and issued a prophetic command to the land of the north to release the Jewish people in the name of the Lord. Within a few days, the Soviet Union unexpectedly agreed to release within one year twelve thousand Jewish people who wanted to emigrate to Israel.[8]

The Second Prayer Mission

Hess led a second prayer mission to the U.S.S.R. in the spring of 1987, with a specific assignment to strike at the root of the Communistic ideology that at the time had enslaved virtually 70 percent of the human race. In Moscow God ministered to the group from Daniel 12:1, revealing that Michael was arising to deliver the Jewish people out of the Soviet Union. It was no coincidence that they went to a major museum in the Kremlin called The Church of Michael the Archangel and prayed for their release.[9]

The team marched Jericho-style around the Kremlin. Then they moved on to Leningrad to visit an atheistic museum, housed in an old church building that was converted into an anti-God memorial. On the lower floor of the church stood a statue of a large, nude male figure surrounded by little cherubs or demons and an eerie portrait of Lenin. These items aptly portrayed the god of Communism. Hess described the twisted scene in detail and explained what God sent the prayer team to accomplish:

> The central focus is a picture of Lenin with all the religions and cultures of the world being subjugated by communism. The cross is broken in two. The American, British, Swiss and other flags are torn in two, and the hammer and sickle triumph over the world. We did another Jericho march around the atheistic museum and with the Sword of the Spirit laid the axe to the spiritual root of communism in the very city where Lenin instituted this demonic ideology in 1917.[10]

By the turn of the century Hess had led ten teams of Jericho-type prayer marches in Russia. Today he is setting his sights toward organizing similar on-site prayer ventures in the United States and other lands.

Canceling the Soviet Constitution

Lightle also took a twelve-member prayer team to Moscow on the seventieth anniversary of the Bolshevik Revolution of 1917. The holiday commemorates the date when Lenin signed the constitution of what became the U.S.S.R. The prayer team's heavenly mission was clear and seemingly impossible: They were sent to cancel the Soviet Constitution signed by Lenin and rewrite a new one based upon God's Word!

After a series of adventures, the twelve prayer commandos gathered in a circle in front of the building where Lenin signed the constitution into law (the building now houses the Bolshoi Theatre). The four KGB agents tailing them were so desperate to learn their plans that one of them accidentally poked Lightle in the back with his elbow as he strained to understand their words, and another was literally cupping his hands to his ears to hear! Lightle wrote, "I don't know why he was doing that. I was praying in the Holy Spirit, and I know he couldn't understand that."[11]

As I taught in my first book, *The Lost Art of Intercession*, "What goes up must come down!" The prayers ascending from a radical remnant of the Body of Christ must have filled to the brim a golden bowl in heaven and started to overflow back down to earth. Many believe the answers to these prayers started to appear in 1988 when Gorbachev changed part of the Soviet Constitution and initiated a total rewrite one year later. By 1990, Jewish people were already emigrating from Russia in unprecedented numbers; but the best was yet to come.

God had one more assignment for the commando prayer team. Because "the Pharaoh of the North," Gorbachev, refused to give up God's people, God had revealed to the intercessors that He was going to shake up the world economy, especially the economy of the Soviet Union and the Communist bloc nations.

Armed with a prophetic word and a key Scripture passage from Ezekiel, the team visited the Econocom Building

127

(roughly the Soviet equivalent of America's Wall Street financial district). On the night of October 17, 1987, the intercessors "prayed judgment concerning the finances of the world, especially in the Communist bloc countries."

Lightle wrote, "When we left the Soviet Union and found out about the stock market crash on Monday, October 19, we understood our prayer."[12] Of course, in a global economy what happens on Wall Street reverberates around the world.

During that same season I was participating with an intercessory team in New York City. The Lord had given me a vivid dream of a crash on Wall Street with the words, *When Wall Street hits 2600, this is a demarcation. Count forty days after.*

By divine direction we were now interceding in New York City exactly forty days prior to the great fall. We had spent hours in prayer that day and then felt released to go on site at the New York Stock Exchange. As we stood in the encased glass balcony overlooking the trading floor, we began to intercede. Then, like an arrow shot from its bow, a prayer was released that hit the target, and we all knew it.

At that moment the time clock changed to 1:26:00 P.M., while at the same time the trading hit 2600. Isn't it amazing to see how God can orchestrate these things? Then, just as the dream had stated, we began to "count forty days after." Sure enough, forty days later the U.S. stock market suffered a devastating but temporary crash. Interesting, isn't it? The Lord had people who did not know one another and who were in two different parts of the world engaged in the same prophetic intercessory activity!

"Identificational Repentance" in Evian

July 6, 1988, marked the fiftieth anniversary of the international travesty that took place in Evian, a small French town situated on the shores of beautiful Lake Geneva. As we discussed in chapter 5, it was there half a century earlier that leaders from 38 nations of the world met at the request of U.S. President Franklin D. Roosevelt. Though they started with good intentions, they ultimately failed to properly answer the question, "How do we rescue the Jewish people from Germany and Austria?" As a result six million Jews perished at the hands of the mad Austrian dictator, Adolf Hitler.

Fifty years later, in what may be seen as a prophetic "year of jubilee" for the beleaguered Jewish people, intercessory and prophetic leaders representing each of the 38 nations that had sent delegates to Evian in 1938 assembled for a prayer conference in Berlin. A small group of them also went to Evian.

The prophetic delegates met together under a mandate from God to conduct solemn acts of "identificational repentance" in Christ's name for the sins committed fifty years earlier against the Jewish people. They were to restore the breach created when their fathers, mothers, forefathers, nations and even the Church itself forsook the Jewish citizens of Germany and Austria in their hour of greatest need.

I ardently wanted to participate in those gatherings because the Lord had placed these issues on my heart years before. Moreover, He had given me a personal mandate to teach and impart to others many of the truths concerning "identificational" intercession and repentance, which resulted in my writing the book *Intercession—The Power and Passion to Shape History.*

The problem was that my wife, Michal Ann, was nine-and-a-half months pregnant with our third child. With the birth of our child two weeks past due, I was not able to attend. Instead I opted to intercede from home at the same hour the delegates began to gather and pray in Berlin.

At 1:17 in the morning, I was praying in my living room in Kansas City, Missouri, confessing the sin American Christians committed when they failed to raise their voices on behalf of the Jewish people in 1939. The intercessors in Berlin were dealing with the same subject at about the same hour.

While I was in prayer, an angel appeared and stood in the doorway of the living room! The angel was dressed in a military uniform, and it looked right at me.

Many different things were revealed in that supernatural encounter that I will not go into at this point, but finally the angel said, "It is time for you to go and lay your hands upon your wife and call forth your son, Tyler Hamilton."

My conviction was that the angelic message was referring to something more and greater than simply the birth of my son, as important and wonderful as that was. The angel arrayed in a military uniform was sent to tell me that it was a time of birthing and it was a time of war.

Sure enough, when I laid hands on Michal Ann she started to have contractions, and our child was born hours later—on 7–7–88. Seven is the number of completion, and eight is the number of new beginnings. On this day we had doubles! In both the natural and the spiritual realm, it was a pivotal day of completion followed by new beginnings, new openings and birthing. Just as birth happens once the birth canal is opened, so the solemn acts of identification, intercession and repentance of the Church on behalf of our historical sins against the Jewish people triggered a completion on the one hand and a "birthing" on the other. It closed the circle of pain and in a moment released new freedom and life.

The natural and the spiritual are often mirrors to one another. As I and others around the world entered into "identificational repentance," a simultaneous new spiritual birth occurred. In the same way, prayer preceded a new era in history. Just before the Berlin Wall fell, Soviet President Gorbachev visited East Germany and told German Chancellor Helmut Kohl that the Soviet Union had abandoned the Brezhnev Doctrine. Moscow would no longer use force to keep its satellite states from adopting democratic forms of government or free-market economies. This was an unprecedented miracle.

The Iron Curtain Starts to Fall

By September 11, 1989, neighboring Hungary had pulled down the Iron Curtain around its borders, and within six months 220,000 East Germans fled to the West through Austria or sought political asylum in West German embassies in Hungary. To put this in perspective, before the miracle of 1989 only a few East Germans managed to escape to West Berlin, and at least eighty people died trying to flee.[13]

The fall of the Iron Curtain had an even greater effect on the immigration of Russian Jews to Israel and Western nations. Russia had a long history of anti-Semitism, but an invisible line was crossed when Soviet leaders chose to persecute the Jewish people living under their control and to deny immigration to Israel.

The refuseniks received worldwide coverage when they opted to risk life and limb to protest the bureaucratic denial of their applications for immigration. Jewish people in Russia knew that simply by applying to leave the U.S.S.R. for Israel they would probably lose their jobs, be denied basic privileges and endure harassment from the KGB and local Communist officials. They also realized that they could possibly face prison time. Nevertheless, thousands of refuseniks applied. They had Eretz Israel on their minds and in their hearts.

The Berlin Wall Comes Down

Sixteen months after the acts of "identificational repentance" were made before God in Berlin and Evian, the Berlin Wall came down. The Iron Curtain of the Soviet Union followed. It marked the beginning of a remarkable decade in which Jewish people could leave Russia and freely return to Israel. Since then more than one million Russian-speaking Jews have moved from the former Soviet Union to the Promised Land, where Russian is now the second most commonly spoken language.

Just as they did in Jericho of old, amazing things happen when God partners with man and when man partners with God. Even walls called immovable start tumbling down. It has happened before, and it will happen again!

8

Acts behind the Scenes

The people who know their God will display strength
and take action.

Daniel 11:32

Supernatural behind-the-scenes acts of intercessory prayer
and prophetic proclamation at God's direction always precede the crumbling of walls, in both the natural and spiritual
realms.

As we discussed in the last chapter, the walls of Jericho fell
flat after seven priests with rams' horns led the people of God
in a silent march around that pagan citadel for six days. They
ended the silent siege on the seventh day with a long trumpet
blast and a corporate shout. They did it all in obedience to
the prophetic direction of almighty God.

In the same way, I believe the seemingly invincible Iron
Curtain and the Berlin Wall collapsed because the people

of God obeyed specific prophetic directions and over many years conducted prayerful behind-the-scenes acts.

Prayer Changes Things!

Dismay and discouragement often overtake anyone who is brave enough to read accounts of the Spanish Inquisition and the World War II Holocaust. We feel powerless to deal with such malevolent hatred.

Nevertheless, do not accept the temptation to give up! The adage "Prayer changes things" is more than a trite phrase, a willful wish or a powerless Christian cliché. I know that on the surface prayer seems like an incredibly ineffective weapon in the face of such malignant hatred and violence toward the Jewish people. Yet I am convinced that if we were ever to realize the true power of Spirit-directed and Spirit-inspired prayer, we would be shocked.

Picture all the water in the Great Lakes combined with the immeasurable volume of the Pacific and Atlantic oceans. Imagine all that watery force held in check behind the trembling walls of a single massive dam by heavily reinforced metal floodgates measuring ten miles or more in height. Now envision a single control button wired to the opening mechanism of this great dam. Even a little toddler would have the strength to release the waters with one expeditious touch, flooding the earth with a deluge matching or surpassing that of Noah's day.

In the same way, the significance of the power of prayer is not based upon the strength or ability of the person praying. Rather, it is rooted in the immeasurable power of God and the awesome force He releases in response to fervent intercession. As the Scriptures declare, "The effective prayer of a righteous man can accomplish much" (James 5:16).

We can now peek behind the curtain of history and see how fervent intercession ushered in God's awesome power to bring down the Iron Curtain and the Berlin Wall. In the years prior to these events, God supernaturally created a unique network of friends and built a worldwide "watch of the Lord." Then with divine precision He launched His secret prayer weapon against the gates of the enemy in the Soviet Union, and then in East Germany.

It is time to give honor to prayer veterans such as the late Gustav Scheller with Operation Exodus; Steve Lightle of Exodus II; Tom Hess with The Jerusalem House of Prayer and many others who laid a foundation of prayer through their pioneer works of rescue and deliverance in Christ's name. Though some of this might seem like "old history," wisdom leads us to review the heroic acts of faith of these consecrated prayer warriors so as to gain courage and insight for the days that lie ahead. As Bill Johnson often says, "Their ceiling becomes the next generation's floor!" This is the beauty of the joining of the generations. With this view in mind, let us proceed to review lessons of history-making prayer.

Let My People Go!

In 1974, Jewish-American businessman Steve Lightle closeted himself away in a fourth-floor room of a Christian drug and alcohol rehabilitation center called Kaffestube in Braunschweig, West Germany. He had already spent several years in Christian ministry in Europe, including a one-year stint at Kaffestube, but something was stirring in his soul. He made up his mind that he would fast and pray until one of two things happened: Either God would change him or he would die in that room.

For six and a half days Lightle prayed, fasted and was visited by angels. Then Jesus appeared in the room and deeply cleansed Lightle's heart, preparing him for a specific task. Lightle received a vision that pointed to a dramatic change in the spiritual climate of Europe. In a book titled *Exodus II: Let My People Go!* he described his vision:

134

I saw a lot of people, and I recognized that they were Jewish faces. And there were so many! Then from a particular viewpoint I saw a multitude of Jewish people—hundreds and hundreds of thousands of them.

Then my angle of vision changed again. This time I saw it from a height that enabled me to see the nation they were in. It was the Soviet Union, and these were Jewish people that were being gathered from different parts of that nation. On many small streets they were gathering from various regions of Russia. They were coming together and began to walk upon a big superhighway that God had built that was bound westward. Somehow I knew this was a highway that only certain people could walk on. Only those that God permitted could get on it. And as they walked they began to come forth out of the U.S.S.R.

At the same time there were ministries that God raised up that were as great or even greater than that of Moses in Egypt. And they began to proclaim unto the Soviet authorities, "Thus saith the Lord God of Israel, 'Let My people go!'" And the Soviets refused. Then God, through these ministries, brought great judgment upon the Soviet Union. The catastrophes were so severe that the whole nation was brought to its knees. Then it was as though the Soviet Union coughed up the Jewish people, and they began to walk on this specially built highway.

As I watched I saw that the highway continued on through Poland, through Warsaw. It continued on through East Germany, through the city of Berlin. From Berlin it crossed over the border into West Germany at Helmstadt into the city of Braunschweig. This highway that had been built by God continued on to the city of Hanover and then into Holland where the Jewish people got on ships and went to Israel.[1]

During the following six years Lightle shared what he had seen only a few times. In 1982, the Lord permitted him to publicly disclose his vision of a second great exodus of the Jewish people from foreign lands to Israel. That is when he discovered that God had been revealing similar messages to Christians around the globe. The message had such great impact that radio and television reporters around the world sought him out for interviews.

When God finally released Lightle to share his experiences in *Exodus II: Let My People Go!* he wrote:

> Right now, in 1983, the Soviet Union has essentially closed all doors so that hardly any of the 2.5 million Jews [living there at the time] are able to return to the land of promise. But God will provoke the "land of the north" to let His people go. The original Exodus out of Egypt will seem like just a shadow of the upcoming dramatic events. No one will talk about the former exodus anymore because of the worldwide impact of the final one.[2]

God Releases Prayer Commando Teams

God began to give specific "prayer assignments" to intercessors around the world. Groups of "prayer commandos" began to travel to key places behind the Iron Curtain to lift up specific prayers and make prophetic declarations at the leading of the Holy Spirit.

In 1982, God intervened in the life of Swiss travel executive Gustav Scheller, who lived in England at the time. Over dinner in a restaurant in northern England, a doctor mentioned to Scheller and his wife, Elsa, that he had just returned from a Festival of Tabernacles celebration in Jerusalem where he heard Lightle speak of a second Jewish exodus. Scheller had been reading the prophets in the Old Testament, and his heart leapt when he heard about Lightle's vision.

Two weeks later the Schellers flew to Jerusalem. They wanted to talk with Lightle but did not know how to contact him. That was not a problem for God. While out on a walk in Jerusalem, the Schellers spotted Lightle. It was a divine appointment with international implications.

The Schellers went on to work with Lightle in the early 1980s. They spread the news throughout the United Kingdom

136

that God planned to return to Israel Jewish people who had lived in the land of the north. With the Cold War still at full throttle, they faced formidable skepticism in the media and even in the Church.

When they held a news conference at the Finnish parliament, the British Broadcasting Corporation (BBC) World Service carried Lightle's challenge across the globe: "It is time that somebody began to tell the leadership of the Soviet Union what the Word of the Lord says: Either they bow their knees to God, or God is going to judge them."[3]

According to Scheller, a major Soviet newspaper mocked Lightle's declaration with the headline "God Brings Russia to Its Knees."[4] The same God who once spoke through a donkey spoke prophetically through a communist newspaper headline!

It was not long before the Soviet Union began to suffer some of the poorest grain harvests in its short history. The superpower tottered on the brink of bankruptcy and in just two and a half years lost three leaders: Leonid Brezhnev, Yuri Andropov and Konstantin Chernenko.

The Impact of the Esther Fast

I suspect the upheaval in the Soviet Union was accelerated in part by a little-known prayer event called The Esther Fast Mandate. God planted the idea in the heart of Canadian minister Clyde Williamson during a Churchwide forty-day fast in January 1983. I never met this man, but I still have a copy of a small book he published called *The Esther Fast Mandate*.

The God-breathed vision captured in this little book had a lasting impact on my life. Here is a brief segment of the prophetic call God issued to the Church through Williamson:

> The Spirit of God is wooing people to do that which Queen Esther did in an absolute fast unto God, a fast in which to seek God for the restoration and deliverance of the people of Israel.

137

And God shall give an appointed time and there shall be those in His Body that shall set themselves aside without food and without drink for a period of three days that God will set forth out of bondage His people (both Israel and the Church) from all over the globe. And they shall come forth by the thousands and by the millions, and His name shall be glorified.[5]

Williamson served as a staff minister with Pastor Ralph Rutledge of Queensway Cathedral in Toronto, Ontario, at the time. The leadership team at Queensway concluded that The Esther Fast Mandate had to be committed to paper and distributed. It was not a one-time call for intervention through fasting but a call for a yearly vigil, listing dates up to the year 2000. (I then picked up the baton in my books *Praying for Israel's Destiny, Prayer Storm* and now *The Coming Israel Awakening* to carry this burden on into the coming generation.)

The Mandate was hurriedly printed in the form of scrolls and distributed to contacts the church already had, but God had bigger plans. Within a short period of time, the news of the Esther Fast traveled around the world. Believers from 73 different nations joined together in a three-day fast for "the release, return, restoration and revival of Israel and the Church."[6] Such an international call to focused prayer was unprecedented, especially in those days when the worldwide prayer organizations we have today did not exist.

Two Jewish holidays, Purim and Passover, occurred during the Esther Fast that year. Jewish people set aside Purim as a time to remember Esther's original fast, which saved her people from annihilation at Haman's hands. Passover honors the night God released the children of Israel from captivity in Egypt. The timing of the initial Esther Fast was crucial because at that time the Soviet Union was allowing only one hundred Jewish people per month to emigrate to Israel. Soviet officials were cracking down on dissidents, and they refused to approve 360,000 applications from Jewish citizens wishing to emigrate to Israel. Moscow would not relent, despite growing pressure from the United States and many other Western nations. Many if not most of the Jewish "refuseniks" who applied to make *aliyah* experienced persecution, and many were imprisoned.

Preparing the Way for Messiah

Tom Hess is another modern prayer pioneer appointed by God for these days. As I mentioned in the previous chapter, he led seven prayer walks into Russia on behalf of the Jewish people in the Soviet Union before the cloud of Communism lifted from her borders and three more since the Iron Curtain fell. During these walks intercessors called out for the release of their Jewish friends from the land of the north.

Hess also helped establish houses of prayer and prayer watches around the world. He still conducts annual international prayer convocations in Jerusalem that draw people from around the world. It has been my privilege to participate in some of his historic behind-the-scenes prayer ventures as far back as the mid-1980s. I am a witness to their incredible effectiveness. Hess described two examples in his book *The Watchmen: Being Prepared and Preparing the Way for Messiah*:

> [In Washington, D.C., in 1986,] I was fasting for a breakthrough in the United States Supreme Court because the Chief Justice was "pro-choice" on abortion (in favor of killing unborn babies). Someone said the results of my fast would be seen on television, which I found hard to believe. But one hour after I ended the fast [of forty days], the Chief Justice of the Supreme Court resigned, and God gave a pro-life Chief Justice, and at the same time another pro-life Justice was appointed to the Court, to everyone's surprise. . . .
>
> Another example was in Russia from 1986–1992—seven times in over seven years to do seven Jericho Marches around the Kremlin in Moscow, one every year. We saw tremendous breakthroughs: the year before we began, only two hundred Jewish people had left Russia for Israel, but since then the wall of

139

communism came down, and in the last ten years over 800,000 Jewish people have come home to Israel! There were numerous groups involved in 24-hour prayer watches, praying and fasting as we went there, and many were praying all over the world.[7]

Delivering a Prophetic Word

I have known Mahesh and Bonnie Chavda for more than thirty years, and I consider them to be treasured friends and co-laborers in the ministry. The Chavdas have a powerful healing and evangelistic work, and they play a crucial role in the world prayer movement, leading the over six hundred Watch of the Lord gatherings that meet on Friday nights in various places around the world.

In 1986, the Lord told the Chavdas they were to deliver a prophetic word to the Jewish people who lived behind the Iron Curtain. Mahesh Chavda traveled from Finland to Moscow. Risking discovery by the KGB, he spoke to refusenik leaders and delivered a prophetic word to an Orthodox Jewish rabbi. He said, "Thus saith the Lord, 'God is going to send a whirlwind of freedom, and this communistic pharaoh is going to let you go. God is going to set you free.'"[8]

The rabbi agreed that God might release his friends, but he assured Chavda that he would never be allowed to leave. Unmoved, Chavda said, "You are the leader; you are going to lead this people out. When the door is open, you take the people to Israel. This is the Word of the Lord."[9]

The rabbi told Chavda, "That is impossible. I am a doctor of mathematics, and I build their rockets. Now I am a rabbi, but because I know their secrets they will never let me go." Chavda asked God to confirm His prophetic word and prayed, "O God of Abraham, Isaac and Jacob, show Yourself here." When he raised his hand the rabbi nearly fell down under the power of God and exclaimed, "The pain is gone!" Chavda learned that the rabbi had been tortured by the KGB and had suffered from chronic rib pain until that moment.[10]

Two years later Chavda was in Jerusalem to welcome home some of the first Russian Jews flown to Israel. The same rabbi's picture appeared on the front page of the local newspaper. He had finally made it to his ancient homeland. I like what Chavda wrote in his book: "For decades the Marxist Communists had said, 'There is no God! There is no God!' Then one day the Lord stood up and said, 'There is no communism.'"[11]

German Believers Interceding behind the Wall

God was also at work among believers in Germany during this season. My West German friend and Christian leader Michael Schiffmann described to me some of the behind-the-scenes events that took place in Germany between the end of World War II and the day the Berlin Wall came down. In a personal email message he wrote:

> After the Second World War, the Federal Republic of Germany was founded; and because of the total breakdown of trust some born-again Christians became part of that first government. The whole government repented for the deeds of the Nazi regime and the Holocaust in one of their first constitutional meetings.
>
> In the fifties and sixties, the Lutheran Order of the Sisters of Mary took a strong stand for identificational repentance in particular for the Holocaust and initiated several public acts on those issues. Many churches responded [through] identificational repentance in their services during the sixties.
>
> In the early seventies, a movie that was broadcast called "Holocaust" made a deep impact into society and showed to the first generation after the war the depth of guilt and released a strong public awareness. This was followed by waves of identificational repentance that touched most denominations and most areas of West Germany.
>
> By the initiative of Ari Ben Israel, a Messianic Jew, and the German Intercessory Movement under the leadership of Berthold and Barbara Becker, together with many differ-

141

ent national leaders, a conference was held that not only caught the attention of the secular media, but that was unique in wideness of range of the churches and denominations attending.

[In] 1985, at the very place [where the former German legislative assembly passed "racial laws" persecuting Jewish people before World War II], about seven thousand German Christians from four hundred different cities [met] together with many representatives from Israel and with many victims of the Holocaust and some government officials. [They] made a public declaration of repentance and remorse that was spoken by all the participants. That very declaration was broadcast and watched by thirty million people.[12]

God Worked through Many Believers

God worked stealthily through obedient believers from many nations to prepare the nations and the Jewish people for the miracle He would soon work before our eyes. He even worked through political leaders such as President Ronald Reagan and British Prime Minister Margaret Thatcher, who took strong stands against the "evil empire" of Soviet rule.

Then there was the work of Pope John Paul II. What a wonderful contribution, both on spiritual and governmental fronts, was made by the man who headed the Roman Catholic Church—the church that had once led the charge against Jewish people during the Spanish Inquisition! It now took the lead in calling for a freedom that would open the floodgates for Jewish people to return to Israel. No other pope accomplished as much as John Paul II to make restoration for the past sins of the Church.

Who but God knows the importance of each behind-the-scenes act of prayer, intercession, repentance or reconciliation that took place in the years before the fall of the Wall and the collapse of the Communist empire to the north? This much is clear: The labors of prayer and intercession we saw before

142

the fall only foreshadowed even greater prayer assignments that would follow.

God Releases a Prayer Avalanche

God released one prayer avalanche to break through the walls, gates and obstructions blocking the return of the Jewish people to Israel from the land of the north. This was the beginning of the fulfillment of Isaiah's prophecy:

> Thus says the Lord GOD,
> "Behold, I will lift up My hand to the nations
> And set up My standard to the peoples;
> And they will bring your sons in their bosom,
> And your daughters will be carried on their shoulders."
>
> Isaiah 49:22

First we carried the Jewish people in the north on our shoulders through prayer and intercession. Then He released a different kind of flood to begin to break down centuries of betrayal, distrust and persecution of the Jewish people by self-proclaimed Christians. He anointed a remnant forerunner group to actually help carry the Jewish pilgrims back home through every means possible. This river of grace in the time of the fishermen would require the Church to stretch out in repentance and serve others as never before.

Oh, let us, the broken and loving Body of the Messiah, carry the descendants of Abraham, Isaac and Jacob in our hearts as well as on our shoulders! Let us know our God, wax strong and release demonstrations by doing daring acts and mighty exploits for the glory of His great name in the earth!

9

Transformation
Altered States of Affairs

Then it will happen on that day that the Lord
    Will again recover the second time with His
      hand
    The remnant of His people, who will remain,
    From Assyria, Egypt, Pathros, Cush, Elam, Shi-
      nar, Hamath,
    And from the islands of the sea.

                                    Isaiah 11:11

The collapse of the Soviet Union's suffocating curtain of terror brought astounding transformations that still affect that
region and the world at large. Most significantly, from the
moment the Iron Curtain began to unravel, the number of
Jewish immigrants making *aliyah* to their biblical homeland
increased dramatically.

    Before the beginning of the end, Russian Jews rarely were
allowed to emigrate, even though the Communist govern-

ment of the Soviet Union was historically hostile toward them and openly treated them as second-class citizens. Just before the fall, as I mentioned in the last chapter, as few as one hundred Jewish people were allowed to leave the Soviet Union annually. The collapse of the Iron Curtain completely changed the situation.

In the thirteen months after December 1989, almost two hundred thousand *olim* ("those going up") flooded out of the former Soviet Union to Israel.[1] By June 2000, one million Jewish people had arrived in Israel from the land of the north. They fled for freedom in automobiles, airplanes, trains, buses and ships. Most were assisted by Jewish or Christian agencies, individuals and groups. It amounts to the emancipation and transportation of an entire people group from one part of the world to another. In missions language, this is referred to as a "people movement." Nothing like it has ever happened on such a massive scale! But far more Jews still need to be reached and rescued.

The Exodus Has Begun and Is Continuing

As I already mentioned, Gustav Scheller and Steve Lightle met in Jerusalem in 1982. They grew closer as they prayed about ways to minister to the Jewish people in the land of the north. They worked with several other intercessors and leaders to sponsor a prayer conference in Jerusalem in 1991. The first session began on the same day the United States had set for Iraq to withdraw its troops from Kuwait.

Despite the danger of military conflict in the region, 120 believers from 24 nations bravely attended the conference to stand in the gap with prayer. War erupted that night. During a week punctuated by SCUD missile attacks and long hours wearing gas masks, God spoke to Scheller. He told him it was time to help bring the Jewish people home.

Scheller shared this with the leader of the conference, Johannes Facius, a Danish church leader and the coordinator of Intercessors International. Facius nodded in agreement. To their surprise, all 120 conference attendees concurred! Delegates donated $30,000 to finance the first flight of Operation Exodus to fly Russian Jews back to Israel. The flights continued with success. But Lightle, who headed the project, had received a vision years before that included ships as well as planes.[2]

Leaving Odessa by Ship

Lightle and Scheller formed the Exodus Shipping Line to transport even larger numbers of *olim* to Israel from Odessa, Ukraine. They entered complicated negotiations with Russian customs officials and Jewish agency leaders from Israel, and then they negotiated with a Greek shipping company for the use of a large ship.

When the Soviet Union dissolved midway through the negotiation process, Lightle and Scheller had to start over again with newly independent Ukrainian customs officials. It did not matter—God had a plan, and they were squarely in the middle of it.

In December 1991, the Exodus Shipping Line overcame every obstacle by God's grace. Lightle described the first trip: "At eleven minutes past midnight, the lines were cast off and we sailed out of Odessa with 476 Jewish immigrants making *aliyah*. This was the first ship since 1948 to take Jewish immigrants to Israel."[3] Many Exodus sailings from the port of Odessa followed, taking thousands of Russian Jewish people home to Israel.

Each time a gap appeared in the "fisher's net" that was drawing these Jewish people of the northern diaspora home, new ministries appeared as if on heavenly cue to meet the need. "Exobus," for example, appeared in June of 1991 to transport stranded *olim* across Belarus from Kiev to the airport

146

in Warsaw, Poland. From that beginning Exobus expanded operations to sixteen bases in four countries. By the late 1990s, Exobus was carrying around one thousand *olim* a month to thirteen airports in five countries.[4]

Refuseniks Finally Leave

When the walls came down, a large number of refuseniks were ready to go. Most of these people of conscience lost their jobs and endured years of persecution simply because they had at one time applied for permission to emigrate to Israel. Year after year, the Soviet bureaucrats denied their requests. In most cases the persecution extended into their places of employment and the local communities. Nevertheless, for years the refuseniks stood against oppression under the Communist regime. Many of them spent time in prison; most of them were Jewish.

When the Iron Curtain finally dropped, these Jewish survivors were eager to leave. The first to leave had prepared their official papers many years in advance and had lived "ready" for years. These people, for the most part, were clearly Jewish in their culture, bloodlines and religious belief.

Many "second-round" Jewish immigrants, however, were barely identifiable as people of Jewish descent or faith. Some could not tell you who Abraham or Moses was. These descendants of Abraham were the product of a secular and antireligious culture in which "being Jewish" evoked images of tattooed numbers on the skin. Since the era of the Russian tsars, many families had changed their Jewish-sounding names or hidden their Jewishness to avoid exile to the Pale of Settlement, an old tsarist community of isolation that segregated Jewish people from the mainstream population.

In many cases it was difficult for these "hidden Jews" to prove their Jewish heritage. Corruption and organized crime in the former Soviet Union—particularly the forging of false iden-

147

tification and immigration papers—led to an unwillingness on the part of Israeli officials to accept many of the new identity papers held by Jewish people wanting to make *aliyah*.

Jewish Immigrants: An Unreached People Group

Some have estimated that nearly 90 percent of the Jewish immigrants entering Israel are totally unreached by the Gospel of Jesus Christ. Many are almost as ignorant of their Jewish heritage and religion. Christian ministries that work closely with Israel to help transport Russian Jewish immigrants to their homeland are careful not to evangelize the *olim*. But the ministries working inside the former Soviet Union among the Russian Jews have had more freedom.

In 1990, before the collapse of the Communist government, Jonathan Bernis led a fact-finding mission to Saint Petersburg (then called Leningrad). The American pastor wanted to assess the condition of the Jewish people in the Soviet Union. During his visit, Bernis was struck by the spiritual hunger of the people he encountered.

Over the next two years Bernis returned to the Soviet Union with other groups and helped establish a Messianic (Jewish Christian) congregation in Minsk. During these trips the Holy Spirit began to speak to him about a unique ministry to the Jewish people in the land of the north. He wrote in his foreword to Sandra Teplinsky's book *Out of the Darkness*:

> By that time, the Iron Curtain had come down. Thousands of missionaries had poured into the former Soviet Union. Only a handful of them, however, were reaching out to the millions of Jews in the land.
>
> I knew God wanted to reach this remnant with the Good News—before they returned to the Promised Land. I also knew He was calling me to play a more significant role in the reaping. I didn't understand how I was to do this . . . then the idea for Messianic Jewish music festivals was born. I knew

148

the Jewish people of Russia were greatly interested in Israel and the Jewish culture. I also knew that Russian people in general had a great love for music and the arts. Organizing a festival of Jewish music and dance seemed to offer the perfect platform for sharing the Good News in a Jewish way with the Russian people.[5]

International Festivals of Jewish Worship and Dance

By May 1993, Jonathan Bernis had founded Hear O Israel Ministries (HOIM) and conducted the first Messianic music festival in Saint Petersburg at the Oktobersky Concert Hall. No one was prepared for what happened there. Bernis writes, "We had no idea what the results would be or how many people would come. So we were all shocked on opening night to find the four thousand-seat hall filled to overflowing."[6]

Even more stunning was the scene following Bernis's short message and altar call. More than 50 percent of the crowd— half of them Jewish—rushed to the front of the concert hall to pray. Many on Bernis's team began to weep as they witnessed an outpouring of the Spirit not often matched in two thousand years since Jewish people became the first Christians in Jesus' day.[7]

HOIM, renamed the International Festivals of Jewish Worship and Dance, subsequently conducted twenty festivals and reached more than 500,000 people in the former Soviet Union. Nearly half of those who attended the festivals were Jewish. The largest festival drew more than 60,000 people to the central football stadium in Odessa, Ukraine, in 1995. More than 200,000 people (approximately 80,000 of them Jewish) responded to altar calls at the festivals. In an email correspondence Bernis wrote, "God is at work among the Jewish people in a way that we have not witnessed since the first century."[8] While Bernis still continues his outreach to the Jewish people in diaspora around the globe, today he is the director of the Jewish Voice ministry, which has a widely watched television broadcast.

Prayer Assignment: Go to Russia

In the summer of 1994, David Fitzpatrick, Avner Boskey, Richard Glickstein and I participated in Bernis's third festival, which was convened in Minsk, the capital city of Belarus (White Russia). We each had been involved in different prayer groups that conducted prophetic intercession for Israel and the Jewish people. But for a season we would be a team with specific prayer assignments. Working hand in hand with Bernis and the festivals, we set out on a prophetic journey that crisscrossed Russia.

The Lord had a specific assignment and a prophetic word for this group. He told us that if we wanted to serve the Jewish people, then we would have to do it in Russia. *This is not an optional trip; this is a strategic alignment,* God revealed to me in a dream. That directive caught us off guard. While we all traveled a lot, relocating half a world away was not something we had envisioned. Nonetheless, we acted on this heavenly assignment. Fitzpatrick, Boskey and Glickstein actually moved with their families to Russia. I continued my task of intercession and networking stateside.

Our assignment was to pray that God would open a way for Jewish people to exit from the land of the north and return to Israel. Belarus, and the capital city of Minsk in particular, marked part of the path leading from Russia to Israel through the great seaport of Odessa.

Most of the other routes required Jewish immigrants to take long detours or pass through nations and regions dominated by fundamentalist Muslims. Since ancient times, the path from the Black Sea through Ukraine and Belarus has been recognized as the southern gateway to Europe, a fact that was not overlooked by the Nazis during World War II. We learned that a lot of atrocities had been inflicted upon the Jewish people of Belarus. In preparation for the festival, we visited some of the sites.[9]

150

Preparing the Way in Minsk

We wanted to find a high place in the city where we could pray. A nonreligious gentleman in Belarus suggested the Mound of Glory. We did not know what it was, but it seemed to make sense.

The Mound of Glory, we discovered, was really a massive hill created by people who carried dirt one handful at a time in processions from their villages all over Belarus. The members of our prayer group walked up on this Mound of Glory and prayed for Jewish people to be able to escape the land of the north.

The day before the festival in Minsk was to begin, Bernis encountered significant resistance from local authorities. Intercessory prayer by the entire festival team played a key role in the crisis, and God made a way where there was no way! In the end, local authorities asked if the festival could be extended another day to accommodate people who had been turned away from overflow crowds!

Minsk was just the beginning of our prayer team's intercessory cycle. During the next three years, we lifted up specific prayers for a variety of locations as God gave them to us.

A Synagogue in Moscow

Once, traveling with a smaller prayer group, we went into Moscow from Minsk. Moscow, a city of ten million people, had only three synagogues. The largest synagogue—the one the presidents and statesmen visit—was attended by only 200 to 250 people. One of the other two synagogues had been firebombed about five months prior to our coming, and we felt that was the place we were to visit.

The sanctuary was boarded up and surrounded by a chain-link fence, but we felt we were to stay and pray. Eventually a couple of us jumped the fence and searched for the grounds-

151

keeper. When we found him, he opened up the facility and gave permission for the entire group to come in.

A Jewish brother from New York picked up something he spotted in the rubble of the burned-out building. Amazingly, it was the complete history of the Exodus, written in Russian. You can imagine what this meant to us, since we had come specifically to pray for a second and even greater exodus from the land of the north. During that trip God knit together the hearts of our prayer team, which was composed of both Jewish and Gentile believers in Messiah.

A Field in Kiev

Other excursions with our Messianic Jewish friends took us to places such as *Babi Yar* ("Grandmother's Ravine"), a field across from Kiev's Jewish cemetery in Ukraine. On September 29, 1941, Nazi troops, assisted by willing Ukrainian soldiers, ordered the city's Jewish residents to strip off all of their clothing and line up in groups of one hundred. Mercilessly, the invading troops raised their machine guns and shot the helpless victims one group at a time. The massacre lasted two days, as long as the gunmen had enough light to see their targets. Witnesses reported that the Nazis literally melted some of their gun barrels.

Thousands of small children who were missed by the bullets of the Nazi machine guns were simply thrown alive into the ravine of death and buried along with their murdered adult family members. Witnesses said so many victims were buried alive that the ground at Babi Yar literally moved for two days after the last gunshot was fired.

When the earth stopped trembling, 33,771 Jewish men, women and children had perished. Even the daily carnage count at the death camps in Treblinka and Auschwitz could not compare with the efficiency of the executioners in Kiev. The horror, however, was not over. During the next year,

65,000 more civilians (mostly Jewish) were brought into Kiev from Nazi-controlled territory throughout Europe. They, too, were murdered and entombed.

When the tide of war turned, officers in the German army ordered Ukrainian prisoners to excavate and obliterate all traces of the remains at Babi Yar. It took several weeks to complete the job. The bodies were incinerated; any bones that survived the flames were crushed and mixed with the earth to hide the evidence of the atrocities committed there.

The only snag in the Nazis' plan was that God witnessed every sinful act committed against His people in that place. He made sure that detailed Nazi documents were preserved and that witnesses to the carnage came forward to describe what happened in 1941 and 1942.[10]

Some of the friends who visited Babi Yar with us had lost grandparents in that massacre. We bypassed the large national monument that had been erected in memory of the atrocity and went directly to the actual site where so many people lost their lives. The place was holy, sovereign and painful at the same time. In consideration and respect for our dear friends who had lost grandparents there, we did not launch any verbal prayers during our visit.

A Messianic Congregation in Kishinev

Several festivals later, in 1996, we embarked upon another strategic prayer assignment in Kishinev, Moldavia, the city where nearly a hundred years earlier Joseph Rabinowitz had established the first Messianic synagogue since the first century (as we discussed in chapter 5). It would mark the culmination of our prophetic intercession efforts for that season of the Spirit, and it was to be one of our most significant prayer assignments.

Throughout our time in Kishinev, the heart of our prayer was that God would anoint the Messianic Jews of this generation with the same radicalism and fire evident in the lives and ministry of Paul, Peter and the other first-century Jewish leaders. We prayed that Jewish people in the land of the north would come back into their full heritage, just as Joseph Rabinowitz did. The contagious devoted zeal that surfaces in certain Jewish followers of Yeshua is amazing.

Once again we were involved in the intercessory and outreach aspects of each festival. Yet we spent a few days scouting around and just listening, as God led us to key points of information and directed us to the exact place we were to launch our prophetic prayer.

Our first goal was to locate the place where Rabinowitz and the Israelites of the New Covenant had worshiped. That was difficult because nearly a century had passed. Many landmarks were destroyed during the pogroms against Jewish citizens of Kishinev in 1903 and 1905, and during the Nazi murder of 53,000 of the city's estimated 65,000 Jews in 1941.[11]

We found the original Jewish synagogue in Kishinev, but it was closed. Rabbi Richard Glickstein, a brother in Christ who was then leading a Messianic congregation in Moscow, found incredible favor on that prayer journey. After Glickstein talked with some people outside the synagogue, we were allowed to go in. As we walked around, we prayed for discernment and crucial information to guide our intercession in Kishinev. Before we left, we felt led to give a donation to the synagogue.

After praying and asking questions, we were ready for the next step in our journey: We had an address!

A Message in a Hole in the Wall

As we entered the neighborhood where we believed Rabinowitz's congregation may have met, we immediately noticed that most of the buildings were relatively new. We knew that meant that the original structures had been bombed during

154

the war. Only one block of older buildings had somehow escaped destruction or extreme damage.

We parked the car in the old section. As we climbed out of the vehicle, we all were struck by the same sight: An old, ten-foot-high concrete wall stretched along the full length of the block, except for one place where a hole had been created. The buildings were perched on top of this foundation.

Our guide led us around to the back of the buildings where a number of doors led to apartments. We made our way to the door of the building we believed was built just above that hole in the foundation wall.

Since we looked like foreigners, we decided to play the part. It would have been unwise and virtually impossible to explain our prayer, so we entered what I call our "dumb, naïve American tourist mode." (This comes under the "Be wise as a serpent and gentle as a dove" principle.)

When we knocked on the door the building owners answered. Through our guide we said, "Hello, we are visitors from America. Could we tour your building?" For emphasis, we added that we had heard it had been used for something or other a long time ago.

The owners were gracious, and the couple invited us in to examine their apartment building. We looked around, but we did not initially see anything that stood out. Then just as we were about to leave Fitzpatrick noticed a door leading to a stairwell to what appeared to be a cellar. There was something about that door that quickened his spirit. When the rest of us saw it, we knew we had to investigate further.

We had already established our identity as dumb American tourists, so we had nothing to lose. We asked, "What's down there? This might be silly as can be, but can we go down in the cellar?"

The couple quickly nodded and motioned for us to freely explore the passageway. They must have been thinking, *Those crazy Americans! What will they want to see next?*

Fresh Oil of Anointing and Fresh Wine of God's Spirit

The stairway was nearly blocked by various items that had been stored for a long time. Nonetheless, we made our way down the stairs and turned right. When we entered the cellar, we looked at each other, amazed. We could see daylight streaming into the room through the hole in the wall we had seen from the street. Old bottles of wine, still packed in their cases, were stacked on a pallet, and empty bottles of olive oil were scattered about on the shelves in the room.

The prophetic symbolism of the scene was almost overwhelming. Immediately we knew this was the place where we would complete our assignment and release "fresh oil of the anointing" and "fresh wine of God's Spirit" into the Jewish people.

Re-digging the Wells

Just as Isaac had his men re-dig the wells of his father, Abraham (see Genesis 26), there is a spiritual concept of re-digging the ancient wells of the anointing of those who walked with God in earlier generations, even in the face of opposition (see Genesis 26:18–22). It was therefore part of our assignment to issue a prophetic on-site prayer to release God's high anointing on His ancient people and to urge them to escape the old walls that were closing in upon them. We were to call forth the apostolic grace of church planting that had originated and rested on that location. We were to call forth the new wine and the fresh oil of the Holy Spirit. (Glickstein ended up going all over the former Soviet states raising up numerous Messianic synagogues.)

This is why the hole in the wall was significant. It was time for God's ancient covenant people to return from the land of captivity to their Land of Promise with the help of the Gentiles who received the New Covenant through the Jewish people. Perhaps it also indicated there was an opening to pray.

156

The Lord had led us to the exact place where He birthed the first Messianic Jewish congregation nearly a century earlier. He took us to their very foundations, to a place still containing prophetic signs of empty olive oil bottles and old wine bottles.

By that time we knew the research portion of our journey was over. We had the information we needed, but we agreed that we were not to pray overtly in this couple's basement. After thanking our bewildered hosts for their hospitality, we returned to the front of the building where the hole breached the old wall. We were in total agreement that this was the spot where the Lord wanted us to pray. Together we released the prayer that we had come to deliver to the city of Kishinev. Out of death and decay would arise a new anointing and fiery zeal to restore the Jews of the diaspora to the God of Israel and to their long-awaited Messiah, Yeshua.

Traveling in Israel with The Caleb Company

Another transformation began to take place after the fall of Communism. It is still transforming Israel and highlighting the importance of Russian Jews making *aliyah*. I discovered this phenomenon in a personal and painful way when Fitzpatrick and I went on a prayer journey to Israel with a group called The Caleb Company.

Dr. Don Finto, the former senior pastor at Belmont Church in Nashville, Tennessee, and author of *Your People Shall Be My People*, had launched the ministry to build upon supernatural favor he had experienced in developing networks and friendships among Messianic leaders of various backgrounds. Finto named the ministry after Caleb, who according to the book of Numbers had a "different spirit." He was a man anointed to look into the Promised Land and take the land without fear of enemies or obstacles.[12]

Five Caleb Company board members, including Fitzpatrick and me, traveled to Israel with Finto. We wanted to discover

God's heart for the nation and the Jewish people. Finto hoped we would grow in our understanding of the Jewish people. He also wanted us to meet with key government and Messianic community leaders from across the Promised Land.

With the Pain Came an Astounding Word

My painful adventure began during a stopover in a remote area north of Tel Aviv. That night I had a peculiar dream in which I was stabbed. The pain of the wound was so agonizing that I awoke to find myself tangled up in blankets and my body literally racked with pain! I did not know whether the attack was physical or spiritual in nature, so I started repenting of anything and everything I had ever done wrong (and a million things I have not done). It was 2:00 A.M., and nothing seemed to alleviate the anguish.

Finally I decided to get help. But I was in so much pain that I could not stand up. I rolled off the bed, hitting the floor with a thud. I was in excruciating pain, but eventually I was able to crawl out of my room into the kibbutzim where we were staying. Then I managed to pound on the door of Finto's room. When he opened the door, he had to look down to figure out who was crazy enough to wake him up at that hour. He immediately contacted our guide and fellow intercessor, Rabbi Avner Boskey, because he spoke fluent Hebrew and also some Russian. They rushed me to a nearby hospital.

I do not remember much of what happened next. My mind was too fuzzy. I later learned that the hospital staff ran a series of tests and gave me powerful painkillers, which had little apparent effect. The pain gradually lifted, but the doctor, who believed I was suffering from kidney stones, gave me more medication, "just in case."

I was ordered to stay in the hospital to recuperate, even though I could now recognize my surroundings. When I met my doctor, I was surprised to discover he was a Russian

Jew. He was so Russian that he could speak only Russian, not Hebrew. I thought to myself, *Well, this is interesting. I have been praying for the release of the Russian Jews, and here I am at the absolute mercy of a Russian Jewish doctor in Israel.*

God Begins to Speak

After I was released, our Caleb Company traveled to a villa (a prayer house) located outside the old walls of Jerusalem. We could see the city from where we stayed. We had barely settled in when the excruciating pain hit me again. Wanting to tough it out, I took the medicine prescribed by my Russian Jewish doctor. Despite the painkillers, I could not sleep. That was all right, because from my window I was able to watch an incredibly beautiful snowfall upon Jerusalem.

In the end, toughing it out did not work. I again had to be taken to a doctor. This time I was checked into Hadassah Hospital. (*Hadassah* is the feminine Hebrew word for "myrtle tree." It is also the Hebrew name of Esther, the queen who in the Old Testament stood up for her Jewish people.)

When I arrived at the hospital I was in agonizing pain. Yet at the same time the Lord was speaking to me. He communicated in dreams, visions and revelations about a variety of issues. He revealed specific plots of the enemy—such as where bombs were planted on the West Bank.

Revelations Come to Pass

I knew these revelations were not the byproduct of medication. My prayer partners and I prayed through each point God had raised. We would cry out for intervention until we received assurances from the Lord that breakthrough had been made.

Invariably each event would show up on the front page of the newspaper the next day.

159

One day we read in the paper that the snow that had fallen in the night had so disrupted traffic that officials had called off school. Israeli security forces subsequently found a bomb-making plant in the West Bank—it was in the exact location God had revealed to me. The paper surmised that the snow had stopped traffic and foiled the plans of the terrorists "for no known reason." But we knew why.

Once again Russian Jewish doctors attended me during my hospital stay. They prescribed more pain pills and more tests. I will never forget the way one of the Messianic Jewish leaders from Jerusalem sat with me the entire day and self-lessly served me.

My Russian-speaking doctors were perplexed with me because on the one hand their X-ray and sonogram exams showed clear evidence that I had been suffering from kidney stones. On the other hand, a second round of tests failed to find anything, and all of my pain simply disappeared. It appears that the Lord simply dissolved it.

God's Purpose Comes through Redemptive Identification

God spoke through Zechariah the prophet and said, "I will make Jerusalem a heavy stone" (Zechariah 12:3). My experience during the Caleb Company's tour of Israel was a warning. I feel that I tasted the reality of the agony and pain mixed with the blessings that come to anyone who dares to identify with the suffering our Messiah endured for us. The Lord also used that trip to Israel as a tool of redemptive identification to help me relate to the pain of the Jewish people and to show me the kind of agonizing prayer needed to bring forth the fullness of God's purposes among the Jewish people.

I find it significant that at two separate hospitals in Israel Russian Jewish doctors treated me. The migration from Russia is beginning to transform Israel. Everywhere we went, we found Russian Jews and heard the Russian language spoken. God is calling His people out of the land of the north in unprecedented numbers! In prophetic retrospect, it is obvious that the "wealth" God is returning to Israel is in the form of Russian Jewish medical doctors, rocket engineers, physicists, musicians, writers, chemists and numerous other highly skilled people.

Teachers of Bible prophecy have speculated for years about various end-time scenarios, but I find it quite amazing that virtually no one fully foresaw the radical changes in Russia preceding the end of the second millennium. Could it be that the biblical predictions of conflict between God and Magog (understood to be the region of the former Soviet Union) might be triggered by divinely engineered jealousy? Will Israel become so Russian due to a potential population of three million Russian Jews that the land of the north will move to supposedly "reclaim its own"? Will jealousy be the "hook" God places in the jaw of Israel's adversary to the north to trigger the ill-fated invasion written about in the book of Revelation (see Revelation 16) that is destined to end in the Battle of Armageddon?

Part 4

A PROPHETIC PROCLAMATION

Gazing into the Future

10

Taking the Pulse of God and His People

> But when He, the Spirit of truth, comes, He will guide you into all the truth; for He will not speak on His own initiative, but whatever He hears, He will speak; and He will disclose to you what is to come.
>
> John 16:13

The more critical the times, the more important is our need to seek God for understanding, knowledge and direction. What is beating God's heart? What is He saying through His written Word? What is He revealing through the voice of the Holy Spirit? What is He doing among men right now? What part are we to play in His plan? As a nurse takes a patient's pulse to determine the heart rate, we are "taking the pulse of God" when we seek God's view of the times.

Sometimes God uses seemingly insignificant events in seemingly insignificant locations to give advance warning or prophetic indications of what is coming on a global or generational scale. God used an ordinary person, for example, tucked away in an insignificant manger in Bethlehem to transform the world.

God is pleased when men and women take the time to understand the issues of the times. He is delighted when we seek to understand the ways He deals with us. The first book of Chronicles said the sons of Issachar were "men who understood the times, with knowledge of what Israel should do" (1 Chronicles 12:32). This kind of knowledge can come only from God.

We are a people who must learn to take the pulse of God, discerning the times in which we live and gleaning from the lessons of past generations. May the sons of Issachar arise for this generation!

A Mission Trip to Austria

In 1996, David Fitzpatrick, a group of friends and I took another mission trip. This time we went to the small city of Wiener Neustadt, south of Vienna, Austria. We were there to lead a prophetic conference. Fitzpatrick and his family had just completed a divine assignment to assist the Avner Boskey family and other leaders of new Messianic congregations in Saint Petersburg and Moscow, Russia. They were ready to return to the United States. When I called Fitzpatrick about the Austria conference he said the Lord impressed upon him that he had to be there. Something special was going to happen. So we made arrangements to rendezvous in Vienna.

A team of German leaders and several intercessory and prophetic friends joined us for this gathering. Rich and Gale Harris, the founders of Living Word Ministries International and the senior ministers of The Front Range S.O.S. (a Denver, Colorado–based congregation and school of the Spirit), also came. The Harrises went with Michal Ann and me on the first prayer tour we led to Israel with Rabbi Boskey of Final Frontier Ministries. They were apprehended by the Holy Spirit on that trip and stayed in touch with us afterward. It was a joy to have them with us for the conference in Austria, but there was much more going on than any of us anticipated.

A wonderful interdenominational church founded by Pastor Helmuth Eiwen and his wife, Uli, in Wiener Neustadt sponsored the conference. Helmuth was originally a Lutheran pastor, but he felt led to establish a pioneer work called the Ichthys Church. This church, like others, sensed a resistance in their region toward the Gospel of the Kingdom and became frustrated that many efforts to bring fresh life to the area failed. The Eiwens and their prayer group had been seeking God for the answer to the questions, "What is wrong with this city?" "What are the hindrances standing in our way and keeping us from making an impact for the Gospel?"

The First Vision: A Small Book Revealed

After seeking the Lord, Uli received several open-eyed revelatory visions. In the first one she saw a small book surrounded by darkness. A bright light suddenly illuminated the book, and in it Uli recognized a part of the old city wall in Wiener Neustadt. The next day they found the old section of the wall—along with something else they never expected. Gail Harris has written a book about the Eiwens' prophetic journey titled *The Gateway to Reconciliation.* In it she recounts:

There they found that six Jewish tombstones had been affixed to the wall as a monument. Next to them was written an inscription: "These tombstones came from a Jewish cemetery in Wiener Neustadt that was closed in 1496."[1]

The Eiwens examined the historical record to see what had happened five hundred years earlier. They discovered that Wiener Neustadt was home to the second largest community of Jewish people in Austria. Unfortunately, that beautiful locale was also the favorite city of Emperor Maximilian I, a member of the Hapsburg dynasty and the ruler of what was called The Holy Roman Empire. Three years after he ascended to the throne, the 34-year-old monarch issued a devastating decree that remained in force for [four] hundred years: "All Jews from Wiener Neustadt must leave the city and for all time and eternity they may not come back."[2]

This royal decree was actually a demonic curse that within 150 years brought cultural and financial destruction to the entire city. The gates of Wiener Neustadt, however, reopened to Jewish people around 1900. By the 1930s, twelve hundred Jewish citizens lived in the city, which was the fourth largest Jewish community in Austria. Then the Nazis annexed Austria in the Anschluss of 1938.

To their horror, the Eiwens discovered that many of Wiener Neustadt's Jewish children had been separated from their parents and sent away. Later the older Jewish citizens had been shipped off to concentration camps where most died. Any survivors from the Jewish community in Wiener Neustadt, therefore, were most likely children during the war. The Eiwens led the leadership of Ichthys Church in repentant prayer for the sins of the past, but somehow they sensed that something more, something personal and public, had to be done.

The Second Vision: A Tree of Healing

Uli received another vision in which she saw a young tree with ancient roots on the city wall in front of the gravestones. The Lord called it a Tree of Healing and compared it to the Body of Christ. He said that it would bring healing to its ancient roots—the city of Wiener Neustadt and the Jewish people who suffered so much in that place.

After receiving a prophetic word from a visiting American minister concerning delegations of Jewish people from all over the world coming to Wiener Neustadt, the Eiwens felt they knew

168

what they had to do. They set out to find Jewish survivors of the Holocaust who originally lived in their city. It was an impossible task, but God intervened to give them the name of a Jewish man living in Israel. He was the son of the last head rabbi of Wiener Neustadt, who had died at the hands of the Nazis.

The Eiwens traveled to Israel to meet this man and tell him what God said they must do. In turn, he helped them contact 25 other Jewish survivors from Wiener Neustadt who were living in Israel. Eventually almost the entire church congregation from Wiener Neustadt went to Israel, where they met in Haifa with a group of survivors!

Holocaust Survivors Return to "Beachhead"

The church in Wiener Neustadt paid for three groups of Jewish Holocaust survivors to return to Wiener Neustadt from Israel and other parts of the world. Each time a group came, the Eiwens and their church congregation asked forgiveness for the wrongs perpetrated during World War II. A supernatural spirit of reconciliation brought healing and close relationships that continue to this day. This reconciliation was monumental.

In the summer of 1995, my oldest son, Justin, and I visited the Eiwens at their home in Wiener Neustadt. We were having breakfast one morning when I began to pray for them. Suddenly in a vision I saw the date June 6 appear across Helmuth's forehead! They told me about a prophetic word they had received the year before that said, "You are people who pray for one specific city, and this city will be a beachhead."[3]

Shortly after our breakfast together the Eiwens were in England, and they received a prophetic reminder that Allied troops had established a beachhead and turned the tide of World War II at Normandy on June 6, 1944. The Eiwens knew that another army, an army of God, was destined to establish a beachhead in Wiener Neustadt: first in the natural and then in the spiritual.

169

On June 6, 1996—six years after the Eiwens established Ichthys Church and five hundred years after Maximilian I banned the Jewish people from the city of Wiener Neustadt— the final group of Jewish Holocaust survivors returned to the city. They heard Helmuth Eiwen ask them, "Please forgive us." Since that group included more than ten Jewish men, a Sabbath service was held at the request of the son of the last head rabbi of Wiener Neustadt before the Nazis came.

Breakthrough Comes at Menorah Service

The Holocaust survivors and their Gentile sponsors gathered in front of the memorial in the old wall of the city—the place where the tombstones of the disenfranchised Jews signified their rejection by men through the decree of Maximilian I and marked the tragic betrayal and death of the Jews of Wiener Neustadt. Then the son of the rabbi, now an elderly grandfather, uttered ancient prayers from God's Word. He and his grandson blew out the candles of a silver menorah brought from Israel for the service. Then the Jewish visitors gave the menorah to the Eiwens as a memorial gift.

Gail Harris described what happened after the service:

> After the Sabbath service, a Sabbath meal was held in the hotel. An inexplicable joy suddenly broke through. They couldn't describe it—it was like an explosion. It began with singing. The men stood up and began to dance with one another. The windows were wide open because it was so hot, and others could hear the singing all over the city. These were the sounds of a people who had been set free. They never would have imagined even being able to laugh in this city. One of the wives said to Uli, "I have *never* seen my husband dance!"[4]

Breakthrough came when Jews and Gentiles lit the candles of the menorah—the candles representative of the light of Jehovah in the ancient holy place of the Tabernacles and the

Temple of Solomon. Like Aaron of old had done, a line was drawn in the sand. The death plague was checked, and life began (see Numbers 16:44–49).

The prophetic action of relighting was a picture of how Gentiles offer again the light we received through Jewish people. I am speaking, of course, of the light of the Messiah, who entered the world and redeemed all men, as the ancient Scriptures said He would. What happened in Wiener Neustadt was a landmark act of identificational repentance reminiscent of the restoration Paul described:

> All Israel will be saved; just as it is written,
> "The deliverer will come from Zion,
> He will remove ungodliness from Jacob."
> "This is my covenant with them,
> When I take away their sins."
>
> Romans 11:26–27

Extending Restoration beyond the Walls of the Church

Unique to the gathering in Wiener Neustadt was how it affected more than just the people inside a church building or the relatively small number of Jewish Holocaust survivors who traveled from Israel. The entire city felt the impact and was deeply involved in this reconciliation and repentance. At the invitation of the mayor, some of the Jewish visitors spoke to students at the local high school. They described what happened to them and their families during the Holocaust. This attracted wide media exposure. In another spin-off from the gathering, a student exchange program was established between the school in Wiener Neustadt and a high school in Bat Yam, near Tel Aviv, Israel. This will influence generations to come. We perceived that there was a "governmental mantle" imparted to Helmuth and Uli Eiwen not only to bring the reconciliation of God to Jewish people and Gentiles, but also to take it to secular institutions and governments.

171

Blowing the Trumpet in Nashville

Three months after the Sabbath service took place in front of the old wall in Wiener Neustadt, the Eiwens brought the silver menorah with them to Nashville, Tennessee, at the invitation of Fitzpatrick and members of our prayer team. I was still living in Kansas City, Missouri, at the time but was deeply involved in prayer for Israel and for the Jewish people who still resided in the land of the north.

Don Finto, Fitzpatrick, a number of other intercessors and I had sensed a strong redemptive gift of God upon the city of Nashville and a place of a stewardship from the Lord for that city to "blow a trumpet" for Israel. Many people in Nashville had done much on behalf of Israel, and our prayer was to plant a spiritual "candlestick" (similar to the "lampstand" in Revelation 1:12) in Nashville on behalf of Israel. I share this not to elevate Nashville but to reveal the spiritual principles involved in our prophetic prayer journey.

Fitzpatrick brought the Eiwens to Nashville on February 13, 1997, for a historic prayer convocation at Finto's Belmont Church. My wife and I flew from Kansas City to attend the event. When the Eiwens spoke God began to move. We lit the menorah candle and asked the Lord to give us, as representatives of the city, a heavenly lampstand on behalf of Israel.

During the service the Lord spoke to me. I even wrote His words in my Bible: *You were born for this city, and this city was born for you.* It was a spiritual ambush. My wife and I had come to support this prophetic act, but the Lord had bigger plans. The following June my family and I moved to the Music City. We reestablished our ministry base in what I have come to call "Worship City, U.S.A." Nashville now also hosts a prayer watch for Israel and Jewish people around the world.

At that time Finto was emerging as a spiritual father and friend to Messianic Jews all over Israel. He became so involved with this God-given mandate that he turned over the pastorate of Belmont, a prominent Spirit-filled evangelical church, to one of his associates. To facilitate his new outreach, Finto launched a ministry he named The Caleb Company.

Passing the Baton

With the lighting of the menorah, what had started in Wiener Neustadt, Austria, had come to Nashville, Tennessee. When that group of intercessors with a heart for Jewish people assembled in Nashville, it became clear to us that what God began in the land of the north was being exported by the Holy Spirit to other cities and nations. If the second great exodus could be compared to a marathon relay, then we were being handed a baton—but it was obvious there would be more than one baton to pass.

In a way, we were permitted by the Lord to help pass batons from Austria and the land of the north. We handed them off first in Nashville, Tennessee, and then in England and Western Europe. After the Nashville conference we prayed at a conference mentioned at the beginning of this book in Sunderland, England, where God lit a candle of anointing and authority to reconcile Gentiles and Jews. This ancient city on the North Sea was the historical shipbuilding center of the British Empire during the era of wooden ships, and in recent years a stream of renewal has broken out in a church there pastored by Ken and Lois Gott. In Sunderland the Holy Spirit linked together the revelations on Israel and the land of the north.[5]

During that period of time, it was as if a time bomb went off in the Spirit as prayers for Russia and God's purposes among the Jewish people exploded. Since that season, the burden of the Lord has been released into many cities, and prayer watches and prayer movements for Jerusalem have been launched. Truly, the Lord has been orchestrating something mighty!

Support for Jewish People Grows

God was also moving others to act on behalf of Jewish people. The World Prayer Center in Colorado Springs, Colorado, for years had conducted a prayer effort they called the 10/40 Window, targeting so-called Third World nations in the 1990s. For the years 2000 to 2005, that effort was expanded to the 40/70 Window, which includes all of Europe and the former Soviet Union. Intercessors were encouraged to pray for the Gospel of Jesus Christ to come forth, for closed hearts to become opened and for demonic powers to be thwarted. Intercessors were also exhorted to call forth God's purposes among the Jewish people in the land of the north and wherever they may reside. Prayer walks and other strategic acts of intercession were built upon the foundation of what others had previously offered up to the Lord.

Perhaps the greatest short-term impact of this new prophetic direction came when members of the Spiritual Warfare Network consulted with Messianic leaders and other Church leaders to draft a historic statement of repentance to the Jewish people in America and the nations of the world. On January 13, 2000, members of the Spiritual Warfare Network presented a wreath and a signed copy of this statement to representatives of the National Holocaust Museum in Washington, D.C. After the statement was read at the presentation, the intercessors ended up on the floor repenting and weeping before God.

I can think of no better way to portray what we believe to be the pulse of God's heart in this generation than to reproduce this statement of repentance and reconciliation in its complete and unedited form.

Acts of Reconciliation in Canada

Our brothers and sisters in Christ in Canada have taken the commitment to stand with the Jewish people even a step

Statement of Repentance to the Jewish People in America and the Nations of the World

Dear Respected Friends in the Jewish Community who share in our common faith in the G-d of Abraham, Isaac and Jacob,

Something is happening in our generation that we deem to be motivated by the Almighty. People of different ethnic backgrounds and national origins are acknowledging the sins of past generations against each other in a desire for reconciliation and peace. The sons and daughters of former slave traders are taking upon themselves the sins of their forbears [sic] and confessing these sins to the sons and daughters of former slaves. You may be aware that a "Reconciliation Walk" was recently taken between Europe and Jerusalem by a group of Christians who were confessing the sins of the devastations of the Crusades.

We know that the Jewish people throughout the centuries have borne the greatest discrimination, the worst persecution and the most barbaric atrocities of all. We, too, have read the histories. We are aware that much of this has been done by Christians or by those who called themselves Christians, sometimes while calling upon the name of Christ.

This is a grotesque misrepresentation of the One who is called the Prince of Peace and who called us to love and to worship our Heavenly Father and to love our neighbor as ourselves. Though the Scriptures we call the New Testament have exhorted us to love, respect and exercise mercy toward you, the ancient people of G-d and G-d's chosen people to this day, we and our forefathers in the Christian faith have rebelled against that

command and have acted out of fear, prejudice, hatred and jealousy. Those who have not so acted have acquiesced by their silence during the times of crusades, pogroms and finally in the terrifying Holocaust.

Nor are we Christian believers in the United States without our own share in this guilt. Not only are many of us descended from the perpetrators of these crimes, but our forefathers stood by without registering complaint when, in the years of the reign of horror in Europe, Jewish refugees were turned away from our shores. Our forefathers turned their eyes away from the death plight of the European Jewish community. Even in recent years, some in the Christian community have often stood in apathy as synagogues have been torched, cemeteries desecrated and Jewish homes and businesses vandalized.

We grieve over these crimes against you, our Jewish brothers and sisters, and in the spirit of Daniel, who confessed the sins of former generations, we confess these horrors as sins and renounce them. We understand from our reading of the Prophet Zechariah that a time will yet come when the whole world turns against Israel. Should such a thing come to pass, many of us want to be numbered with those few Gentile Christians through the centuries who have risked their lives to protect you. We commit ourselves to standing with you in the strength of G-d, whatever the cost.[6]

175

Declaration from the Church in Canada

We, as a Body of concerned Christians representing the many streams of the Church in Canada, humbly make this Declaration to the survivors of the Holocaust and the Saint Louis ship. In the merciful prompting of God, we have been on a long prayerful journey of several years to bring us to this historic occasion. Our sincere expressions today are the fruit of much travel, numerous consultations, sacrificial giving and active involvement of thousands of Christians across Canada.

We express our deep sorrow and genuine repentance for the sins of our forefathers and the subsequent atrocities you have personally suffered. We are grieved that in May 1939, Canada rejected the St. Louis ship, carrying more than 900 Jewish men, women and children looking for a place of refuge from the Nazi regime in Europe.

We are shamed by the memory of Canada not honouring the commitment to bring one thousand Jewish children from a refugee camp in France to our shores in November 1942.

We admit that these two deplorable episodes were the result of strong anti-Semitic sentiment within Canada. The passive silence of the Canadian Church supported the government's tragic policies and decisions.

We identify with the sins of the past regarding the Holocaust, and we ask the forgiveness of you and all Jewish people. We endorse the pledge of our Prime Minister, the Honourable Jean Chretien, during his April 2000 visit to Yad Vashem: "As Prime Minister of Canada, I pledge to you that Canada will take a leading role to ensure that such atrocities never happen again."

• We warmly express our love to you and to all Jewish people in Israel and in the global Diaspora.

• We denounce any unbiblical beliefs within the Church that result in harmful attitudes and actions toward the Jewish people.

• We commit to stand with the Jewish people for righteousness and justice in all nations.

• We pledge to continue our intercession for Jewish people by heeding King David's exhortation in Psalm 122:

Pray for the peace of Jerusalem: "May they prosper who love you. May peace be within your walls, and prosperity within your palaces." For the sake of my brothers and my friends, I will now say, "May peace be within you." For the sake of the house of the Lord our God, I will seek your good.

November 5, 2000
Ottawa-Hull, Canada

further. On November 5, 2000, a historic gathering convened in Ottawa. Participants held a time of repentance and reconciliation with survivors of the ship *Saint Louis*, which in May 1939 was turned away from Canadian shores—along

176

with the nine hundred Jewish men, women and children who were aboard. Three hundred believers representing the Church came together in humility to ask for forgiveness for the shameful deed.

Among those who spoke on behalf of the Canadian Church were David Mainse, host of the *100 Huntley Street* television show; Archbishop Gervais, representing the Canadian Council of Bishops; and Doug Blair, nephew of former deputy immigration minister Fred Blair. Ken Hall from West Ottawa Christian Community chaired the gathering.

A Beat Is Pulsating in the Body of Christ

All these acts of reconciliation indicate that a shift is occurring in the heart of God's people. I feel a beat pulsating with the rhythm of God's heart in the Body of Christ.

These changes are wonderful! But more must happen. Change is coming. Change must come. The winds of change are blowing!

Change is on the way!

11

The Mordecai Calling
A Gaze into the Future

> For if you remain silent at this time, relief and de-
> liverance will arise for the Jews from another place
> and you and your father's house will perish. And
> who knows whether you have not attained royalty
> for such a time as this?
>
> Esther 4:14

The dark spirit of anti-Semitism—or what may be called "the spirit of Haman," named after the man who plotted to exterminate the Jewish people in the days of King Artaxerxes of Persia (see the book of Esther)—is on the move across the world today.

We Christians have a dangerous tendency to consider biblical narratives such as the story of Esther, Mordecai and Haman as myths or children's stories. On the contrary, these

178

stories are real and still instructive to us today. The Bible declares, "All Scripture is inspired by God and profitable for teaching, for reproof, for correction, for training in righteousness" (2 Timothy 3:16).

This ancient spirit of genocide still lives. It yields only to the power of God, and that power can be released only by a people who, like Esther's uncle Mordecai, pray and fast and even put themselves at personal risk.

A Divine Appointment in Berlin

The reality of this age-old nemesis of the Jews was driven further home to me in 1992, during one of my first trips to the central European nations right after the fall of Communism. After ministering in the nations formerly known as Yugoslavia and Czechoslovakia, I rode a train from Prague in the Czech Republic to Berlin, Germany. I traveled alone because I needed some special time to seek the Lord. Being a "Goll" of German descent, I have for years carried a heart for the German-speaking world, desiring that the wrongs of the past be righted.

I took advantage of the free time on the train to read Dr. David Yonggi Cho's book *Daniel: Insight on the Life and Dreams of the Prophet from Babylon*.[1] The book cover featured a striking image of a beastlike character. I was intrigued by this mosaic depiction of the ancient Isthar Gate of Babylon and pondered about what it meant. I even wondered if there was a purpose in my reading the book at that time.

Cho had written a remarkable phrase in the text: "In order to make a nation stand upright, the evil prince which is behind the nation must be driven away through prayer. The demon which seeks to steal and kill an individual or a family must also be bound in prayer."[2] The principles revealed in this book flowed right into the revelations presented in the second book I read on that long train trip, *Engaging the*

Enemy: How to Fight and Defeat Territorial Spirits by Dr. C. Peter Wagner.[3]

Guided by the Holy Spirit to the "Seat of Satan"

Although I had visited Germany previously, I knew only a few phrases in German. I had never been to Berlin. I did not even know where to get off the train or how to find lodging. But my Guide, the Holy Spirit, knew the layout of the land quite well.

My train trip ended at the Berlin Wall. I made it to a hotel, and then I did not leave my room for nearly three days. After being holed up in prayer, I sensed God releasing me to walk through the city to pray. That was when I literally stumbled across a section of the larger Berlin Museum called the Pergamon Museum, a place I did not know existed. (Pergamon is another name for Pergamum.)

In the book of Revelation, the Spirit said to the angel of the church of Pergamum,

> I know where you dwell, where Satan's throne is; and you hold fast My name, and did not deny My faith even in the days of Antipas, My witness, My faithful one, who was killed among you, *where Satan dwells.*
>
> Revelation 2:13, emphasis mine

As far as I know, this is the only mention in the Scriptures of a physical site where Satan's throne could be found. Pergamum was also called the place where the adversary dwelled or lived. It was not surprising to learn that in the original Greek, *pergamum* literally means "fortified, fortress or castle."[4]

I went into the Pergamon Museum and was shocked to find myself staring at the exact beastlike idol pictured on the front of Cho's book! But this was the original, the real thing. How could it be?

I soon learned that sometime between 1878 and 1886 (close to the time Joseph Rabinowitz met the Messiah and took the Good News from the Middle East back to his home in Eastern Europe), German engineer and archaeologist Karl Humann excavated the ruins of Pergamum in what is now Turkey. Most of what is called the Great Altar of Zeus was removed from Pergamum and shipped to Germany's Berlin Museum.[5] The stone sections of the Altar of Zeus remained in storage until they were reconstructed stone by stone. The completed work is called the Pergamum Altar, and it now resides in the section of the Berlin Museum called the Pergamon Museum.

The Pergamon Museum also contains Athena's Temple and a model of ancient Babylon's Ishtar Gate and Processional Way. They represent with chilling power the ancient enemy of Israel and the God of Israel. Here, right in front of my eyes, were the original artifacts from ancient Babylon.

After just reading about Daniel, the prophet to Babylon, in Cho's book, I entered this authentic, reconstructed pagan shrine the Bible describes as "the seat of Satan." I literally had walked into a building only to be confronted by the very pagan deity—the genuine original image—that I saw pictured on the front of Cho's book on Babylon and Daniel's prophecies. This was the actual graven idol to which men bowed and worshiped in Pergamum when John received the warning in the book of Revelation!

To put this in context, the day I stepped into the reassembled Altar of Zeus in Berlin, the children of Israel were again in captivity—but this time in the land of the north. They had reached the end of another seventy-year period (compare Daniel 9:1–19 with Jeremiah 25:11; 29:10), and another conquering nation was in turmoil after touching the "apple of God's eye." Not only did the Jewish people begin their journey homeward in Daniel's day at the end of seventy years, but the walls of Soviet Communism also came tumbling down at exactly the seventy-year mark of their origins! And there

I was, staring at the restored ruins of the time about which Daniel spoke. I wanted to maximize this once-in-a-lifetime "divine appointment."

Spiritual Roots of Anti-Semitism

I felt it was time to intercede quietly in the Spirit. I softly prayed that the same God who had enlightened Daniel would now enlighten me. As I waited upon God, the proverbial light began to go on. Massive pieces of a jigsaw puzzle started to fall into place. I was beginning to understand what God had orchestrated.

Could the spirit of anti-Semitism having a base of operation here in Germany have some connection with this occultic high place being reestablished? Could this be one of the spiritual strongholds that empowered Hitler's reign of terror? I mused. I listened. I learned.

I knew that in order to view the future accurately, we must have a proper reading of yesterday's headlines and an accurate pulse on today. I wondered, *What do we see when we gaze into the future? Where are we at this point? What are the current conditions in the nations of the world? Is the spirit of anti-Semitism at work again? What signs could give us some clues?*

From that initial revelation in Berlin, God has continued to reveal to me the spiritual pulse of His heart for His chosen people today. He has revealed to me how this brooding, anti-christ, anti-Semitic spirit is raising its ugly head all around the world, just as it has in the past. And whenever there is a major threat to God's Kingdom, God also counters it. Conflict is turned to great purpose. God always has a plan, and He always reveals it to His servants the prophets (see Amos 3:7). The more I pray and seek God's face, the more I sense a prophetic word rising in my heart for the nations concerning the need for an Esther anointing and a Mordecai anointing in the Church.

182

Jews Targeted in Russia

In the years that followed, pressures began to mount in Russia. Anti-Semitism once again arose with a vengeance. Fire bombings, persecution and violence began to occur on a regular basis. Anti-Semitic terrorists vandalized Jewish synagogues and cultural centers and attempted to assassinate leading Jewish figures. Russian Jewish leaders claimed that an "increasing number of [Russian] political figures . . . have with impunity issued anti-Semitic statements as part of their effort to win popular support."[6] Even the number of Jewish people allowed to receive visas to emigrate to Israel was legally reduced.

Richard Glickstein had been working with Messianic congregations in Moscow. As Russians began to show greater animosity toward Westerners and to blame the United States for their economic woes, Glickstein, a Jewish American, could have become a target of harassment. Glickstein moved his family from Moscow to Germany where he worked with a pocket of Russian Jews. Then he relocated to Finland so he could be postured to help the growing number of Russian-speaking Jewish people wanting to leave the former Soviet states. Today my friend has relocated to New York to reach out to American Jewry. He is one of many modern-day Mordecais who are being positioned for what is about to come—the second great exodus!

Targeted in Austria, Hungary and the United States

Austria, the nation that gave us some of the great composers, philosophers and artists, also produced Adolf Hitler and the Nazi movement. In 2000, a far-right political party headed by alleged Nazi-sympathizer Joerg Haider was allowed to join the ruling coalition of the Austrian government. The move sent shock waves throughout Europe.

The Jewish people both in Austria and neighboring Hungary have since felt the growing threat of anti-Semitism once again breathing down their necks. In recent years, the ruling party in Hungary's capital, Budapest, has been headed by Laszlo Kover. Rabbi David Levine calls Kover "blatantly anti-Semitic."[7]

Even the United States has felt the pangs of growing anti-Semitic violence. On the Saturday before Palm Sunday 1999, three of the five Jewish synagogues in Sacramento, California, were firebombed. Rick Stivers, who like Glickstein had moved to Moscow with his family to seek God's heart for the Russian Jews, at one point visited one of the burned-out synagogues while fire marshals, police and the FBI were still conducting their investigations. He collected pieces of the burned synagogues. He and his wife, Annie, kept them in their home and have used them as a prayer reminder to cry out to the Lord on behalf of the Jewish people. Stivers commented, "I wondered if in the last fifty years there had been any other city in the world that had seen three synagogues torched in one day."[8]

A Growing Concern about the Fate of the Jewish People

The Lord often has spoken to my wife, Michal Ann, through prophetic dreams, and many of her dreams have come to pass. My concern for the Jewish people in the land of the north grew even greater when Michal Ann began to have consistent, vivid dreams about a new European holocaust. This is what Michal Ann saw in one of her dramatic dreams in the summer of 2000:

> I saw thousands of Jews trying to escape from within European countries. In this dream they not only were trying to escape through Finland and across the North Sea to England, but they also were trying to head south through Italy to the Mediterranean Sea. [Their route] included Russia, Germany, France, Austria and the whole European scene.

184

These countries were providing transportation so the Jews could escape, but their policy toward anyone who wanted to pursue the Jews was: "Whoever wants to go after them may do so. However many you kill is fine. Our official statement is that we are allowing them to leave, and we are providing transportation. Whatever happens to them in transit is not our responsibility."

There were many different modes of escape, but in every case I saw tremendous numbers of people being killed. It was horrible.

I saw railway boxcars filled with Jewish people—just like the images of Jews herded into Nazi boxcars during the Holocaust of World War II. They were packed like sardines. In some cases it seemed like someone had purposely pulled out old train cars from the World War II Holocaust and made these Jews get into those same boxcars. They also had rigged the sliding doors to these boxcars so they would stay open. Then I saw automobiles filled with modern neo-Nazis in uniforms driving alongside these train cars and killing as many people as they could with their guns.

At a later point I saw that only a handful of Jews had survived the train trip. I also noticed that in some of the boxcars hangman's nooses had been tied to supporting beams. As many as fifty nooses were in a car, and some of them had been used to hang Jewish victims. Their bodies were cut down, but the Nazis left the ends of the nooses hanging in the boxcars to terrorize all the people who might try to escape in the future.

They also used a taxidermy procedure on three Jewish bodies, and their stuffed skins hung in the nooses. Anyone riding in the boxcars was jostled by the carcasses throughout the train ride. I remember riding in one of the cars and bumping up against one of those bodies while looking into its face. It was just horrible.

Then the scene changed, and I saw Jewish people trying to escape in automobiles. Once again I saw carloads of uniformed neo-Nazis pulling alongside them. The Jews were fleeing for their lives, and they had little with which to defend themselves.

I remember one carload of Jewish people in particular because they actually fought back with some boat oars they had found. The only thing they could think to do was to wait until these Nazi soldiers had pulled up alongside.

When the neo-Nazis pulled up alongside the Jews, they rolled down the window to point their guns. The Jews stuck their boat oars through the window and jabbed them into the chests of the soldiers, crushing their sternums. In their desperation, they had no choice but to brutally defend themselves.

Every time the Jews tried to defend themselves, it was with hand tools and in hand-to-hand combat. The enemy always had cars and guns.

It seemed that Italy had decided to open up a portion of its border to the Jews. Many, however, were still being killed—thousands upon thousands. I found myself praying in the dream, "Open the door! Open the door and let them go!"

Finally the few straggling refugees who made it through the gauntlet of escape seemed to arrive at their destination—a large green pasture that was totally surrounded by a dense planting of scrubby oak trees. In one way it seemed like it could be a good defensive place, but to me what seemed to be the issue was that those trees constricted a possible path of escape should one become necessary. And I had a foreboding sense that the neo-Nazis were still following and that the Jews had no real security at all.

I was one of these refugees, along with two of my children, because in the dream I was Jewish. We experienced these things alongside the Jewish people.

The Jews were provided with some empty, rough cabins, but I do not know if they had any small cots or blankets. It just seemed that all the Jews had were the things they had brought with them.

This was definitely a dream about the Jews being hunted, but it had a twisted, "sporting edge" to it. The Nazis let them think they were escaping, but they were really just playing a mental game with them.

The enemy let them run while driving them with fear. They wanted to see how many they could track down and kill, and they wanted to see how they would react.[9]

God sometimes gives us glimpses of unpleasant things not to paralyze us with fear but to energize us to pray in faith. I fell to my knees in even greater intercession for my Jewish brothers in the land of the north and other nations.

A Fresh Focus on Esther

In February 2000, I spoke at The Lord of the Harvest conference in Hanover, Germany. The theme of this event came from the Lord's words in Matthew 9:38: "Therefore beseech the Lord of the harvest to send out workers into His harvest."

I was slated to speak each of the first two nights of the three-night conference. In a dream I had before I traveled to Hanover, however, the meeting on the second night took a different direction because of the weighty presence of the Spirit of the Lord during the worship time. I dreamed that I would be given "a trumpet to blast" on the third night. (This was not a desire on my part to have a third night at the podium. I speak so often in so many places that my itch to preach was scratched many years ago.)

As I had dreamed, on the second night of the conference the anointing of God settled upon us as we worshiped. Many in the audience were on their faces seeking the Lord, as His presence among His people was both sweet and convicting.

In that atmosphere of high anointing I felt led to read the book of Esther in its entirety. I had read it scores of times before but never under these circumstances. Within the first few verses, I realized I was seeing Esther's story with a different set of spiritual lenses. This time I focused on Mordecai instead of Esther. The Lord wanted me to see and understand the role Mordecai played in that time of crisis. Sure enough, I was asked to address the conference on the third night. When I spoke, I told the people, "Rarely do I stand in what I would call the 'office of a prophet' to give a word to a nation. But I believe the Lord would have me give a prophetic word to the nation

187

of Germany." I then proceeded to tell them that God wanted to raise up Mordecais for this generation to prepare Esther, figuratively representing the corporate Church in its proper role as deliverer and intercessor for the Jewish people.

On that third night of the meeting in Hanover, after a sanctified time in God's presence at the close of my message, I gave a word to Germany: "The Russians are coming." I explained that a God-sent Russian invasion of Jewish people was about to descend on the nation of Germany. It would be the Germans' opportunity to right history. I stood in brokenness, reminding the audience that German people and the slumbering Church worldwide had slaughtered the Jews before—but we could give them safe harbor today and in the future. It was a prophetic word to an entire nation—a Mordecai and Esther call.

Mordecai and Esther: A Fresh Perspective

I am convinced that we are destined to relive the book of Esther in this generation! In the book of Esther, Mordecai warned the queen about Haman's plot against the Jewish exiles (see Esther 3–4). Let's take a deeper look at this call of God on the man Mordecai. What was his God-given task? What was his divine assignment?

Mordecai's job was to raise up and prepare Esther for her hour of influence before the king. Mordecai raised Esther as his own daughter. He did not bow down or pay homage to Haman but worshiped only the one true God. He intercepted Haman's scheme of the enemy and revealed it with wisdom to those in authority. He walked in prophetic counsel and instilled courage in Esther.

Esther, properly tutored and mentored by the counsel of Mordecai, seized the moment through prayer and fasting. Alongside Mordecai, Esther entered into an urgent act of crisis intervention: a three-day fast from food and drink of any kind.

188

No one casually enters into this kind of a fast. A life-and-death crisis is a good reason; so is a direct command from God.

Then Esther launched an all-out appeal to the king for the deliverance of her fellow Jews from their sworn enemy. Esther was anointed to intervene and stand in the gap, yet she had to walk in cooperation with the preparation of Mordecai, the spiritual authority that God placed in her life. Her intervention would not have succeeded unless she had first cooperated.

If there had been no Mordecai, then there would have been no Esther. If there had been no Esther, then genocide of an entire generation would have occurred!

We Must Learn to Walk Together

Prayer gave Esther the right of approach, helping create the favor that extended the scepter of grace, and gave her privileged access to the supreme earthly authority, the king. God was the true authority, but He chose to work through Mordecai to alert Esther to her destiny and the timing of her intercessory acts on behalf of the Jewish people.

In an hour of crisis, intercessors and those in authority (spiritual and secular) must learn to walk together. Today, as in Esther's day, millions of lives are at stake. Just as intercessors cannot afford to walk an independent road, so spiritual leaders must avoid the temptation to walk and lead in exclusivity, reserving their outreach, leadership and spiritual resources solely for their own gatherings. A marriage must occur between the watchmen on the walls and the gatekeepers of every city.

In the Old Testament the gatekeepers were elders who sat at the gates. Today they are the spiritual and physical governmental authorities and are to act in a spiritual sense as gatekeepers of His presence.

Biblically, watchmen on the walls were posted in high places to watch every route of approach and announce ahead of time the identity and purpose of those who approached the city.

189

Watchmen today are the intercessors. They are to watch and see what the Lord is doing locally and among the nations. Spiritually, they are posted in high places to watch and announce ahead of time the identity and purpose of those who approach the community of God—whether the visitors are ambassadors of goodwill or enemies approaching with evil intent.

Watchmen do not always have the authority to apply the revelation or even to issue the warnings; by God's design their revelation and intercession must be submitted to the governmental authorities who sit at the gates. These gatekeepers, both secular and spiritual leaders, then must determine whether to bar the gates or to open them wide. No matter what opinions or experiences we may have, it is clear from God's Word that these two essential ministries must learn to walk together.

To put it more clearly, the evil, anti-Semitic Haman spirit is once again moving eagerly to wipe out the Jewish people. The Church (Esther) may or may not be ready. It is the job of the watchmen—the Mordecais—to recognize the dangers approaching and inform the Church before it is too late, so that she can fill her God-ordained role of saving His chosen people.

A Historic Window of Opportunity

People gifted with prophetic vision and insight came to understand that Jewish people—in this case Russian Jews—were approaching another season of crisis. This Mordecai and Esther call is not limited to German believers; this is a historic global window of opportunity for the Church to arise and wash the stains and spots out of our bridal garment. This is our chance to right history. Like a nurse with a fully loaded needle, the Holy Spirit wants to inject into the global prayer movement the burden of the Lord for the Jewish people. We need a potent injection of God's heart into our heart! That is why God wants to raise up a Mordecai anointing to prepare Esther for a time of intervention.

190

After my prophetic word to the Church in Germany, Chuck Pierce, who was serving as the executive director of the World Prayer Center and vice president of Global Harvest, talked with me about this word. He was in Europe when he sent me the following email message:

> Since I am here in Europe, I will pray through this issue. One strong word we received before leaving on this trip had to do with Haman—how [he] was waiting and watching. I have pondered it much. Therefore, I will believe with you that the Mordecai and Esther anointing will begin to arise all across Europe to overthrow the noose being prepared.
>
> The other portion of the word was, "Tell Esther not to come forth until Mordecai releases her and tells her when." I will pray about timing.[10]

My mandate and heavenly burden became clear. It involved releasing a cry and making a loud, divine declaration: Let the Mordecais and Esthers of the Church come forth! Let these men and women take their stand for God and for the Jewish people. There is no better time than now! We were born, anointed and set in place for "such a time as this."

The Church must throw out life preservers of prayer and fasting to save the Jewish people who are at risk of being overtaken by a rising flood of unreasoning anti-Semitism. I am not talking about something that is going to come; no, it has already begun! In fact, it is spiraling out of control in hot spots around the world, especially in the former Soviet bloc.

When we speak comfort to God's covenant people, we honor Him. We want the Jewish people to discover and receive their Messiah; but one of the first steps is to reach out in prayer, fasting, love, compassion and practical assistance, particularly to help them safely return to their ancient home of Israel.

Serious crises call for serious strategies. Unbridled attacks from the enemy require our most powerful weapons of warfare. Desperate times demand desperate measures!

We must somehow tap into deeper veins of prayer.

Such a longing has compelled me to look back at historic times of effective crisis intercession. What was it that worked for our spiritual ancestors when they faced their most difficult trials? I found some answers in Wales.

A Visit with Samuel Howells

Trevor and Sharon Baker, friends of mine who live in England, had graduated from Swansea Bible College, also known as the Bible College of Wales. They arranged for me to meet with Samuel Howells, the only living son and successor of the great intercessor Rees Howells.

Sue Kellough, a proven prophetess who was serving on the board of directors for our ministry, came with me. Howells, who had succeeded his father as president of the Bible college, was 86 years old when we had tea with him on the Swansea campus. He showed us "the blue room" where many historic prayer meetings had taken place during the dark years of World War II. An elderly lady who had participated in all of those prayer gatherings also attended the tea.

Before the door had opened in Wales, I had already visited other places on the historic crisis intercession map. I had led a group to Herrnhut, Germany, the site of the Moravian community and prayer movement that conducted an unprecedented round-the-clock prayer watch that was unbroken for more than a hundred years. The Holy Spirit had descended upon the Moravians in an unforgettable manifestation of divine impartation.[11]

It became clear that this time (in the 21st century) the Lord had another plan. This was to be a quieter, personal impartation. Why He would choose such a strategy soon became apparent.

During our "divine appointment" in Wales, I asked Howells some vital questions, knowing that his family and the

192

intercessors at the college had a proven anointing to pray for intervention.

In his book *Rees Howells: Intercessor*, author Norm Grubb recounts how Howells and students at Swansea Bible College had interceded during crucial moments at the end of World War II. They received divine revelation about Nazi movements and aerial invasion schemes, and then they prayed using the writings of the Old Testament prophets. At the last minute Nazi bombers turned back without any apparent reason. "There seemed no reason why the Luftwaffe should have turned home just at the moment when victory was in their grasp," records the Swansea Bible College website. "But we know why."[12]

The Key to Authority in Prayer

As soon as we settled down to tea, I asked, "Mr. Samuel [the proper way to address Samuel Howells in Wales], how is it that your father got this revelation? How did he and the people know what to pray for? I know it was not by newspaper [reports], and I know it was not by radio. How did he know what armies were in what locations? How did he know what battles to pray through and when? Did it come by dreams or visions? How did it come?"

Howells did not immediately answer my question. The son of the great intercessor turned to me and simply said, "Don't you think it is time for another crumpet?"

He freely talked about other things. He answered questions and carried on a dialogue without hesitation, but his demeanor changed when I turned to him again and asked, "Mr. Samuel, how is it that your father and all the intercessors in that period of time knew what to pray for? What was the key of authority that the Lord gave you for intervention in that period of time?"

Again, Howells looked at me and said, "Don't you think it is time for a little more tea?" It was as if he did not hear the questions I asked and would not give the answers I yearned to hear.

I grew bolder. A third time I inquired, "Mr. Samuel, I must know! Did an angel come and announce these things? How did they know? Did it happen by spiritual gifts or through illumination of the written Word? How did they know of the battles and when and how to pray?"

Still he gave no answer. "Enough of this," Howells said, refusing to satisfy my query.

Then Sue Kellough, older and more tenacious than I, approached Howells. She dropped to her knees, peered up at the veteran intercessor and gave it one last try: "Mr. Samuel, our nation is in great need, and [with] the days that lie in front of us we are in great need of the kind of prayer that your father and you and these people have known in the past."

A tear trickled down his cheek as he looked into our eyes: "You must understand, the Lord's servant [that is how he referred to his father] was possessed by God."

Kellough and I wept. Then we asked Howells to pray for us. Later we learned that Howells rarely met with people, and I have been told that he rarely prayed for people when he did meet with them. Nevertheless, he laid his hands upon us and asked the Lord to grant to us the authority of "identification" and "intercession."

He asked the Lord to give us the place of purity in prayer, that our hearts would become aligned with God's purposes and that we would pray out of God's heart. He prayed simply, concluding with the prayer that it would all be centered in Jesus.

What a timely, strategic appointment! Mr. Samuel Howells has now moved on to his heavenly reward.

But I left Swansea Bible College that day knowing I had taken part in a divine appointment. This was greater than a mere prayer technique. Howells had reluctantly shared with me a truth that few people are willing to implement in their lives: The most effectual fervent prayer comes when the Lord

Himself takes possession of His people. We are not our own. We were bought at a price. We are being called to be possessed with and by God.[13] This revelation answered all my questions about the key to effective crisis intercession.

I later came across the text of a letter from Dr. Kingsley Priddy of Swansea Bible College. It was reproduced in the appendix of Gustav Scheller's book *Operation Exodus*:

> You see, intercession is not prayer, nor even very intense prayer. Anyone may pray, and pray earnestly, for something, and yet not be committed to be irrevocably responsible, at any cost, for its fulfillment. The intercessor is.
>
> In intercession there is identification with the matter or persons interceded for. The intercessor is willing to take the place of the one prayed for; to let their need become his need; to let their need be met at his expense and to let their suffering become the travail of his own heart.
>
> That is how the Lord Jesus "made intercession for the transgressors" (Isaiah 53:12). "He was numbered with the transgressors," and "He was wounded for (their) transgressions" (verse 5). He had to be "identified" with sinners; He secured their pardon by vicariously paying the debt that they owed.[14]

The Mordecai Call

The antichrist spirit of Haman has loosed a fresh plot to destroy the Jewish generation of today. The events of recent years bring me back to the same important questions: Have enough intercessors heard the sound of the shofar? Have enough of us not only listened but also obeyed the summons? Are we stirring ourselves to respond? Are we moving toward the next (and last) great awakening? Will enough of us be awakened in time?

The biblical Mordecai and Esther are gone. The season of Joseph Rabinowitz is over. Now it is time for someone in this generation to step forward, shout and signal to His shipwrecked people to flee to the Rock. As each generation passes on, another must carry the baton. The Holy One of Israel is once again looking for a man, for a woman, for a people to stand in the gap on behalf of His ancient covenant people.

God is seeking Mordecais and Esthers to step forward. He is calling people of prayer to stand in the gap in this generation. It is time to cry out to the Church with a solemn call to a yearly fast—an Esther Fast—for the salvation and preservation of the Jewish people around the world. In the name of Jesus Christ, I call forth the Mordecais to prepare Esther, which is the Church, for her greatest hour of selfless intercession for the Jewish people.

True deliverance comes in the realm of the Spirit, not in the realm of man. God is offering an opportunity for the Body of Christ to arise. A window of opportunity has opened, enabling the Church to right history before the throne of almighty God.

I was born for such a time as this. So were you!

Signs and Wonders Will Follow

When God delivered Israel from Egypt with the first great Exodus, He did it through sovereign acts of supernatural intervention. The Hebrews were not delivered from Pharaoh's grip by swords, chariots or mighty armies; they were delivered by God's hand. Supernatural signs and wonders were the tools of their release!

Most of the Jewish people who have made *aliyah* since World War II did not arrive in Israel through signs and wonders. They have migrated to Israel by plane and by ship. They have made their exodus because of the sacrifices of men. A few miracles occurred along the way, but most of the breakthroughs happened as the result of hard work and astute maneuvering through political mazes.

God will continue to use all of these means to free His people. There have been and will continue to be multiple phases of His great work. But my strong conviction is that the completion of the second great exodus is destined to eclipse the first, and it will again come about through the supernatural contending of altars.

We see "the altar of the occult and the demonic" rising around the world. At the same time, an authentic staff of God is being lifted through the prayers and selfless obedience of the Church. By this means, the supernatural authority of God will once again swallow up the counterfeit powers of the enemy.

The present era of the fishermen is coming to a close. Another era of the hunters is already beginning. The gentle awakening is giving way to a rude awakening (see chapter 2). As it was in Egypt during the first great Exodus, the Jewish people will be pushed out by the hands of the hunters and by the prophetic and the apostolic display of great signs and wonders—all for the glory of God.

We have seen miracle after miracle come to pass in recent years on behalf of the Jewish people in Russia. Everything occurred in response to prayer. There is no other explanation for the rapid disintegration of what was the world's second-ranked superpower. There is no other rationale for the fall of the Berlin Wall after decades of unrestrained terror and bondage. The truth is: Prayer changes things!

"Let My People Go"

With great power and authority, God's people are declaring to the land of the north: "Let My people go! Let My people go!" At such a time as this, we must ask: Where are the Corrie ten Booms and Fritz Graebes, the righteous Gentiles of our day who are willing to identify so closely with the plight of the Jewish people that they will put themselves on the line to see them saved and preserved from destruction? Where are the Dietrich Bonhoeffers who will stand up and declare the truth about God's love for their Jewish neighbors, even in the face of public disapproval and personal danger?

Are we willing to stand and make a difference? Then we must become possessed by God! Do we want to be close to the heart of God? Then we need to love the things that He loves, and that specifically includes His covenant people.

Now is the time for Mordecai to rise up and for Esther to be prepared. We must catch the Mordecai anointing and be people who prepare the corporate Esther, the Church, for this critical time. We need to call forth the same anointing for crisis intercession that was upon Rees Howells at Swansea Bible College during World War II.

Together, we can make history before the throne of God through the power of effective intercession!

12

What Then Shall We Do?

The burden of the word of the LORD concerning
Israel. Thus declares the LORD who stretches out
the heavens, lays the foundation of the earth, and
forms the spirit of man within him, "Behold, I am
going to make Jerusalem a cup that causes reeling to
all the peoples around; and when the siege is against
Jerusalem, it will also be against Judah. It will come
about in that day that I will make Jerusalem a heavy
stone for all the peoples; all who lift it will be severely injured. And all the nations of the earth will
be gathered against it. . . .

"In that day the LORD will defend the inhabitants
of Jerusalem, and the one who is feeble among them
in that day will be like David, and the house of David
will be like God, like the angel of the LORD before
them. And in that day I will set about to destroy all
the nations that come against Jerusalem.

"I will pour out on the house of David and on the
inhabitants of Jerusalem, the Spirit of grace and of
supplication, so that they will look on Me whom they

have pierced; and they will mourn for Him, as one
mourns for an only son, and they will weep bitterly
over Him like the bitter weeping over a firstborn."

Zechariah 12:1–3, 8–10

This phenomenal prophecy from Zechariah indicates that
the day is coming soon—perhaps immediately, perhaps in a
little while, but soon—when God will act decisively on behalf
of Jerusalem and her inhabitants. This is the day the world
has been waiting and aching to see. In that day, every one of
God's promises will be fulfilled. Are we ready? Do we have
oil in our lamps (see Matthew 25:1–13)? Can we hasten that
day? How can we prepare?

Throughout this book I have tried to present an overview
of the history of and God's plan for His people. But I also have
tried to give you a glimpse of some specific ways God has
been working among the Jewish people and among Gentile
believers while His prophetic clock moves toward the *kairos*
moment when His plan for Jerusalem will be consummated.
This is the message I have been preaching and teaching everywhere I go.

Despite what it may look like, Israel has not fallen so far
from God that it can never return. In fact, its falling away was
ordained by God as a measure of grace to us, the Gentiles.
Paul said it this way: "He redeemed us in order that the blessing given to Abraham might come to the Gentiles through
Christ Jesus, so that by faith we might receive the promise
of the Spirit" (Galatians 3:14, NIV).

The Gentiles are being embraced by the Jewish Messiah in
part to make Jews jealous (see Romans 11:11). Gentiles are
not "natural branches" on God's family tree, but rather "wild
olive shoots" who must recognize that they have been grafted
into His tree. God's plan is to graft the "natural branches" into

200

their own olive tree once again (see Romans 11:24), resulting in the reality that "all Israel will be saved" (Romans 11:26).[1]

With a firm grasp of this reality, we can pray and we can act as God gives us the grace and guidance to do so. We can make it a priority to ask Him to give us our personal assignments. The Lord Himself, our Commander in Chief, will show us where to stand and what to do. If we are going to align ourselves with the God of Israel, then we are going to have to align ourselves with His prophetic promises of salvation for the Jewish people and His promise to restore the city of Jerusalem in both a physical and a spiritual sense.

By prayer and action we can help prepare the army of Ezekiel 37—the dry bones of Israel—to rise to life again as a prophetic army that has come at last into its destiny. To do that, we need to keep urging the Church as never before to be filled with the Holy Spirit and to be led by Jesus Christ. Like Winston Churchill before World War II, we need to plead with our countrymen, "Wake up! Wake up before it is too late! The enemy is at the gates!" Getting people to wake up can become arduous business, as Churchill discovered, but if enough people join us in saying "Wake up!" then others will wake up and report for duty.

If our urgent prayers and declarations are not enough to wake up both the Church and Israel, then God Himself will do it (and He already is doing it, to a large extent) by allowing disasters and terrifying threats to proliferate. One way or the other, we will be shaken awake. We will not be able to ignore His voice. Our hearts will be softened, and we will become willing to follow the One who was pierced for our transgressions.

Apostolic Appointments

The beginning of the 21st century saw the birth of a new apostolic movement that is raising up effective ministries and planting new churches in record numbers. As a result, a veritable army of young people on fire for God is advancing on the kingdom of darkness, fueled by day-and-night prayer.

At the center of this church-planting movement, I believe, are the awakened or Messianic Sephardic Jews (those whose forefathers came from the region of Spain and Portugal) who now live in diaspora throughout much of Latin America. In chapter 6, you read about the Spanish Inquisition and the fate of Jews in Europe. This group of Messianic Sephardic Jews will be central to righting those wrongs of the past. As God moves upon these Sephardic Jews, they will retrace the trail their ancestors took from Europe to the New World. They will converge upon Spain and Portugal, where such evil atrocities prevailed in past centuries. Once back in their native lands, these Messianic Jews will take part in radical acts of intercession. They will break generational curses, extend prayers of forgiveness for past wrongs and reclaim what Satan has stolen. Empowered by the Holy Spirit, they will write a new page of history.

But the apostolic mission of the Jewish people goes even further. Missiologists believe that the final frontier of evangelism targets Islam and Hinduism. I contend that the eventual "secret weapon" of this evangelistic thrust is empowered Hebrew Christians. The devil cannot hold his ground against Messianic apostolic evangelists who are backed by a truly supernatural Church. The people of Israel must become a living, humble army whose Messiah has come, and they must advance on their knees alongside the Church of the living God, which must become a radical representation of the Lord she names as the Christ.

Thus in this end-time season the apostolic reformation springs from a radical Church—not merely a religious institution whose programs are maintained without the transforming, powerful presence of God. The Church is apostolic in the sense that it was established upon the "foundation of the apostles and prophets" (Ephesians 2:19, 20). It has been sent

202

to take territory. Besides planting churches and establishing new works to expand the Kingdom of God on the earth, the Church also has been sent to bring divine order to godless chaos through the authority and name of the Prince of Peace, Jesus. Today's Church is beginning to display all of the characteristics, power and anointing demonstrated in the first-century Church of the book of Acts. Instead of being a powerless monolith that preserves the lifeless vestiges of a dead religion like some museum of failed faith, this is the Church of the living God that moves in supernatural signs and wonders. When God's Word is declared, the Lord Himself confirms it through signs and wonders (see Mark 16:20).

Through this 21st-century apostolic movement that combines the Gentile Church with the Messianic believers, God will be revolutionizing every one of our national, ethnic and political definitions. He is and will be pushing us beyond the denominational walls that we have worked so long to construct and maintain.

In previous centuries, the Church sat back in fear or apathy; even worse, it took the lead in persecuting the Jewish people in ignorance or outright hatred. Never again. I declare that this time the Church will take the lead in crisis intervention through intercession, carrying the Jewish people on our shoulders in fulfillment of the ancient prophecy:

> Thus says the Lord GOD,
> "Behold, I will lift up My hand to the nations
> And set up My standard to the peoples;
> And *they will bring your sons in their bosom,*
> And *your daughters will be carried on their shoulders."*
>
> Isaiah 49:22, emphasis mine

God's Mandate for the Church

I believe that we must possess five vital components to fulfill this particular mandate of God on the modern Church:

203

Discernment

This is an age of transition, and we must be shrewd as serpents and innocent as doves (see Matthew 10:16; 1 Chronicles 12:32). If we ask God for wisdom, then He will give it to us (see James 1:5). Inquire of the Lord so that the eyes of your heart will be enlightened with the Spirit of wisdom and revelation (see Ephesians 1:17–19).

Preparation

Scripture, especially the book of Proverbs, urges us to anticipate the future and be prepared for it. We prepare for the changing seasons, we take measures to avoid danger and we count the cost before we build something or go to war. Correspondingly, it is our responsibility to prepare for the final return of the King of kings.

Financial Commitment

An immense exodus to Israel has already taken place, but the exodus ahead of us will eclipse anything the world has ever seen. The Scriptures tell us that as the hunters are released in the former Soviet states and Europe, the Jewish people who remain will run for safety. When that second great exodus takes place, somebody needs to greet them with food, clothing, shelter, transportation and other assistance. These things cost money. Christians can support many organizations that offer help to the Jewish people, including the ones mentioned in the appendix called "Referral Ministries."

The Word of God

One of the most spiritual ways to help these Jewish pilgrims is to provide the life-giving truth of the New Testament to them in their own languages. Just as doctors need medicine and builders need lumber, Christian relief workers need appropriate "bridge tools" to help introduce these Jewish people to their Messiah. Invest in ministries that help provide the Word for the Jewish people.

Radical Prayer and Fasting

Radical prayer is Bible-based and crisis-oriented. It is persistent (see Luke 18:1–8). As never before, the Jewish people need justice and legal protection from their dark opponent and ancient adversary, Satan. As Daniel did, we are to cry out and fast before God on behalf of the Jewish people (see Daniel 9:3). Truly effective crisis intercession is launched from the biblical foundation of fasting. God's Word provides the greatest examples in Esther and Mordecai, who called a solemn three-day fast from all food and drink in a time of life-and-death crisis (see the book of Esther). Once again, God is calling us to an Esther fast on behalf of His ancient covenant people.

Destiny of Israel and the Church

Before his death in 2003, Derek Prince, a longtime friend of Israel, published a book called *The Destiny of Israel and the Church*. He reaches the following conclusions, which serve to sum up the message of *The Coming Israel Awakening*:

> The . . . analysis of the destiny of Israel and the Church, as unfolded in the Scriptures, leads us to certain important conclusions.
>
> First, the only reliable source of light upon the current situation in the Middle East is provided by God's prophetic Word. If we do not seek the light that comes from this source, we will inevitably find ourselves in the dark, subject to many forms of confusion and deception.
>
> Second, the destiny of both Israel and the Church has been determined by God in eternity on the basis of His foreknowledge. Its outworking in time is guaranteed by the irrevocable covenants which God has established with each of them.

Third, for all the good that God has promised to Israel and the Church, both are equally and totally dependent upon God's grace, which can be appropriated only by faith.

Fourth, tremendous tests and pressures lie ahead for both Israel and the Church, but those who faithfully endure will be privileged to share God's Kingdom with Him throughout eternity.

Fifth, Christians from Gentile backgrounds owe their entire spiritual inheritance to Israel. One appropriate way for them to acknowledge their indebtedness is to stand by Israel in the midst of their present pressures and to uphold them with faithful intercession.

Sixth, the peoples of the Middle East will never know true justice or lasting peace until they are submitted to God's appointed ruler, the Lord Jesus Christ.[2]

Prince, who influenced my life enormously, spoke often about the much-anticipated parallel restoration of both Israel and the Church.[3] But he emphasized the fact that it would be only through prayer and intercession that this could be accomplished, and that the key—the only key—to spiritual success would be to follow the plan of God. Jesus is the Head of the Church, and as such He has initiated a time of restoration that is making real changes in both Israel and the Church. We need to assent to His plan, pray for it and work with it.

Psalm 102:14 speaks of the servants of God taking pleasure in the very stones of Jerusalem. Even if you have never visited Jerusalem in person, you probably know that most of the city is built of stone. Those who love Jerusalem are insistent and persistent in their prayers for the city they love. They cry out in watchman-prayer day and night. They know that if they do not do it, then those very stones will cry out instead (see Luke 19:40).

This time of parallel restoration is being balanced against the time of desolation that has been leading up to it. First comes the desolation; then comes the restoration. Last comes the Judgment. The time of the end is near. It is easy to see if you know the signs of the times. Look around you. The fig tree is supposed to be bearing fruit. The vine is supposed to be mature. We are not all the way there yet, but we are moving into the final season.

Throughout the Bible, especially within Jesus' teaching in the gospels, we see fig trees and vines. The fig tree represents the Jewish people. The vine represents the Church. Whenever the fig tree and the vine are devastated and their crops are decimated, a time of restoration always occurs. Read the short prophetic book of Joel, for example, to see what I mean.

We and the generations before us have lived through one desolation after another. Now we are moving into the final and most glorious parallel restoration of them all. One way or the other, we will be involved. Why not be involved in a way that both hastens and advances the day of His coming while also pleasing the Lord Himself? Yes, it is time for a great awakening for both Israel and the Church!

A Personal Call

"From the days of John the Baptist until now the kingdom of heaven suffers violence, and the violent take it by force" (Matthew 11:12, NKJV). True and lasting peace for Jerusalem—and for the rest of the earth—must be appropriated through violence. Can you hear the sound of approaching hoofbeats? Are you ready for what lies immediately ahead—conflict, heart cries and blood? Are you anticipating the victory, joy and final fulfillment that will follow?

Have you received your personal summons to the battlefield? Your battlefield may be as close as the chair in which you are sitting as you finish this book. Like any army, this one includes soldiers who remain at home base, even in their prayer closets, supporting and opening the way for others who are on the front lines. It also includes supply trains, finance managers, armament manufacturers and more. (To mount the walls of intercession from your own home, join our Prayer Storm efforts where we pray together weekly using the modern technology of the Internet and Web-based teaching to pray for all the descendants of Abraham.[4])

On the other hand, your battlefield may be as far away as across the ocean. To know where to serve, you must receive a personal summons. Ask the Lord of the harvest to send workers into the harvest (see Matthew 9:37–38; Luke 10:2), and ask Him to set you to a specific task.

Unified and gathered together with many others who also hear from Him, we can prepare and accomplish the massive mission set before us, which is to bring in the great and final harvest of all history. The sons of Abraham, both by blood and in spirit, have been waiting for this day. This is the great Israel Awakening, and the glorious shofar sound is echoing across all the nations—as far as the Land of Promise!

On May 11, 2008, in cooperation with the Global Day of Prayer, I had the honor of participating with thousands of others in The Call Jerusalem. Twelve hours of nonstop worship and prayer led by Gentile and Jewish believers calling upon the name of the one true Lord declared that a new worldwide Pentecost is coming. The nations are waking up! The Church is awakening! Yes, Israel shall be awakened!

As I complete the penning of this book, I can see the vision once again. I see that angel in radiant white garments glowing with the presence of the Almighty. His shofar blew a sound into me. It woke me up! Perhaps that angel, or one under its charge, will awaken you to the prophetic destiny of Israel and the Church in these last days.

Can you hear the sound? It is time for the greatest awakening the world has ever seen—in Israel and in the Church!

Will you be a part?

Appendix A

Come Humbly to Israel!

Don Finto

As a non-Jewish believer who has come to some understanding of the purposes of God for the nation of Israel and the Jewish people in this end-time generation, let me encourage you to consider several things as you pursue connections with Jewish friends, acquaintances and co-workers and look forward to an upcoming visit to Jerusalem.

Come humbly to Israel; come humbly to Jerusalem. This is the Land of your inheritance. Here Jesus was born, lived, taught, ministered, was crucified as a common criminal and buried, rose from the dead, ascended from the Mount of Olives where He will return as King/Emperor/Supreme Ruler over all nations in a future world empire of peace (see Acts 1:11; Zechariah 14:9).

Israel is the only nation of the world whose land deed was signed by the Almighty Himself. Look at His words to Abraham, Isaac, Jacob and Joshua in Genesis 15:18–21; 26:3; 35:12 and Joshua 1:4, and His words through the psalmist in Psalm 105:8–11. The Land belongs to Abraham's descendants through Isaac and Jacob (Israel) in perpetuity, even though she will not have full possession until she is walking in the commandments of God (see Deuteronomy 28:15, 36, 41, 63).

Jesus predicted that Jerusalem would be destroyed and "taken as prisoners to all the nations" (Luke 21:24, NIV). Ezekiel 37:1–11 described Israel as dry bones that would be resurrected and into whom the breath of God would enter. Jeremiah called the return of Israel "out of all the countries where he had banished them" a greater miracle than the Exodus from Egypt (see Jeremiah 23:7–8, NIV).

God sees Jerusalem as "the center of the nations, with countries all around her" (Ezekiel 5:5, NIV). "Whoever touches you [Jerusalem] touches the apple of [God's] eye" (Zechariah 2:8, NIV). Even the boundaries of the nations somehow relate to the tribes of Israel (see Deuteronomy 32:8).

Believers in our day are learning to honor the host nations on every continent. Israel is the host nation of all nations. Of no other city does the Lord say, "Give yourselves no rest, and give him no rest till he establishes Jerusalem and makes her the praise of the earth" (Isaiah 62:6–7, NIV). No other city has a divine injunction to be remembered in prayer (see Psalm 122:6).

You, as a believer in Jesus, are grafted into the Jewish olive tree (see Romans 11:17). Grafted in, not replacing. This is our family of faith. Even Jewish people who have not yet come to faith in their Messiah are a part of our yet-to-be-redeemed family.

Enjoy the diversity of Abraham's sons and daughters who have been returned from two thousand years of exile from over a hundred nations and languages. Listen as people speak the language of Moses and the prophets. Enjoy especially the fellowship with your Jewish brothers and sisters whose eyes and hearts have been opened to their own Messiah.

Go to be blessed, but also go to bless others. Walk in the blessing God spoke to Abraham. "I will bless those who bless you, and whoever curses you I will curse; and all peoples on earth will be blessed through you" (Genesis 12:3, NIV). Israel was created as a blessing to all nations, but you have now become a part of that heritage, so you are both to receive and to carry the blessing wherever you go.

Those of us who have learned to love Israel and the Jewish people must, however, never forget her blood cousins, the Arab nations, the sons and daughters of Ishmael and other related peoples. Ishmael was not Abraham's son of the covenant and was sent away from his family home at an early age, but Abraham also blessed him and his descendants. "*As for Ishmael*, I have heard you: *I will surely bless him*" (Genesis 17:20, NIV, emphasis mine).

The surrounding Arab nations also have a destiny in God. Egyptians and Assyrians (which would represent today's Iraq, Syria and other nations adjacent to Israel) are also a people of destiny. They, along with Israel, will one day be a blessing to the whole earth (see Isaiah 19:23–25). Be alert to both Jewish and Arab believers who are united and often risking their lives to see that their people learn of their common Redeemer.

Ours is a unique day in history, the day predicted by Jesus, the day for which the prophets and apostles yearned:

1. Israel will be returned from centuries of exile and established as a nation. The return from Egypt was from the south, the return from Babylon was from the east, but this return is from the north (think Russian Jews), south (Ethiopia), east and west (think America and other Western nations) (see Isaiah 43:5–6).

   Israel entered into exile as two distinct nations: the northern kingdom of Israel and the southern kingdom of Judah. But the prophets knew they would come back united as one. Jeremiah, Hosea and Ezekiel all foresaw our day when she would return as one people (see Jeremiah 3:18; Hosea 1:11; Ezekiel 37:20–22).

Eighty percent of those who have returned from the nations are secular Jews, often with very little faith and little knowledge of their own God. Some may wonder why Israel has come back in our day, since so many of the Jewish people are no longer committed to their God, but Ezekiel made it clear that Israel's return from exile would not be because she had become righteous, but rather "for the sake of my holy name, which you have profaned among the nations where you have gone" (Ezekiel 36:22, NIV).

Jeremiah knew Israel's return would not be a time of peace. "Cries of fear are heard—terror, not peace," was his description. "Why do I see every strong man with his hands on his stomach like a woman in labor, every face turned deathly pale?" (Jeremiah 30:5–6, NIV).

This return from the nations is often described in great detail. Jeremiah spoke of "women in labor" (31:8, NIV) who would be among the returnees, a reference applicable to both Ethiopian and Yemenite Jews who gave birth en route. Isaiah foresaw airplanes and ships bringing back the "captives" (see Isaiah 60:8–9).

2. "Jerusalem will be trampled on by the Gentiles until . . ." (Luke 21:24, NIV) were Jesus' words that day on the Mount of Olives. In other words, the Gentiles would dominate the city for a season, but the Jews would be back. That coming back happened in the Six-Day War of 1967 when Israel again took sovereign control of the city of Jerusalem.

3. For the first time since the first century, tens of thousands of Jewish eyes are opening to the Gospel of Yeshua/Jesus, just as predicted. God told Isaiah Israel's eyes would be closed "until the cities lie ruined and

without inhabitant, until the houses are left deserted and the fields ruined" (Isaiah 6:11, NIV). Isaiah's "until" is fulfilled in our day; Jewish eyes are opening to their Messiah.

Congregations/synagogues of Jewish believers have sprung up all over the world, with over a hundred groups inside Israel alone.

Hosea described a time when Israel would be "many days" without a king and without a sacrifice. "Afterward the Israelites will return and seek the LORD" (Hosea 3:4–5, NIV).

Ezekiel foresaw a time when "you, my people, will know that I am the LORD, when I open your graves and bring you up from them" (Ezekiel 37:13, NIV).

The apostle Paul spoke of a "hardening in part until . . ."(Romans 11:25, NIV) indicating that at a future time Israel's eyes would open.

And Jesus told the Jewish leaders of His day that they would not see Him again until they were ready to receive Him (see Matthew 23:39).

The predicted future time is now!

4. The amazing awakening of faith among nations long held in darkness is yet another sign that we are living in prophecy-fulfilling days. Both Paul and Ezekiel connect this international revival of faith to the return of the Jewish people, and Jesus specifically says that every nation (*ethnos*—ethnic group) of the world must hear the Gospel of the Kingdom before the end (see Romans 11:12; Ezekiel 36:23; Matthew 24:14).

As we ponder world evangelism, we would do well to remember the words of the first century's most prominent evangelist. "First for the Jew," Paul reminded the Romans (see Romans 1:16). Though Paul was called to the Gentiles, he always went first to the Jewish synagogues to witness to his own people before turning to the Gentiles in that very city (see Acts 13:5, 14; 14:1;

213

17:2, 10, 17; 18:4; 19:8). I am convinced that all of our worldwide evangelism will prosper if we will place the Jewish people in the proper priority in our ministry and in our witness.

5. The Church from the nations has a growing awareness of her relationship to the Jewish people. For centuries the Church loudly proclaimed that Jewish people must give up their Jewishness to become "Christians." Believers in the nations assumed the Lord had severed relationship with the nation of Israel. But in recent years the Church has come to see that we are now "fellow citizens with God's people" (Ephesians 2:19, NIV), that we are "heirs together," "members together," "sharers together" with the Jewish people (see Ephesians 3:6; 2:14).

As you look forward to your time in Israel, let me encourage you to rethink the way in which you relate to the Jewish people and offer some suggestions for expressing your faith while walking among them.

The Jewish people are the "parents of our faith." When Malachi spoke of the hearts of the fathers being turned to the children, and the children to their fathers (see Malachi 4:6), he was referring to family relationships. But there is another sense in which these words refer to us from the nations as we relate to the "parents of our faith," the Jewish people.

Jewish people are turning to acknowledge their own Messiah. Perhaps we have become accustomed to thinking of Jewish "converts" to the faith. Though this is true—in the sense that "convert" means "to turn," and that all of us who have come to Jesus have turned [from sin]—there is another sense in which Jewish people do not "convert" when they come to faith. They are simply returning to the God of their fathers.

Jewish believers prefer to use the words "congregation" or "synagogue" rather than "church." The whole Christian world speaks freely of "the Church," but the Greek word for church (*ekklesia*) can also easily be translated "congregation." To the Jewish ear, the word *church* evokes scenes of the Crusades, when Jewish people were locked in their synagogues and burned to their death; pogroms, when Jewish people were required to reside only in certain areas and were subjected to repeated persecution; the Inquisition, when "Christian" rulers of Spain led the charge to confiscate Jewish wealth and drive the Jews from their country; and the Holocaust, spawned and executed in "Christian" Germany, Austria and Poland. Think, therefore, in terms of "congregations" of Jewish believers, even "synagogues" rather than "churches." It is just a matter of terminology, but it shows love and respect for our centuries-long persecuted Jewish family.

Christ is the transliteration of the Greek *Christos*, meaning "Anointed One." In speaking of Jesus, Jewish believers prefer to use the Hebrew equivalent, *Messiah*. Even the name *Christ* brings up memories of persecution and horror to the Jewish mind. *Christ-killers* was a derogatory term spoken over countless Jewish people through the centuries. "Die in the name of Christ!" was often scrawled across the death chambers of Europe during the years of the Nazi reign of terror. Jesus, however, made it clear that it was not only the Jewish leaders who would be responsible for His death, but that the Son of Man would also be "handed over to the Gentiles" who would "mock him, insult him, spit on him, flog him and kill him" (Luke 18:32, NIV).

Messiah is so Jewish and scriptural! In deference to the soul of the Jewish nation, which has suffered so much at the hands of "Christians," I choose to refer to Jesus as "Messiah," especially when speaking to my Jewish friends.

Most of the Jewish believers I know do not refer to themselves as "Christians." The term *Christian* has little meaning in today's world. It may simply imply that one was born into a family that has been nominally "Christian" for generations. In other words, there are "Christian atheists" or "Christian

215

skeptics" who have no faith at all in God, in His Word or in His Son. In the New Covenant Scripture, the name *Christian* appears only three times, and in each of those incidents it was a name that others applied to the believers of the day (see Acts 11:26; 26:28; 1 Peter 4:16).

Christian Zionism—the belief that Israel has a right to be in the Land of her inheritance—is a growing phenomenon in our day. Believers from the nations are beginning to bless Israel. But even among Christian Zionists, there is great diversity, with sometimes totally unbiblical teaching.

1. Some would have us believe that the Jewish people do not need their own Messiah—that God has a different plan for them. This would be hard for the apostle Paul to accept. He said, "I could wish that I myself were cursed and cut off from Christ for the sake of my brothers, those of my own race, the people of Israel" (Romans 9:3–4, NIV).

2. Others believe that the Jewish people will come to faith one day, but that this is not their day. No need to tell them about Yeshua, since all Israel will eventually be saved. These people believe that Jesus did not intend to be the Messiah of Israel the first time He came and that event awaits future fulfillment. The apostle Peter, however, would have differed. "God has made this Jesus, whom you crucified, both Lord and Christ," he told the gathered people from the nations on that first Shavuot (Pentecost) after the resurrection (Acts 2:36, NIV).

3. Christian Zionists have wonderfully sown millions of dollars into the land of Israel, bringing in millions of believers from around the world and establishing great storehouses of humanitarian aid. This is right and good. Paul said that since we have received spiritual blessings from the Jewish people, we "owe it" to them "to share with them" our material blessings (see Romans 15:27). But Paul also adds, in speaking to the Galatians, that we

216

should always especially remember "those who belong to the family of believers" (Galatians 6:10, NIV). Not only are we related to Israel and the Jewish people, but we also are doubly connected to those in the family of faith.

As you interact with Jewish brothers and sisters and actually travel the Land, listen to the voice of the Holy Spirit. Speak when He calls you to speak, and be silent when He calls you to be silent. Plant seeds of salvation, water the seeds already sown, and yes, be ready to reap the harvest. Remember that it is the work of the Holy Spirit to draw people to Himself. We are simply His instruments to do His bidding in the process.

Come to Israel! Come humbly!

Come under the blessing! Be a blessing (see Genesis 12:1–3)!

Obey the biblical injunction regarding prayer for Israel (see Psalm 122:6; Isaiah 62:7)!

Pray for the eyes of the Jewish people to be opened to their Messiah (see Isaiah 6:8–13)!

Include also the Arab family in your prayers (see Genesis 17:20; Isaiah 19:19–25)!

Do not forget the special connection to "those who are of the household of the faith" (Galatians 6:10).

Walk forth in the "mystery revealed"—Jew and Gentile together in Messiah Yeshua/Jesus (see Ephesians 3:6)!

For more information about Don Finto or to order one of his books, *Your People Shall Be My People*, or *God's Promise and the Future of Israel*, go to the website of The Caleb Company (www.calebcompany.com).

Appendix B

Overview of Israel's History

November 29, 1947. The United Nations (U.N.) partitions Palestine into two independent states—one Jewish and the other Arab. Arab nations renounce the Jewish state and vow to seize all of Palestine by force.

May 14, 1948. The British Mandate for Palestine expires. A Jewish Declaration of Independence is signed, proclaiming the State of Israel.

May 15, 1948. Arab nations surrounding Israel suddenly attack the world's newest nation. (This Pan-Arab force includes armed forces from Egypt, Transjordan [present-day Jordan], Syria, Lebanon and Iraq.)

January 7, 1949. A cease-fire agreement ends Israel's War of Independence. (However, in an armistice agreement signed July 1949, the Arab League closes its frontiers to

Israel and declares itself "in a permanent state of war" with Israel.)

January 25, 1949. The first Knesset (Israeli Parliament) meets in Jerusalem and elects Chaim Weizmann (the Jewish chemist who helped Great Britain prior to the Balfour Declaration) as its first president.

May 11, 1949. Israel is admitted to the United Nations.

1948–51. The Knesset enacts the Law of Return, which states, "Every Jew has the right to come to this country as an immigrant." Israel's population more than doubles with 684,000 new arrivals from North Africa and the Middle East and the airlift of entire Jewish communities from Yemen (43,000) and Iraq (113,000).

1951. World Zionist Congress meets for the first time in Jerusalem.

1952–56. West Germany signs a reparations agreement to pay the State of Israel $719 million for material losses to Jews under Nazism and $100 million to individuals. Arabs continue to be actively hostile, with three thousand clashes between armed Arab forces and Israeli soldiers.

Egypt, Syria and Jordan sign a military pact to defend one another in the event of war (with Israel).

October 1956. Egypt nationalizes the Suez Canal and cuts off international shipping through it. Faced with Arab threats of war, Israel launches a preemptive attack called The Sinai Campaign, with support from Britain and France (who fear their shipping will be endangered).

March 1957. Israel withdraws from Sinai. U.N. peacekeeping troops are sent to ensure the Suez Canal remains open to most international—but not yet Israeli—shipping.

1958–59. End of first decade as a new state: Jewish population reaches 1.8 million, raises the standard of living and achieves agricultural self-sufficiency. Arab and Druse communities share in progress, participate in free elections and have their own representation in the Knesset.

Israel provides technical and scientific assistance to emerging nations in Africa and Latin America; many of them establish embassies in Jerusalem and support Israel in the U.N.

1964. Pope Paul VI becomes the first pope to visit Israel, though Israel's statehood is not recognized by the Vatican.

The Palestinian Liberation Organization (PLO) is founded in Egypt with the express goal of destroying Israel through armed struggle. Yasser Arafat soon becomes head of this terrorist organization.

1967. Prelude to The Six-Day War. Al Fatah, a Palestinian terrorist organization, sends trained terrorists into Israel for sabotage. Kibbutz settlements in Galilee are bombed by Syrians.

May 14, 1967. Egyptian leader Nasser moves large numbers of troops into Sinai.

May 16–June 4, 1967. Nasser expels U.N. peacekeeping forces from Sinai, blocking shipping lanes in the Gulf of Aqaba, and announces that Egypt is "prepared to wage war on Israel." Jordan and Iraq place their military forces under Nasser's command.

June 4, 1967. Six-Day War starts. Israel mobilizes for defense, leaving older men, women and children to keep necessary, basic services going, bring in agricultural harvests and pack export orders.

June 5, 1967. Israel bombs airfields of Egypt, Syria, Jordan and Iraq, destroying 452 planes in three hours! Israeli ground forces move against Egyptian forces in the Sinai at four points. Israel notifies King Hussein that it will not attack Jordan if his troops will keep the peace. In response, Jordanian troops open fire on Israel along the entire armistice line and occupy U.N. headquarters in Jerusalem.

June 6–7, 1967. Israel counterattacks and takes all of Jerusalem, including the Old City, for the first time since A.D. 70.

June 9, 1967. Israel drives Syrians from the heavily fortified Golan Heights, penetrates Sinai to Suez Canal and takes Gaza Strip. Israeli naval forces capture Sharm el Sheikh on the Red Sea.

June 10, 1967. Cease-fire called after Israel's miraculous victory against overwhelming odds. Israel establishes free access to Jewish, Christian and Muslim holy sites and removes barriers between East and West Jerusalem. The result is an unprecedented awakening of Jews abroad to Israel's importance for world Jewry.

1967–73. The war of attrition brings on continual harassment by Egypt on Sinai borders and increasing Soviet involvement in Egypt, including Soviet planes, anti-aircraft missile bases and troops.

Prelude to Yom Kippur War: Egyptian and Syrian troops gather on cease-fire lines. Israel begins mobilization of reserve forces on eve of Yom Kippur (Day of Atonement).

September 5–6, 1972. The Munich Massacre occurs, in which Palestinian terrorists break into the Munich (Germany) Olympic Village, kidnapping and killing eleven members of the Israeli Olympic team.

October 6, 1973. Yom Kippur War: Israeli Cabinet meets on the holy day itself, confirms Prime Minister Golda Meir's decision not to make a preemptive air strike, despite "unmistakable signs of imminent attack." The purpose is to make the responsibility for aggression unmistakably clear. As the Israeli Cabinet is meeting on Yom Kippur, Arabs attack on two fronts at 2 P.M.

October 7–25, 1973. Israel stops advance on both fronts within two days, but at a heavy cost, including high casualties.

October–November 1973. The "Oil War" begins after the cease-fire; Arab nations dramatically reduce oil supplies to the West.

January 18, 1974. Egypt and Israel sign a disengagement agreement. U.S. officials (evidently unaware of biblical prophecy and the spiritual history of the region) claim it is the first step toward permanent peace in the Middle East.

May 1974. Syria and Israel sign a disengagement agreement, and Israeli forces withdraw slightly west of the cease-fire lines on the Golan Heights.

September 1975. Israel withdraws from portions of the Sinai, and Egypt reopens the Suez Canal to Israeli shipping for the first time since 1951.

January 1976. Syria takes advantage of civil war in Lebanon to move troops into Lebanon and join forces with the PLO. With much of southern Lebanon under their control, they bombard northern Israel with Soviet Ketyusha rockets.

July 1976. Israeli forces stage a daring rescue operation and free more than one hundred hostages from Arab terrorists in a hijacked plane in Entebbe Airport in Uganda.

July 1977. Israeli Prime Minister Menachem Begin presents a plan for Middle East peace to U.S. President Jimmy Carter in Washington.

November 1977. Egyptian President Anwar Sadat visits Jerusalem at the invitation of Prime Minister Begin to initiate direct peace talks.

September 1978. Prime Minister Begin, President Sadat and President Carter meet at Camp David, Maryland, to formulate peace accords.

1979. In response to increasing Israeli civilian casualties, Israel begins preemptive strikes against terrorist bases in southern Lebanon.

March 26, 1979. Israel and Egypt sign a treaty in which Israel agrees to relinquish the Sinai Peninsula to Egypt in exchange for peace. They agree to recognize and respect each other's right to live in peace within secure and recognized borders and to establish regular diplomatic relations.

1981. PLO and Syrian forces bombard northern Israel daily, forcing residents, including children, to spend weeks in bomb shelters. Israel responds by bombing the PLO headquarters in Beirut.

June 7, 1981. Israel destroys Iraq's Osirak nuclear facility and neutralizes Iraqi nuclear weapons capacity through Operation Opera.

January 7, 1982. Foreign Minister Yitzhak Shamir meets with Pope John Paul II.

April 25, 1982. Prime Minister Begin returns to the Sinai Peninsula to meet with President Mubarak of Egypt.

June 4, 1982. The attempted assassination of Shlomo Argov, Israel's ambassador to Britain, triggers Operation Peace for Galilee, an Israeli invasion of southern Lebanon to remove

223

PLO Ketyusha rockets and dismantle their Soviet-armed terrorist camps.

September 16, 1982. Lebanese Maronite-Christian soldiers enter Palestinian refugee camps in West Beirut and slaughter hundreds. One week later, 400,000 Israelis (10 percent of the entire population) gather in Tel Aviv to demonstrate their horror and demand a commission of inquiry.

October 1982. Arafat is exiled from Lebanon to Tunisia, which serves as PLO headquarters until 1993.

November 23, 1983. Israel trades 4,765 terrorists for six Israeli soldiers held prisoner by Arafat's Fatah terror forces.

June 28, 1984. Israel trades 291 Syrian prisoners for eleven Israeli soldiers (five of them deceased).

January 4, 1985. Operation Moses airlifts six thousand Ethiopian followers of Judaism to Israel.

May 20, 1985. Israel trades 1,150 terrorists for three Israeli soldiers held by Ahmed Jibril's PLO-related forces.

October 1, 1985. Israel bombs the PLO Headquarters in Tunis in response to the murder of Israeli yachters in Cyprus.

December 27, 1985. Seventeen El Al airline passengers are murdered and 109 wounded by PLO attacks at airports in Rome and Vienna.

February 11, 1986. Anatoly Sharansky, a Russian Jewish human rights activist who had been imprisoned for many years in Russia's notorious labor camps, is finally freed by the U.S.S.R. and arrives in Israel.

April 17, 1986. Agents of the Syrian Air Force attempt to smuggle a suitcase bomb onto an El Al London-to-Tel Aviv flight, but security guards discover and successfully dismantle the bomb.

July 22, 1986. Prime Minister Shimon Peres pays a surprise public visit to King Hassan of Morocco.

October 26, 1986. Mordechai Vanunu is kidnapped back to Israel by agents of Israel's legendary Mossad security apparatus, after accepting a bribe to publicize information about Israel's purported nuclear capabilities.

February 15, 1987. Yosef Begun, a so-called "prisoner of Zion," is freed from Russian imprisonment after being sentenced in 1983 to twelve years in prison/exile for distributing anti-Soviet propaganda. (Begun had applied to leave Russia twelve years earlier, but his application was denied.)

October 15, 1987. Ida Nudel, a prisoner of Zion, arrives in Israel following sixteen years of refused permission to leave Russia.

December 9, 1987. The Intifada, an organized Palestinian revolt against Israeli occupation of the Gaza Strip, begins. By the end of December, 21 Palestinians are dead and 179 wounded; 41 Israeli soldiers and 27 civilians are wounded.

March–April 1989. Abu Jihad, Arafat's military deputy, is killed in his Tunis home by commandos purported to be Israeli elite troops. Abu Jihad had masterminded an attack on a bus full of civilians (mostly mothers) in southern Israel and was guiding the Intifada revolt. (Israel has never claimed responsibility.)

July 6, 1989. Islamic Jihad terrorist forces Jerusalem-bound bus into a gorge, killing 16 and wounding 27.

225

July 27, 1989. Israeli commandos kidnap Hezbollah leader of south Lebanon, Sheikh Obeid, as a bargaining chip in negotiating the release of three Israeli soldiers held captive in Lebanon.

1989–94. More than 500,000 Jewish immigrants reach Israel.

February 4, 1990. Nine Israeli tourists are killed and seventeen wounded by Muslim fundamentalists in a tourist bus on the way to Cairo.

May 1, 1990. The Jewish Agency, which oversees Jewish immigration to Israel, reports record numbers of Russian Jews leaving the U.S.S.R. Over the next decade, more than 820,000 Jews emigrate from the former U.S.S.R. to Israel.

August 2, 1990. Iraq invades Kuwait, and Israel distributes gas masks to all citizens in anticipation of a chemical weapons attack by Iraq.

September 8, 1990. Muslim fears that Jews are building a Third Temple on the Temple Mount in Jerusalem lead to a riot in which thousands of Arabs attack an Israeli police station. Twenty-six Jews are injured, 140 Arabs are injured and 21 Arabs are killed.

December 12, 1990. The U.S.S.R. and Israel restore diplomatic ties.

January 17, 1991. During U.S.-led Operation Desert Storm against Iraq, Saddam Hussein fires eight SCUD missiles into Israel, causing much damage. In all, 39 SCUDs are fired. More than nine thousand apartments and hundreds of businesses are damaged, three hundred people are slightly injured and one person is killed. Israel assents to American requests not to respond. On February 25, a cease-fire is declared.

226

May 25, 1991. Operation Solomon brings 14,000 Ethiopian followers of Judaism to Israel in forty airlifts within 35 hours.

October 30, 1991. The Madrid International Middle East Peace Committee meets, discussing "land for peace."

January 24, 1992. Israel and China establish full diplomatic relations.

March 1992. The terrorist group Islamic Jihad bombs the Israeli Embassy in Argentina, killing 22 and injuring 252.

June 23, 1992. Yitzhak Rabin is elected Prime Minister of Israel, defeating Yitzhak Shamir.

September 13, 1993. Lacking support by the Israeli public, the U.S.-brokered Oslo Accord (Oslo I) is signed between the PLO and Israel. This accord is understood as promoting land for peace and expressing the PLO's desire to solve disputes in a peaceful manner.

February 25, 1994. Lone activist Baruch Goldstein kills 29 Muslims and wounds a hundred in an attack on a Muslim service in Hebron's Machpelah Cave on Purim, the Feast of Esther. Two of his friends had been murdered on December 6 by terrorists.

June 12, 1994. Lubavitch Rabbi Menachem Schneerson, head of the Chabad Hasidic stream, dies at age 92. Many of his followers believed that he was the messiah and would be resurrected.

July 1, 1994. Arafat arrives from Tunisia (via Egypt) to cheering crowds in Gaza and four days later in Jericho.

July 18, 1994. Terrorists detonate a car bomb, blowing up the Jewish community center in Buenos Aires, Argentina. Thirty-seven are killed and 59 are missing.

July 26, 1994. Terrorists detonate a car bomb at the Israeli Embassy in London, injuring thirteen.

October 19, 1994. A Hamas suicide bomber blows up a Tel Aviv bus, killing 22 and injuring 44.

October 26, 1994. Israel and Jordan sign a peace treaty.

December 10, 1994. Yitzhak Rabin, Shimon Peres and Yasser Arafat are awarded the Nobel Peace Prize.

January 22, 1995. Two Islamic Jihad suicide bombers blow themselves up at Beit Lid junction, killing 21 and injuring 34.

July 24, 1995. Seven Israelis are killed and 32 injured by a suicide bus bomber in Tel Aviv.

August 21, 1995. Five are killed and 107 injured in Jerusalem suicide bus bombing. Both bombs were built by Yihye Ayash, the "Engineer."

October 25, 1995. Fathi Shkaki, one of Islamic Jihad's leaders, is killed by gunmen in Malta.

November 4, 1995. Prime Minister Yitzhak Rabin is assassinated by Yigal Amir, a 26-year-old law student and opponent of the Oslo Accords.

January 5, 1996. The "Engineer" is killed by a booby-trapped cell phone in Gaza.

February 25, 1996. Twenty-seven Israelis are killed and 78 injured by two suicide bombs in Jerusalem and Ashkelon.

March 3, 1996. Eighteen Israelis are killed and dozens injured by a suicide bus bomb in Jerusalem.

March 4, 1996. Fourteen Israelis are killed and 157 injured by a suicide bomb at Dizengoff Center, Tel Aviv, on the Feast of Purim.

May 29, 1996. Binyamin Netanyahu becomes Prime Minister of Israel.

September 24, 1996. An archaeological tunnel along the Western Wall opens in Jerusalem. Rioting by Muslims spreads with tens of thousands attacking Israeli forces. Forty-one Israeli soldiers and 69 Palestinians are killed.

January 15, 1997. Israel redeploys in Hebron, according to the Oslo Accords.

March 13, 1997. A Jordanian soldier kills seven eighth-grade schoolgirls on the Island of Peace, between Jordan and Israel on the Jordan River.

July 30, 1997. Thirteen Israelis are killed and 120 injured by Hamas suicide bombers in Jerusalem.

October 23, 1998. Prime Minister Netanyahu and Yasser Arafat sign the Wye River Memorandum, consisting of steps to implement Oslo II (signed September 28, 1995).

May 4, 1999. Deadline set forth in Oslo I passes without establishing the permanent status of a Palestinian entity.

July 1999. Labor Party leader Ehud Barak is elected Prime Minister of Israel.

September 4, 1999. Sharm el-Sheikh Memorandum, signed by Ehud Barak and Yasser Arafat, extends deadline for implementation of Oslo I. It also attempts to restart stalled negotiations and ensure compliance with Oslo I and II and the

Wye River Memorandum. Deadline for completion is set for September 13, 2000.

September 5, 1999–May 22, 2000. A flurry of diplomatic activity between the Israelis and Palestinians attempts to push forward the peace process.

March 21, 2000. Pope John Paul II visits Israel. He is credited by Israel with unprecedented and significant improvement in Catholic-Jewish relations.

May 2000. Israel withdraws its peacekeeping forces from the strategic military "buffer zone" in southern Lebanon, resulting in the proliferation of the terrorist group Hezbollah.

May 22, 2000. Barak cuts off talks with Palestinians due to violence in Arab-occupied Israeli territories.

June 6, 2000. U.S. Secretary of State Madeleine Albright meets separately with Barak and Arafat to push for the resumption of negotiations.

July 11–25, 2000. At Camp David summit meetings initiated by U.S. President Bill Clinton, Barak offers the following: Israeli withdrawal from virtually all of the West Bank and all of the Gaza Strip to create a Palestinian state; the removal of isolated Jewish settlements and transfer of resulting vacated lands to Palestinian control; the exchange of other Israeli lands for certain West Bank settlements that would remain under Israeli control; and Palestinian control over East Jerusalem, including most of the Old City and the Temple Mount. In summary, Barak's offer concedes to approximately 95 percent of Arafat's demands. Refusing Barak's offer or further negotiation, Arafat walks out of the meetings without making a counteroffer.

September 27, 2000. Palestinian terror attack in Gaza kills an Israeli soldier.

September 28, 2000. With legal permission of Palestinian officials, Ariel Sharon visits the Temple Mount. In protest of his visit, an uprising of terror begins against Israel, known as the Al Aqsa Intifada.

September 28, 2000–September 2005. Terrorism inside Israel escalates dramatically. The Palestinian Authority Communications Director states this uprising was planned weeks earlier, when Barak offered to meet 95 but not 100 percent of Arafat's demands at Camp David. The Al Aqsa Intifada continues "officially" until September 2005. More than one thousand Israelis are killed by terrorism during this period.

2000–2006. First wave of *aliyah* (Jewish immigration to Israel) from the West occurs. More than eleven thousand Jewish immigrants move to Israel from France, with more than seven thousand from North America and ten thousand from Argentina.

March 7, 2001. Ariel Sharon is elected Prime Minister of Israel.

April 30, 2001. U.S. Senator George Mitchell releases an analysis of the causes behind the Al Aqsa Intifada, known as the Mitchell Report. It concludes Sharon's visit to the Temple Mount was not the cause of the Intifada. The report is intended as an effort to restart peace negotiations and calls for the Palestinians to stop violence as a precondition to further negotiation.

October 2, 2001. George W. Bush becomes the first U.S. president to publicly call for establishment of a Palestinian state, stating, "The idea of a Palestinian state has always been part of the vision."

January 3, 2002. Israel intercepts the cargo freighter *Karine A*, carrying fifty tons of weapons shipped from Iran to the Palestinian Authority.

March 27, 2002. Suicide bombing at the Park Hotel in Netanya during a Passover observance kills 28 Israelis and injures many more. Days later Israel launches Operation Defensive Shield to dismantle terror nests in Jenin (West Bank).

March 29, 2002. Records are discovered implicating Arafat in the continued financing of terrorism, including his order for weapons associated with *Karine A*. As a result, Israel confines him for the remainder of his active life to his headquarters in Ramallah.

June 24, 2002. President Bush declares there can never be a Palestinian state while Arafat is leader of the Palestinians and no longer considers him a partner in the peace process.

January 2003. Prime Minister Sharon wins a landslide re-election on a platform that includes condemnation of the notion of Israeli withdrawal from Gaza.

April 30, 2003. The United States, in cooperation with Russia, the European Union and the U.N. (known as the Quartet), presents its Roadmap to Peace to Israel and the Palestinian Authority. The plan is a performance-based, goal-driven plan, with clear phases, timelines and benchmarks. It involves reciprocal steps by the two parties in the political, national security, economic and humanitarian spheres. The goal is to create a Palestinian state, based on the premise that this will resolve the Israeli-Palestinian conflict.

November 11, 2004. Yasser Arafat dies in France from an undisclosed illness, and within hours Mahmoud Abbas is chairman of the PLO Executive Committee.

January 9, 2005. Abbas is elected President of the Palestinian Authority.

August 15, 2005. At Prime Minister Sharon's direction, Israel unilaterally withdraws from Gaza, forcibly evicting Jewish citizens who fail to leave voluntarily. This causes a significant rift in Israeli society. Shortly thereafter, Kassam rockets are launched regularly in terror attacks from Gaza into the western Negev, particularly Sderot, and continue to the date of this writing.

September 2, 2005. The International Atomic Energy Agency announces that Iran has been concealing development of nuclear technology.

December 24, 2005. Ultraorthodox, Jewish anti-missionaries opposed to the Gospel (who for decades have harassed and caused varying degrees of persecution against Messianic Jews) physically attack Jewish believers during a congregational Sabbath service in Beersheba.

January 4, 2006. Sharon suffers a severe stroke, ending his political career and leaving him in a coma.

January 25, 2006. The terrorist group Hamas is elected as the majority representative of the Palestinian Authority.

April 24, 2006–present. President Ahmadinejad of Iran announces to the world, "Israel cannot logically continue to exist." He regularly and publicly reiterates this statement, to the date of this writing.

May 4, 2006. Ehud Olmert, a protégé of Sharon, is elected Prime Minister of Israel.

June 25, 2006. Israeli soldier Gilad Shalit is kidnapped in Gaza by Hamas.

June 28–November 26, 2006. Israel Defense Forces intermittently strike Hamas in Gaza as a result of increased Palestinian Kassam rocket fire into western Israel.

July 12–August 14, 2006. Hezbollah attacks northern Israel, killing three Israeli soldiers and kidnapping two others. Israel and Hezbollah fight a war in southern Lebanon and northern Israel. A U.N. ceasefire creates a peacekeeping force in Lebanon to disarm Hezbollah and ensure Israeli withdrawal. Israel withdraws, but Hezbollah is not disarmed. Two Israeli soldiers remain prisoners as of this writing.

2006–2007. Israel's economy grows faster than that of any Western nation.

June 7–15, 2007. Hamas wins military and political control over Gaza through a civil war with the Fatah party of President Abbas. As a result, Abbas loses control over Gaza. Sharia (Islamic) law is established in Gaza.

September 6, 2007. Israeli Air Force bombs suspected nuclear reactor development site in Syria.

October 7, 2007. After receiving several Islamic death threats, Rami Ayyad, Arab Christian manager of the only Christian bookstore in Gaza, is found murdered.

November 27, 2007. U.S. President Bush convenes a summit in Annapolis, Maryland, to jumpstart the peace process between Israel and the Palestinian Authority.

January 1, 2008–present. More than two thousand rocket and mortar attacks are launched from Gaza into the Negev. Negotiations between the governments of Israel and the Palestinian Authority continue.

March 6, 2008. A Palestinian from East Jerusalem opens fire on students at Yeshiva Mercaz HaRav in Jerusalem, killing eight.

March 22, 2008. A terrorist bomb disguised as a Purim holiday gift is delivered to the home of a Messianic Jewish family in Ariel, severely injuring their teenage boy. At this writing, it appears the perpetrators were ultraorthodox, Jewish anti-missionaries. In the months that follow, national and international interest in Messianic Jewish faith in Israel significantly increases.

April 2008. Prime Minister Olmert announces his intent to divide Jerusalem and concede governmental control over much of the city either to Palestinians or an international peacekeeping force.

May 2008. Israel's sixtieth anniversary is honored in an unprecedented manner when vast numbers of Christians come for celebrations and prayer gatherings.

May 14, 2008. After sixty years of statehood, Israel's population stands at approximately 7,282,000. Approximately 5.5 million Israelis are Jewish, representing about 43 percent of the world's total Jewish population.

May 28, 2008. Prime Minister Olmert is implicated in an international finance scandal that threatens to remove him from office.

June 2008. Indirect peace negotiations begin between Israel and Syria in Turkey. Included are discussions of Israeli withdrawal from the Golan Heights.

235

July 2, 2008. A Palestinian terrorist and resident of East Jerusalem drives a bulldozer into cars, buses and pedestrians in downtown Jerusalem, killing three Israelis and wounding 45.

July 30, 2008. Under pressure of criminal investigation, Prime Minister Ehud Olmert resigns from office, effective September 2008.

Author's Note: This overview of Israeli history was developed from information compiled and provided by Avner Boskey and from information appearing in Derek Prince's book *The Last Word On the Middle East* (Chosen, 1982), pages 143–53. Special appreciation to Kerry and Sandra Teplinsky for their invaluable expertise in revising and adding to this timeline, particularly regarding more recent history.

Appendix C

Images of Historic Revivals and Movements of the Holy Spirit

To make *The Coming Israel Awakening* more complete, I wanted to add a section on revivals and movements of the Holy Spirit in Church history. As I sought the Lord concerning my desire for this, an amazing book, *Images of Revival*, by Richard and Kathryn Riss, was put into my hands. The following material was adapted from this book, which was published by Destiny Image. Thanks go to Richard M. Riss and Destiny Image for the use of the material, which I have updated and revised in part.

An amazing historical correlation can be found in what I call "parallel restoration" of the Jewish people to the Land of Israel and the outpourings of the Holy Spirit, particularly in modern-day Church history. I trust you will benefit from this short overview on some important revivals and awakenings, especially in the history of Western Civilization.

A.D. 30	The Day of Pentecost (see Acts 2).
51–54	Athens and Corinth, under Paul of Tarsus (see Acts 15:36–18:22, Paul's "Second Missionary Journey").
54–58	Ephesus (see Acts 18:23–21:19, Paul's "Third Missionary Journey").
61–65	Rome (Paul, Peter, Luke, Mark and others) and Ephesus (the apostle John).
c.150	Phrygia and Asia Minor
178	Lyons (Iranaeus)
202–30	Alexandria (Origen)
300s	Pachomius (d. 346); "Desert Fathers," Antony of Egypt (d. 356), John of Egypt (d. 394), Martin (d. 397)
420s	North African revival. See Augustine, *City of God*, book 22.
601	England, under Augustine of Canterbury. See Bede, *Ecclesiastical History*, chapter 31.
1100s	England, under Bernard of Clairvaux (d. 1153), Hildegard of Bingen (d. 1179).
1221–31	Anthony of Padua, Dominic, Francis of Assisi.
1494–98	Florence, Italy, under Savanarolla.
1500s	France, under Farel and Viret. See Edwards, 135.
1517	Protestant Reformation: Germany, under Martin Luther and Ayr, Scotland, under John Welch (son-in-law of John Knox). See Gillies, 167–70.
1596	Scottish General Assembly under preaching of Robert Bruce of Edinburgh; General Assembly of Scotland: May 12, 1596 (Synod of Fife met at Dumfermine; James Melville presided). See Gillies, 157.

1625   West of Scotland. See Edwards, 135; Fleming, 103–4; and Gillies, 197. This was the "Stewarton Sickness" (1625–30) under David Dickson of Irvine, who ministered 1618–42. See Keith Hardman, *The Spiritual Awakeners*, 33, quoting Thomas McCrie, *Sketches of Scottish Church History* (London: Blanchard & Ott, 1846), 1:190–93. See Gillies, 182, 197, 198. See also *Narratives of Revivals of Religion* by Presbyterian Board of Publication, 1842, part IV (56–65).

1625   North of Ireland, Ulster. See James S. Reid, *History of the Presbyterian Church in Ireland, Vol. 1.*

1626   North of Ireland, Josiah (Josias) Welch, at Sixmile-water, Temple, Patrick. See Gillies, 168, 202; *Narratives*, part VII (102–21); and Reid, *History.*

1630   Kirk of Shotts, Scotland, on June 21, under John Livingstone ("Livingstone of Shotts"). Also, Robert Bruce of Kinnaird at Edinburgh, summer 1627, and Inverness. See Gillies, 171, 176–77, esp. 179, 198ff. See also Humphrey, 29–33, and *Narratives*, part IV (65–73).

1650–61   Scotland. See Gillies, 202.

1665   London, at the time of the Plague. See Gillies, 124.

1679, 1683, 1696, 1712, 1718   Northampton, Massachusetts, under Solomon Stoddard.

1704–05   Taunton, Massachusetts, under Danforth. See Humphrey, 63–64.

1720s   New Jersey under Frelinghuysen. See Hardman, *Spiritual Awakeners*, 47–59.

1727	Moravian Revival on August 13, at Hernhut in Berthelsdorf, Germany, under Count Nikolaus von Zinzendorf.
1730–33	Freehold, New Jersey, under John William Tennant. See Humphrey, 64.
1734ff.	Northampton, Massachusetts, under Jonathan Edwards.
1739–43	See Gillies, 305–37 (Britain) and 337–433 (America). See also Humphrey, 46–93.
1742	Cambuslang, Scotland, on February 18, under William McCulloch and George Whitefield. This spread everywhere. See Gledstone's *George Whitefield, M.A., Field Preacher,* and Gillies, 433ff. and 441–62. See also *Narratives,* parts I, II, III (5–55).
1744	Native Americans under David Brainerd.
1749	Nieukerk, Holland, on November 19, under Gerardus Kuypers.
1763–64	New England. See Hardman, *Spiritual Awakeners,* 119.
1759–63	New England, under John Wesley. See Wesley, *Works, Vol. 13,* 344–63.
1776–77	Martin Boos (1762–1824). Revival crowned his preaching at Wiggensbach, Germany, and Gallneukirchen, Austria, in 1776–77.
1787	Hampden-Sydney College, Virginia, under its president, John Blair Smith. See Hardman, *Spiritual Awakeners,* 106, 119.
1788	Virginia—Interdenominational. See Hardman, *Spiritual Awakeners,* 133.
1792–99	New England. See Hardman, *Spiritual Awakeners,* 119.

1798, 1800   Moulin, Scotland, under Alexander Stewart. See *Narratives*, part VI (85–101).

1800   Kentucky's Caneridge Revival in June; spreads across America.

1805   Williams College. See Hardman, *Spiritual Awakeners*, 152.

1812, 1814   Island of Skye, Scotland (Hebrides). See *Narratives*, part X (159–84).

1812–13   Island of Arran, Scotland, under Neil McBride. See *Narratives*, part V (74–84).

1815–18   America. See Humphrey, 259–63.

1816–17   Breadalbane, Scotland, under John McDonald of Urquhart.

1820–25   Central and Western New York State. See Humphrey, 263.

1821   Connecticut and Massachusetts under Asahel Nettleton. See Humphrey, 232–36 and 242–58.

1824, 1835   Island of Lewis, Scotland. See *Narratives*, part VIII (122–38).

1825–27   Oneida County, New York, under Charles G. Finney. See Hardman, *Spiritual Awakeners*, 176.

1830–31   Rochester, New York, under Charles Finney. See Hardman, *Spiritual Awakeners*, 184.

1831   General outpouring of the Spirit in America. See appendix to *Sprague's Lectures on Revivals*.

1832   New York City, under Charles G. Finney, according to T. L. Cuyler. See *History of Broadway Tabernacle* by Susan Hayes Ward; also Hardman, *Spiritual Awakeners*, 184.

1839	Kilsyth, Scotland, July 23, under William Chalmers Burns—sparked by retelling of the story of Kirk of Shotts. See Gillies, 556ff., also *Narratives*, part XI (185–98).
1840	Heemstede, Netherlands, under Nicholaas Beets.
1840	Baltimore, New Haven, Hartford and Boston, under Rev. Jacob Knapp. See E. N. Kirk, *Lectures on Revivals*, 142.
1844	Moettlingen, Germany, under J. C. Blumhardt.
1857–58	Hamilton, Ontario, and New York City (Laymen's Prayer Revival) with Jeremiah Lamphere releasing Worldwide Awakening.
1859	Ulster, Ireland. See William Gibson, *The Year of Grace*.
1859–60	England, Scotland, Ireland, Wales.
1865	America. See Kirk, *Lectures on Revivals*, 142.
1871	South Wales. See Eifion Jones, *The Welsh Revival of 1904*, 11.
1873–74	Scotland and Ireland, under Moody and Sankey. See MacRae, 102–30; also Hardman, *Spiritual Awakeners*, 203–4.
1875	England, under Moody and Sankey. See Hardman, *Spiritual Awakeners*, 204–6.
1875–77	Brooklyn, Philadelphia, New York, Chicago and Boston, under Moody and Sankey. See Hardman, *Spiritual Awakeners*, 206–7.
1885ff.	Localized revivals in America under Maria B. Woodworth-Etter. Power gifts released through Alexander Dowie in Zion, Illinois.

1904–5   Welsh Revival with Evan Roberts—sparked a worldwide revival. Topeka, Kansas, outbreak of the gift of tongues. Los Angeles (North Bonnie Brae Street, Azusa Street) with William Seymour and many others, which went worldwide in its aftermath. Korean outpouring. See Hardman, *Spiritual Awakeners*, 212.

1920s   Signs and Wonders movement with John G. Lake, Aimee Semple MacPherson and others, which resulted in mass crusades and new denominations and released many miracles, healings, signs and wonders.

Mid-twentieth-century Evangelical Awakening. Billy Graham, Chuck Templeton, William Branham, Gordon Lindsay, Oral Roberts, T. L. Osborn, etc. Healing and Latter Rains revivals. Also includes the Hebrides Revival in Scotland (1949).

1960–70s Charismatic renewal in mainline denominational churches (worldwide). Overlapping Jesus People Movement in southern California with Lonnie Frisbie and Chuck Smith and others, which scattered around the world.

1970–80s Global Prayer Movement launched with Yonggi Cho and Prayer Mountain in Korea; Intercessors for Great Britain, America and many nations formed.

1980s   Emergence of the Third Wave Movement and Church Growth Institute with John Wimber, C. Peter Wagner, James Robison, Jack Deere and hundreds of others impacting leaders worldwide. Spiritual Warfare Network with Peter Wagner and Cindy Jacobs; the birthing of prayer and fasting for revival around the world.

1988   The birthing of the modern day prophetic movement in Kansas City, Missouri; Charlotte, North Carolina; Florida; Ohio and other locations simultaneously.

1992ff.   Late-twentieth-century Awakening (worldwide). Claudio Freidzon, Carlos Anaconda and many others in Buenos Aires, Argentina; Rodney Howard-Browne in the U.S.; John Arnott and Randy Clark in Toronto, Canada (January 20, 1994); John Kilpatrick and Stephen Hill in Pensacola, Florida (Father's Day, 1995). New Apostolic Reformation and the forming of new apostolic worldwide church planting networks. Lou Engle and The Call prayer and fasting movement launched across the nations. Mike Bickle and the International House of Prayer goes 24/7/365.

2004   Pray for the Peace of Jerusalem Day on the first Sunday of October by Robert Stearns and Jack Hayford going worldwide.

2005   Global Day of Prayer launched in South Africa with Graham Powers resulting in millions gathering across the nations for worship and intercession.

2008   The Call Jerusalem, on May 11.

Bibliography to Appendix

Conant, William C. *Narratives of Remarkable Conversions and Revival Incidents Including a Review of Revivals From the Day of Pentecost to the Great Awakening in the Last Century*. New York: Derby & Jackson, 1858.

Edwards, Jonathan. *A Faithful Narrative of the Surprising Work of God in the Conversion of Many Hundred Souls in Northampton, Massachusetts*. New York: Dunning and Spalding, 1832.

Evans, Eifion. *The Welsh Revival of 1904*. London: Evangelical Press, 1969.

Gibson, William. *The Year of Grace: A History of the Ulster Revival of 1859*, 2nd ed. Edinburgh: Andrew Elliot, 1860.

Gillies, John. *Historical Collections of Accounts of Revival*. Fairfield, Pa.: Banner of Truth Trust, 1981. Reprint of John Gillies, *Historical Collections*, ed. Horatius Bonar. Kelso: John Rutherford, 1854. First published 1754.

Gledstone, James Patterson. *George Whitefield, M.A., Field Preacher*, 2nd ed. New York: American Tract Society, 1901.

Hardman, Keith. *The Spiritual Awakeners*. Chicago: Moody Press, 1983.

Humphrey, Heman. *Revival Sketches and Manual*. New York: American Tract Society, 1859.

Kirk, Edward Norris. *Lectures on Revivals*. Boston: Congregational Publishing Society, 1875.

MacRae, Alexander. *Revivals in the Highlands and Islands in the Nineteenth Century*. Stirling: E. Mackay, 1906.

M'Crie, Thomas. *Sketches of Scottish Church History*, 4th ed. Edinburgh & London: John Johnstone, 1841.

Narratives of Revivals of Religion in Scotland, Ireland, and Wales. Philadelphia: Presbyterian Board of Publication, 1842.

Reid, James Seaton. *History of the Presbyterian Church in Ireland*, 3rd ed. London: Whittaker and Co., 1853.

Sprague, William B. *Lectures on Revivals of Religion*. New York: Daniel Appleton & Co., 1833.

Ward, Susan Hayes. *The History of the Broadway Tabernacle Church From Its Organization in 1840 to the Close of 1900, Including Factors Influencing Its Formation*. New York: The Trow Print, 1901.

Appendix D

Dates of Purim and the Esther Fast

Purim is a Jewish holiday observed in celebration of God's supernatural deliverance of the Jewish people from Haman's genocidal plot to destroy them in the time of Persia's King Artaxerxes. The holiday was held on the 14th of Adar (according to the Jewish calendar) in the unwalled cities and on the 15th of Adar in the cities that were walled in the time of Joshua.

Esther called for a nationwide three-day fast preceding her intervention on behalf of the Jewish people. She entered the royal throne room on the third day (see Esther 4:16–5:1). The Church, the spiritual Esther, can undertake this same fast to intercede once again on behalf of the Jewish people for deliverance from Haman's plot.

Note: All Jewish holidays begin at sundown on the evening before the date shown.

Year	Feast of Purim	Esther Fast Dates
2009	March 10	March 8–10
2010	February 28	February 26–28
2011	March 20	March 18–20
2012	March 8	March 6–8
2013	February 24	February 22–24
2014	March 16	March 14–16
2015	March 5	March 3–5
2016	March 24	March 22–24
2017	March 12	March 10–12
2018	March 1	February 27–March 1
2019	March 21	March 19–21
2020	March 10	March 8–10

Do not undertake the Esther fast unless you are in good health and follow accepted guidelines for starting and ending the fast. To undertake a complete Esther fast, do not eat or drink (except for Holy Communion) for the duration of the three days. If necessary, you may adapt the type of fast to fit your life and schedule.

The purpose of fasting is so that you can devote yourself without reservation to extra prayer and Scripture reading. Below you will find a list of Scriptures that you might find helpful. Use the Scriptures to guide your prayers, and be specific when you pray. Include prayers for yourself, asking God to direct and empower you in your own ministry in the Body of Christ. Then pray for reconciliation in your own personal relationships as well as among groups, regions and nations on the earth.

Scriptures for Prayer

Genesis 12:1–3; 35:11–12
Deuteronomy 30:1–4
Psalm 102:1, 13; 105; 106:44–47; 122:6; 137:4–6; 147:1–2

Isaiah 11:10–12; 14:1–2; 27:12–13; 40:1–5; 41:8–11; 42:22;
43:1–13; 44:3–6; 45:2–6; 46:3–4; 49:8–10, 22; 51:14;
57:18; 59:21; 60:4, 8–9; 62:4–7, 10–12

Jeremiah 16:14–16; 23:3–8; 30:10, 16–17; 31:7–11, 31–34,
37

Ezekiel 20:33–35; 34:11–16; chapter 36, especially vv. 8,
17–18, 24–28; 37:12–14; 39:27–28

Hosea 3, 4, 11, 14

Amos 9:11–14

Micah 4:6–7

Zephaniah 2:1–2, 6–7

Romans 11:11–12; 12:17–18; 15:27

Ephesians 3:6

Appendix E

Scriptures for Praying for Israel

The material in this section is adapted from an appendix of my book, *The Prophetic Intercessor* (Chosen, 2007).

Foundational Scriptures about Israel's future: Hosea 1:10; Jeremiah 31:8–10

Scriptures about *aliyah*, the return to the Land: Jeremiah 16:14–15; 23:7–8; 30:3; Isaiah 11:11–12; 43:5–6

Scriptural response to prophetic words about Israel: Jeremiah 31:10–14; Isaiah 12:1; 49:13; 51:3; 52:9; 61:2; 66:13; Romans 16:26–27

Biblical Intercessory Prayers for Israel

From the Life of Moses

- Exodus 32:11–13, 32 (Moses' cry to the Lord based on the Hebrews' reputation and His in the earth, and on His covenant, as well as for His glory's sake)

- Deuteronomy 9:18–19, 25–29 (Moses' fasting for forty days for intervention in a time of great crisis)
- Deuteronomy 30:1–10 (the proclamation of restoration as taught to the sons)
- Numbers 14:13–19 (a plea for God to demonstrate His power, followed by an intense cry for pardon according to God's great lovingkindness)

From the Life of Solomon

- 1 Kings 8:46–53 (a simple prayer for God to forgive as He has done before)

From the Life of Nehemiah

- Nehemiah 1:4–11 (a compassionate plea before God for the forgiveness of His people)

From the Lives of Asaph and the Sons of Korah

- Psalm 44 ("Rise up, be our help . . . redeem us!")
- Psalm 74 (an appeal against the devastation of the land by the enemy)
- Psalm 79 (a lament over the destruction of Jerusalem and a cry for help)
- Psalm 80 ("Save us! Restore us! Revive us!")
- Psalm 83 (a prayer for the Lord to confound their enemies)
- Psalm 85 (a prayer for God's mercy upon the nation)
- Psalm 123 ("Be gracious to us, O LORD, be gracious to us")

From the Life of Joel

- Joel 1:8, 13–14 (a call to a solemn assembly)

- Joel 2:12–17 (an intercessory cry to "spare Your people, O LORD")

From the Life of Isaiah

- Isaiah 63:15–64:12 (a desperate prayer for mercy and help)
- Isaiah 58:1 ("Cry loudly, do not hold back")
- Isaiah 62:1, 6 ("For Zion's sake I will not keep silent, and for Jerusalem's sake I will not keep quiet. . . . All day and all night they will never keep silent")

From the Life of Jeremiah

- Jeremiah 14:7–9, 17–22 ("O LORD, act for Your name's sake! Truly our apostasies have been many, we have sinned against You")
- Jeremiah 15:5 (a plea in the midst of judgment)
- Jeremiah 9:1 ("I . . . weep day and night")
- Lamentations 3:43–51 ("My eyes pour down unceasingly, without stopping, until the LORD looks down and sees from heaven")
- Lamentations 5:19–22 ("Restore us to You, O LORD, that we may be restored")

From the Life of Daniel

- Daniel 6:10 (praying three times each day)
- Daniel 9:1–19 ("O Lord, hear! O Lord, forgive! O Lord, listen and take action! For Your own sake, O my God, do not delay, because Your city and Your people are called by Your name." Daniel's prayer of confession on behalf of his people is our biblical model to follow today)

251

Reasons to Pray for Israel

- Israel is still the apple of God's eye and His inheritance, close to His heart (see Deuteronomy 32:8–11; Zechariah 2:8; Psalm 33:11–12; 148:14; Romans 11:29).
- God says that His servants should pray with compassion over Israel's condition (see Psalm 102:13–17).
- God commands us to give Him and ourselves no rest until He establishes Jerusalem and makes her the praise in the earth (see Isaiah 62:1, 6–7).
- God's heart travails for Israel's salvation. If we receive His heart, then His heart will travail through ours (see Romans 9:2–3; 10:1, 14).
- God commands us to seek the spiritual and physical good of the Israeli people and to pray for the peace of Jerusalem (see Psalm 122:4, 6–9; Romans 1:16; 2:9–11; 15:25–27).
- The Jewish people's acceptance of Messiah Jesus will lead to life from the dead—worldwide revival of unprecedented magnitude (see Isaiah 27:6; Romans 11:15).
- Jesus linked His Second Coming to Israel's national turning to Him (see Matthew 23:39).

Practical Prayer Suggestions

- Perform acts of identificational repentance. Cry out to the Lord with brokenness that our Father would forgive us, the Church, for our apathy and fear and for not speaking up and acting with righteousness in past times of history.
- Pray for an awakening. Ask the Lord to awaken the global Church of Jesus Christ in this hour to the immediacy and urgency of this message. Intercede that the Lord

252

would raise up modern-day Esthers, Josephs, Daniels and Deborahs "for such a time as this."

- Pray for an extension of time. Petition the Lord for an extension of a time of mercy and freedom so that the Jews from Russia and elsewhere may flee to Israel.

- Pray for protection. Pray for places of safety and refuge to be raised up in anticipation of times of persecution of the Jewish people. Intercede that the enemy's plans would be thwarted and that God's destiny for the Jewish people would be fulfilled in this generation.

- Pray for a movement of signs and wonders. Petition the Lord to release an increase of His presence with a movement of signs and wonders. Pray that the blinders would fall off the eyes of the Jewish people and that they would recognize and receive Jesus Christ as their sovereign Lord.

Appendix F

Referral Ministries

A number of ministries have demonstrated a genuine heart for Israel over the years. Their emphases are varied: prayer, inspirational teaching, compassionate humanitarian aid, hosting reconciliation events and rallies and helping Jewish people make *aliyah*. This list highlights some of the ministries with which I am familiar, but in no way is it an exhaustive list, as the Lord is raising up many other ministries that align with God's heart for Israel in this hour.

The Caleb Company (Don Finto)
68 Music Square East
Nashville, Tennessee 37203
www.calebcompany.com
The Caleb Company supports Jewish believers by helping with restoration and reconciliation as well as with financial support. It also helps the Church embrace its Hebrew roots.

Derek Prince Ministries
DPM-USA
P.O. Box 19501
Charlotte, North Carolina 28219
www.derekprince.com
This ministry continues the Bible teaching ministry of the late Derek Prince, much of which concerns Israel.

Exobus Project—USA Headquarters
P.O. Box 16871
Washington, D.C. 20041
www.exobus.org/
This ministry operates a fleet of buses to transport Jewish people making *aliyah* from their homes in other countries to major airports, ports or transportation hubs where other transportation awaits them.

Final Frontier Ministries (Avner and Rachel Boskey)
www.davidstent.org
From the Beersheva area of Israel and with offices in Nashville, Final Frontier Ministries is "dedicated to stirring up the creative arts, worship, intercession, evangelism and the prophetic within a Jewish and Israeli matrix."

House of David (Curt Landry)
P.O. Box 452407
Grove, Oklahoma 74345
www.houseofdavid.us
This is a prophetic (signs and wonders) international television ministry with a focus on the nation of Israel.

International Day of Prayer for the Peace of Jerusalem (Robert Stearns, Eagles' Wings)
http://ew.us.churchinsight.com/Group/Group.aspx?id=100 0001667
This event is held annually on the first Sunday of October, coinciding with the season of Yom Kippur.

Israel Prayer Coalition (James W. Goll)
www.encountersnetwork.com/israel_prayer_coalition
Israel Prayer Coalition is a network of ministries of intercession, compassion and humanitarian aid to Israel. It also offers prayer-focused Israel tours and strategic calls to prayer, including "The Cry," prayer and fasting during Purim.

Israel Relief Fund (David and Anne Dreiling, James W. Goll, Dave Fitzpatrick)
1511 Diamond Ct.
Franklin, Tennessee 37064
www.israelrelief.org
IRF connects humanitarian aid partners together on behalf of the poor in Israel and collects funds to cover transportation-related costs for sending donated relief supplies to Israel.

Jerusalem House of Prayer for All Nations (Tom Hess)
P.O. Box 31393
91313 Jerusalem, Israel
www.jhopfan.org
This ministry operates prayer tours of Israel, prayer convocations, the Watchman's School of Ministry and All Nations World Wide Watch Jerusalem.

Jewish Voice Ministries International (Jonathan Bernis)
P.O. Box 81439
Phoenix, Arizona 85069-1439
www.jewishvoice.org
Bringing the Gospel to the Jew first and also to the Gentile through television, medical outreaches, seminars and large-scale Messianic outreach festivals, this ministry also partners with other ministries to establish and operate Messianic Jewish Bible institutes and to plant and strengthen congregations.

Light of Zion (Sandra and Kerry Teplinsky)
P.O. Box 27575
Anaheim Hills, California 92809
This ministry mobilizes intercessory prayer for Israel, provides a house of prayer in Israel, offers financial aid to needy Israeli believers, teaches seminars on Israel and the Jewish roots of Christianity and will be doing medical ministry in Israel.

MaozIsrael Ministries (Ari and Shira Sorko-Ram)
United States address:
P.O. Box 535788
Grand Prairie, Texas 75053-5788
istandwithisrael.com
The Sorko-Rams pastor a Messianic congregation in Tel Aviv. The benevolence outreach of MaozIsrael is called "I Stand with Israel."

Messianic Jewish Communications and Jewish New Testament Publications, Inc.
P.O. Box 615
6120 Day Long Lane
Clarksville, Maryland 21029
www.messianicjewish.net
This is a Messianic Jewish publisher who published the *Complete Jewish Bible* and many other resources.

Messianic Vision (Sid Roth)
P.O. Box 1918
Brunswick, Georgia 31521
www.sidroth.org
A radio and television ministry.

One New Man Call (Reuven and Mary Lou Doron)
P.O. Box 164
Hayfield, Minnesota 55940
www.onenewman.injesus.com

The Israel Fund of One New Man Call provides support to Messianic believers in the land of Israel.

Operation Exodus—Ebenezer Emergency Fund International—Ebenezer Aid Fund (founded by Gustav Scheller)
5a Poole Road
Bournemouth BH2 5QJ, England
www.operation-exodus.org
This ministry helps Jewish people make *aliyah* by providing transportation to airports via bus, train, car and domestic flights, as well as field working teams and humanitarian aid.

Revive Israel (Asher and Betty Intrater)
www.revive-israel.org
This ministry fosters revival in the land of Israel via personal evangelism, discipleship training and congregational planting. It is centered around Jerusalem and Tel Aviv.

The Road to Jerusalem (Bill McCartney)
700 N. Colorado Blvd. #152
Denver, Colorado 80206
www.roadtojerusalem.org
Part of ICCM, The International Coalition of Christians and Messianic Jews.

Succat Hallel (Rick and Patti Ridings)
www.jerusalempraise.com.
This ministry gives 24/7 prayer and praise in the city of Jerusalem. The primary facility overlooks Mount Zion and the Old City of Jerusalem. Succat Hallel means "Tabernacle of Praise" in Hebrew.

Tents of Mercy (Eitan Shishkoff)
P.O. Box 1018
Kiryat Yam 29109
Israel

This ministry plants Messianic congregations and provides humanitarian aid in Israel in order to be an "oasis" in the desert.

Tikkun Ministries International (Dan and Patty Juster)
P.O. Box 2997
Gaithersburg, Maryland 20866-2997
www.tikkunministries.org/
This ministry is "a network of emissaries in Israel and around the world who are working toward the restoration of Israel and the unity of Jew and Gentile in the Body of Messiah."

Toward Jerusalem Council II
U.S. office:
6304 Beltline Road
Dallas, Texas 75254-7867
www.tjcii.org
This ministry is "an initiative of repentance and reconciliation between the Jewish and Gentile segments of the Church."

Vision for Israel—Joseph Storehouse (Barry Segal)
U.S. office:
P.O. Box 7743
Charlotte, North Carolina 28241
www.visionforisrael.com
This ministry provides weekly aid for needy Jewish and Arab people living in Israel, orphans, widows, homeless, handicapped, senior citizens, new immigrants and victims of terrorism.

The Watchman International (TWI) (Lars Enarson)
U.S. address:
P.O. Box 94
Lake Mills, Iowa 50450
www.thewatchman.org
The Elijah Prayer Army and more. Motto: "Prepare the way of the Lord."

Watchmen on the Wall/Eagles' Wings Ministry (Robert Stearns)
P.O. Box 450
Clarence, New York 14031
http://ew.us.churchinsight.com/Group/Group.aspx?group_id=1000001702
This ministry provides an intensive training program to equip intercessors to pray "day and night" for Israel. It includes a prayer pilgrimage to Israel.

Watchmen on the Wall (WOW)—Aglow International (Jane Hansen Hoyt)
123 2nd Avenue South, Suite 100
P.O. Box 1749
Edmonds, Washington 98020-1749
This is an educational and equipping seminar adapted from Robert Stearns's Eagles Wings Ministry. It equips women to intercede for Israel.

Wilbur Ministries (Paul Wilbur)
10920–27 Baymeadows Road
Suite 127
Jacksonville, Florida 32256
This is a concert ministry that provides instructional seminars.

Notes

Chapter 2: The Gradual Awakening

1. I'm indebted to Avner Boskey for much of the factual and perspective-building information in this chapter and the next. Avner is from Canada and was educated in Canada, the United States and Israel. He lives with his American-born wife, Rachel, and four sons in the Beersheva area of Israel. Both Avner and Rachel have been a part of the Messianic Jewish music scene and have ministered through church planting, teaching, intercession and counseling. See the website for his ministry, Final Frontier Ministries, at www.davidstent.org. Avner Boskey is the author of the book *Israel: The Key to World Revival* and a booklet entitled *A Perspective on Islam.*

2. James W. Goll and Lou Engle, *The Call of the Elijah Revolution* (Shippensburg, Penn.: Destiny Image, 2008), 225–26.

Chapter 3: The Parallel Awakening

1. I derived much of the framework for this overview of Church history from my notes from an excellent presentation at the meeting of the Toward Jerusalem Council II (www.tjcii.org). This council was an initiative of repentance and reconciliation between Jews and Gentiles held in Dallas, Texas, at the turn of the 21st century.

2. Iain H. Murray, *The Puritan Hope: A Study in Revival and the Interpretation of Prophecy* (Edinburgh, Scotland: Banner of Truth Trust, 1971), 41–43, 45.

3. Ibid. Murray quotes William Perkins, *A Commentarie upon the first five chapters of the Epistle to the Galatians* (1617), 159; and elsewhere in his writings, e.g., "A Fruitful Dialogue Concerning the End of the World," *The Works of W. Perkins* (1618), vol. 3, 470.

4. Ibid. Murray quotes Richard Sibbes, *The Complete Works of Richard Sibbes*, vol. 1 (1862), edited by A. B. Grosart, 99.

5. This fact is noted in the Rabinowitz entry on the "Brief List of Most Famous Messianic Jews," posted on the German-language Israel in Prophetischer Sicht website, http://www.israelinprophecy.org/GERMAN/live_site/brief_list-most_famous_messianic_jews.html.

6. Don Finto, *Your People Shall Be My People* (Ventura, Calif.: Regal, 2001), 127–28. Finto is quoting "The Theology of Israel's Fiftieth Birthday," *Teaching from Zion* (Jerusalem: Netivyah Bible Instruction Ministry, 1998).

7. Ibid., 43–44.

8. According to Ralph Winter and the Center for World Missions in Pasadena, California, as cited in Finto, 43.

9. Statistics from the Lausanne Taskforce on Evangelism, as cited in Finto, *Your People*, 44.

10. From "What is TJCII?" on the website of the Toward Jerusalem Council II (www.tjcii.org/what-is-toward-jerusalem-council-ii.htm).

11. Cited by Don Finto in an October 2007 presentation entitled "Divine Intervention" at the Encounters Ministry Israel Awakening Conference in Nashville, Tenn.

12. Ibid.

13. Archives of *Israel Today*, story originally published April 10, 2007, under the title "Rabbi Reveals Name of the Messiah" (www.israeltoday.co.il/default.aspx?tabid=128&view=item&idx=1347).

Chapter 4: The Hunters Are Coming

1. This was the external audible voice of God, not an internal impression or thought.

2. Derek Prince, *The Last Word on the Middle East* (Lincoln, Va.: Chosen, 1982), 73.

3. Sandra Teplinsky, *Why Care About Israel?* (Grand Rapids: Chosen, 2004), 237.

4. See, for example, news articles such as Babak Dehghanpisheh and Christopher Dickey, "Devoted and Defiant," *Newsweek*, February 13, 2006, 28 (www.newsweek.com/id/57035), and Greg Myre, "Israeli Official Says Hamas Has Made Abbas Irrelevant," *New York Times*, February 27, 2006 (www.nytimes.com/2006/02/27/international/middleeast/27mideast.html?ex=1298696400&en).

5. Ismail Haniyah, as quoted by Geoffrey Smith in "Haman, Hamas and the Bishop of Jerusalem," *CFI Interactive*, March 13, 2006 (www.cfi-interactive.co.uk/audiofiles.php?viewmessage=39&PHPSESSID=2788ae).

6. James W. Goll, *Praying for Israel's Destiny* (Grand Rapids: Chosen, 2005), 92–93.

7. Ibid., 94–95.

8. James W. Goll, "Understanding Purim" (www.encountersnetwork.com/email_blasts/march_2008_prayerstorm11.htm).

Chapter 5: The Birth of a Nation

1. Lance Lambert, *The Uniqueness of Israel* (Eastbourne, England: Kingsway, 1991), 55.

2. Ibid.

3. Merrill C. Tenney, *New Testament Survey* (Grand Rapids: Eerdmans, 1961), 45. In addition, Lambert, 160, mentions Emperor Hadrian's attempt to rename Jerusalem and remove every trace of Jewish history from it.

4. James Goll, "Say to the North," *Engage* newsletter, 2002.

5. Kai Kjæ-Hansen, *Joseph Rabinowitz and the Messianic Movement: The Herzl of Jewish Christianity* (Grand Rapids: Eerdmans; and The Stables, Carberry, Scotland: The Handsel Press Ltd., 1995), 17–18.

6. My narrative of Joseph Rabinowitz's supernatural revelation on the Mount of Olives has been reconstructed from several sources, including transcripts of actual messages and the report of a student attending a meeting in Leipzig, Germany, on February 13, 1887, where Rabinowitz gave his testimony. According to author Kai Kjæ-Hansen, the details contained in this student's report "are probably the closest we can get to a description of Rabinowitz's conversion." Ibid., 19.

7. Ibid., 22.

8. Ibid., 33.

9. Ibid.

10. Ibid.

11. Lambert, *Uniqueness*, 129–30. Quoting Theodor Herzl, *The Jewish State*, trans. S. D'Avigdor, 15.

12. Ibid., 79.

13. Ibid., 130, emphasis mine.

14. Herzl, diary for September 3, 1897; quoted in Tom Hess, *Let My People Go! The Struggle of the Jewish People to Return to Israel* (Washington, D.C.: Progressive Vision, 1988), 116.

15. Ramon Bennett, *Saga: Israel and the Demise of Nations* (Jerusalem: Arm of Salvation Press, 1993), 149–50. The specific application of acetone in the manufacture of cordite is briefly described in *Merriam Webster's Dictionary*, 10th Ed., s.v. "cordite."

16. Ibid., 150, emphasis mine.

17. Hess, *Let My People Go!* 57.

18. Quoted in Bennett, *Saga*, 150.

19. Ramon Bennett, *When Day and Night Cease* (Jerusalem: Arm of Salvation Press, 1992), 92.

20. James W. Goll, *The Prophetic Intercessor: Releasing God's Purposes to Change Lives and Influence Nations* (Grand Rapids: Chosen, 2007), n.p.

21. Steve Lightle, *Operation Exodus II* (Tulsa, Okla.: Insight Publishing, 1999), 154.

22. Ibid.

23. Ibid., 158.

24. Ulf Ekman, *The Jews: People of the Future* (Minneapolis: Word of Life Publications, 1993), 70.

25. Gordon Lindsay, *The Miracle of Israel* (Dallas: Christ For The Nations, Inc., 1987), 46.
26. Ibid.
27. Ibid., 47.
28. Ibid., 51.

Chapter 6: Touching the Apple of God's Eye

1. Tom Hess, *The Watchmen: Being Prepared and Preparing the Way for Messiah* (Charlotte, N.C.: Morningstar Publications, 1998), 168; also Hess, *Let My People Go!*, 18.
2. John Hagee, *Final Dawn over Jerusalem* (Nashville, Tenn.: Thomas Nelson, 1998), 58–60: "I want you to see that church policy shaped the policy of the Third Reich. When Hitler signed the Concordant with the Roman Church, he said, 'I am only continuing the work of the Catholic Church.'" The author provides a shocking sixteen-point comparison of church policies and their tragic Nazi counterparts. I must mention that Hitler did not limit his admiration to the anti-Semitic leanings of the Roman Catholic Church—he was also a great admirer of Martin Luther, and particularly of the anti-Semitic writings characteristic of his later years.
3. Michael L. Brown and Don Wilkerson, *Our Hands Are Stained with Blood* (Shippensburg, Penn.: Destiny Image, 1997), 91, citing Eliezer Berkovits, "Judaism in the Post-Christian Era," reprinted in Frank Ephraim Talmage, *Disputation and Dialogue: Readings in the Jewish-Christian Encounter* (New York: Ktav/Anti-Defamation League of B'nai B'rith, 1975), 287ff.
4. Ibid., 10–11; from quotes cited by Malcolm Hay, *The Roots of Christian Anti-Semitism* (New York: Liberty Press, 1981), 27.
5. Ibid.
6. Ibid., 11.
7. Dell F. Sanchez, *The Last Exodus* (San Antonio: Jubilee Books, 1998), 42–43.
8. Ibid., 43.
9. Bernard Hamilton, *The Crusades* (Gloucestershire, U.K.: Sutton Publishing, 1998), 1–2.
10. Ibid., 4.
11. Hagee, 47–48, citing Jonathan Riley-Smith, ed., *The Oxford Illustrated History of the Crusades* (New York: Oxford University Press, 1995), 81. According to Hamilton, *Crusades*, 3, Pope Urban made it easy for knights and professional soldiers to defend the faith against Muslims in Jerusalem and Jews at home by fashioning a specialized crusade indulgence for them. This new quick version dispensed with the usual bread-and-water fasts and acts of public humiliation. All they had to do to get a papal indulgence for sins of violence was "make a solemn vow in the presence of a priest, confess their sins to him and wear a red cross on their cloaks."
12. Ibid., 48.
13. Brown and Wilkerson, *Hands Are Stained*, 12; citing Edward H. Flannery, *The Anguish of the Jews: Twenty-Three Centuries of Anti-Semitism* (New York/Mahwah: Paulist Press, 1985), 90–91.

14. Ibid., 13–14; citing Hay, *The Roots of Christian Anti-Semitism*, 76, 81, 86–87.

15. Hagee, 50; citing Hay, *The Roots of Christian Anti-Semitism* (USA: Anti-Defamation League of B'nai B'rith and Alice Ivy Hay, 1981), 37. Brown and Hagee each drew from the same work by Malcolm Hay, but evidently they used versions published under different publisher imprints.

16. Sanchez, *Last Exodus*, 63.

17. Sanchez, *Last Exodus*, 14–15, with reference to Tarshish in 2 Chronicles 9:21 and 1 Kings 10:22.

18. *The Doubleday Dictionary for Home, School and Office*, s.v. "Sephardim."

19. Sanchez, *Last Exodus*, 28.

20. Ibid., 43–45.

21. Ibid., 44–58.

22. Ibid., 59.

23. Hagee, 53.

24. Ibid.

25. Brown and Wilkerson, *Hands Are Stained*, n.p.

26. Sanchez, *Last Exodus*, 83–85.

27. Ekman, *The Jews*, 70–71.

28. Brown and Wilkerson, *Hands Are Stained*, 89–90; citing Benjamin Shlomo Hamburger, *False Messiahs and Their Opposers* (Hebrew; B'nai Brak, Israel: Mechon Moreshet Ashkenaz, 1989), 19. The quotation at the end of the paragraph is from Rav Shimon Walbah, a leading Orthodox rabbi in Israel.

Chapter 7: When the Walls Came Tumbling Down

1. The Commonwealth of Independent States (CIS) was formed in December 1991, after a tripartite agreement among Russia, Ukraine and Belarus created the nucleus of the new political center of the former U.S.S.R. It marked the end of Mikhail Gorbachev's political career as general secretary of the fallen Communist party and the temporary rise of former Moscow Communist party chief Boris Yeltsin.

2. Microsoft Encarta Online Encyclopedia 2000, s.v. "Berlin Wall."

3. Lightle, *Operation Exodus II*, 20–21, 27–29; and Gustav Scheller with Jonathan Miles, *Operation Exodus: Prophecy Being Fulfilled* (Tonbridge, England: Sovereign World, 1998; distributed in U.S. by Renew Books), 29–30.

4. Lightle, *Operation Exodus II*, 45–47.

5. Ibid.

6. Scheller, *Operation Exodus*, 7.

7. Lightle, *Operation Exodus II*, 55–59.

8. Hess, *Let My People Go!*, 34–36.

9. Ibid., 36.

10. Ibid., 36–37.

11. Lightle, *Operation Exodus II*, 105.

12. Ibid., 106–7.

13. Deutsches Historisches Museum: Berlin. "A Concrete Curtain: The Life and Death of the Wall and Part 5: The Fall" (www.wall-berlin.org/gb/chute_tex2.htm).

Chapter 8: Acts behind the Scenes

1. Steve Lightle with Eberhard Muehlan and Katie Fortune, *Exodus II: Let My People Go!* (Kingwood, Tex.: Hunter Books, 1983), 66–67.
2. Ibid., 229.
3. Ibid., 28–29.
4. Scheller, 27–28.
5. Clyde Williamson with James Craig, *The Esther Fast Mandate: A Call to End-Time Intercession for the Release, Return, Restoration and Revival of Israel and the Church* (Etobicoke, Ontario: Almond Publications, 1987), 29.
6. Ibid., cover.
7. Hess, *The Watchmen*, 11–12.
8. Mahesh and Bonnie Chavda, *Watch of the Lord: The Secret Weapon of the Last-Day Church* (Lake Mary, Fla.: Creation House, 1999), 144–45.
9. Ibid.
10. Ibid.
11. Ibid.
12. Michael Schiffmann, from a personal email communication received on February 25, 2000.

Chapter 9: Transformation

1. Scheller, 43.
2. Ibid., 46–47.
3. Lightle, *Operation Exodus II*, 181.
4. Information cited from the September 2000 *Exobus Project Update*, the official newsletter of the Exobus Project based in Hull, England. This ministry operates with a staff of volunteers from many different countries. For more information see appendix F.
5. Sandra Teplinsky, *Out of the Darkness: The Untold Story of Jewish Revival in the Former Soviet Union* (Jacksonville Beach, Fla.: HOIM Publishing, 1998), foreword by Jonathan Bernis, p. xii.
6. Ibid., xii–xiii.
7. Ibid.
8. In a 1994 interview, Jonathan Bernis said that HOIM has held festivals in Moscow, Saint Petersburg, Nizhny Novgorod, Novosibersk and Kiev, Russia; Minsk, Belarus; Kishinev, Moldova; Riga, Latvia; Budapest, Hungary; and Donesk, Vinnitsa, Zaparoshya, Nikaliev, Zhitomir and Odessa, Ukraine. He also has led festivals in India and Argentina. Fifteen Messianic Jewish congregations in Eastern Europe have been founded or strengthened through the festivals. The largest congregation, located in Kiev, has about eight hundred members. For more information concerning Hear O Israel Ministries, visit the ministry's website: Jewishvoice.org.
9. Teplinsky, *Out of the Darkness*, 80; citing Zvi Gitelman, "Soviet Reactions to the Holocaust, 1945–1991" in *The Holocaust in the Soviet Union*, Dobrozycki and Gurock, eds., 3. Teplinsky, an attorney, wrote, "It is not widely known that approximately one-third of the six million Jews killed in the Holocaust were living under Soviet rule at the onset of World War II."

10. The massacre at Babi Yar is well documented. Some notable sources for more detailed information include: Simon Wiesenthal Center, ed., *Babi Yar: 1941–1991* (Los Angeles: Simon Wiesenthal Center, 1991); and *Encyclopedia of the Holocaust* (New York: MacMillan Publishing Co., 1990), vol. 1, s.v. "Babi Yar."

11. Kjæ-Hansen, *Joseph Rabinowitz*, 68.

12. Caleb was described as a man with "a different spirit" in Numbers 14:24. He is recognized as one of only two men in his generation with the ability to look past the enemies, obstacles, doubt and unbelief and clearly perceive the will and plan of God for His people.

Chapter 10: Taking the Pulse of God and His People

1. Gail Harris, *The Gateway to Reconciliation: A True Story of the Love of God for His People the Jews as Told to Us by Pastor Helmuth and Uli Eiwen as They Lived It* (Evergreen, Colo.: Evergreen Publications, 1997), 5.

2. Ibid.

3. Ibid., 15.

4. Ibid., 14.

5. See the public statement issued through the Generals of Intercession (GI) titled *A Word upon Entering the New Millennium: Apostolic Council of Prophetic Elders, November 30, 1999*: "There will be a great harvest of Jews which will begin during this decade. This will particularly affect the Russian Jews around the world. There will be what some missiologists term a 'people movement' among them. There will also be a persecution of Jews in Russia that . . . will notably escalate during the fall of 2000. This is so serious that it requires an immediate response from the Church in prayer. We believe that it is the devil's strategy to precipitate another holocaust, and that this prayer will help open a window of escape for those [who] feel called to leave, and a protection to those who are called to stay (Jeremiah 16:15, 16)."

6. If you have questions or comments regarding this statement, please write to Generals of Intercession, P.O. Box 49788, Colorado Springs, CO 80949. The framers of this statement have observed the Jewish custom of omitting key letter(s) to honor the holy name of the Almighty by reproducing it only in part in written form.

Chapter 11: The Mordecai Calling

1. Paul Yonggi Cho, *Daniel: Insight on the Life and Dreams of the Prophet from Babylon* (Lake Mary, Fla.: Creation House, 1990). Paul Yonggi Cho later changed his name to David Yonggi Cho.

2. Ibid., 144.

3. C. Peter Wagner, *Engaging the Enemy: How to Fight and Defeat Territorial Spirits* (Ventura, Calif.: Regal, 1995).

4. James Strong, "Greek Dictionary of the New Testament," *Strong's Exhaustive Concordance of the Bible* (Nashville, Tenn.: Abingdon, 1980), "pergamum," 4010, 4444, 4456, 4463.

5. "Humann, Karl," *Encyclopaedia Britannica* (www.eb.com).

6. Paul Goble, "Russia: Analysis From Washington: Rise Of Anti-Semitism In Russia" (Radio Free Europe / Radio Liberty), July 28, 1999 (www.rferl.org/nca/features/1999/07/f.ru.990728125607.html).

7. Rabbi David Levine, who lives in Budapest, Hungary, email message, February 6, 2000. A good background report on Joerg Haider can be found at the Anti-Defamation League's website: www.adl.org/backgrounders/joerg_haider.html.

8. Rick Stivers, email message, June 22, 1999. Stivers had visited the B'nai Israel Synagogue in Sacramento. He wrote, "I just knelt and wept at the yellow crime scene tape that kept me ten feet away from the building, the water still flowing at my feet through the heaps of charred cinders all around me. I picked up a handful of the blackened remains and stuffed them in a paper lunch bag. I wanted to remember. My hands turned black, but it was okay. My elder brother's entire building was black; my hands would help me remember."

9. Michal Ann Goll recorded the dream in her diary and told me the details.

10. Chuck Pierce, from a personal email communication, 1999.

11. For more information about this unforgettable prayer journey to the Moravian Prayer Tower, read James W. Goll, *The Lost Art of Intercession: Restoring the Power and Passion of the Watch of the Lord* (Shippensburg, Penn.: Destiny Image, 2007).

12. "The Battle of Britain," The Bible College of Wales, Swansea (http://members.netscapeonline.co.uk/philaedwards/history.htm).

13. If you are serious about "effectual fervent prayer," then I encourage you to pick up copies of the following books: Norman Grubb, *Rees Howells: Intercessor* (Fort Washington, Penn.: Christian Literature Crusade, 1952); and Doris M. Ruscoe, *The Intercession of Rees Howells* (Fort Washington, Penn.: Christian Literature Crusade, 1988).

14. Scheller, *Operation Exodus*, 150–51.

Chapter 12: What Then Shall We Do?

1. Goll, *Praying for Israel's Destiny*, 149.

2. Derek Prince, *The Destiny of Israel and the Church* (Milton Keynes, England: Word, Ltd., 1992), 129–30.

3. For the ideas in the remainder of this short section, I am indebted to Derek Prince, whose audiotape, *Israel and the Church: Parallel Restoration*, has been released by Intercessors for America (www.ifa.org).

4. See www.prayerstorm.com.

Glossary of Terms

aliyah. The Hebrew word for the return of the Jews to their ancient covenant homeland in Israel. It literally means "going up."

anti-Semitism/anti-Semitic. Intense dislike, hostility, hatred or discrimination against Jewish people, religious practices, culture or ethnicity.

Ashkenazi-Ashkenazim. A name that in its more popular use describes those Jewish people originating in northwest Europe, particularly Germany, central Europe, eastern Europe and Russia. It has become a designation of culture and way of life for Jewish people from those areas, as contrasted with the Sephardi culture.

Day of Atonement. The most holy day for the Jews, an annual day of fasting, penitence and sacrifice for sin. Before the destruction of the Temple, the high priest would enter the holy of holies on the tenth day of the seventh month of the Hebrew calendar and offer sacrifices for the sanctuary, the priests and the people. This foreshadowed the entrance of Jesus, the Great High Priest, who offered Himself as our eternal sacrifice once for all, having purchased for us eternal salvation. This day, also known as Yom Kippur, is observed today with fasting and confession of sins.

diaspora. A dispersion of a people from their homeland, such as the Jewish people being sent out of Egypt in the time of Moses or their desperate flight from Jerusalem and Israel in the latter years of the Roman Empire—in fulfillment of the prophecy of Jesus Christ.

Eretz Israel. This Hebrew term means "the land of Israel."

Gentile. This Hebrew word literally means "nation," but it is used to describe any person who is neither of Jewish origin nor an adherent of Judaism. (See *righteous Gentile.*)

Hasid-Hasidism (also *Chasid-Chasidism*). A popular religious movement within Judaism that began in the latter part of the eighteenth century. At first it was bitterly contested by orthodoxy, but it was finally accepted and recognized. It was characterized by religious ecstasy, mass enthusiasm, a close-knit and cohesive community life and charismatic personalities in leadership.

Holocaust. The word is derived from Greek and means "a whole burnt offering; wholesale sacrifice to destruction." It is the name given to the most tragic period of the second Jewish exile. It spans a period of twelve years, from 1933 to 1945. The last six years of this period, 1939–45, were the worst. It was the Nazi-inspired "final solution" to the so-called Jewish problem, and it called for the systematic liquidation of the Jewish people. It is conservatively estimated that at least six million Jews died in this period.

hunters and fishers. "'Behold, I am going to send for many fishermen,' declares the Lord, 'and they will fish for them;

270

and afterwards I will send for many hunters, and they will hunt them from every mountain and every hill and from the clefts of the rocks'" (Jeremiah 16:16). Fishermen are benevolent messengers sent to the Jewish people to encourage, woo and entice them to obey God's call to flee foreign lands and return to Israel. They are benevolent because they wish only good upon the Jewish people. Their mission is to extend mercy and deliverance to a divine destiny and from impending danger. Hunters, on the other hand, operate under the influence of the spirit of Haman or some other satanic force, to hunt down and round up every Jewish person they can find with only one ultimate goal—absolute annihilation of the Jewish people.

neo-Nazi. This term describes new Nazis: those today who agree with or follow the programs and principles of Hitler's Nazi party, particularly his extreme anti-Semitism.

olim. Those "going up" to Israel from other lands.

pogrom. This Russian word meaning "destruction" or "devastation" describes the organized or officially encouraged slaughter of Jewish people through militia-led riots in Russia, the Ukraine, Poland, Romania and parts of eastern Europe (particularly during the time of the Russian tsars).

priest. One who pleads the needs of the people before God. In the Old Testament a special tribe, the Levites, was set apart for this purpose. In the New Testament each believer in Christ is a priest unto the Lord.

replacement theology. The theological teaching that God is finished with the Jewish people and that the Church has replaced Israel in the plan and purpose of God. According to this view, God's promised blessings to Israel in the Hebrew Scriptures are now the exclusive property of the Church

271

because God has cursed and rejected Israel. The Church is seen as the new or true Israel because of the role the Jewish people played in the rejection and crucifixion of Jesus the Messiah. It is clear, however, that Jew and Gentile worked together to crucify the Savior of the world and that He died to bring forgiveness and new life to both through His own death and resurrection.

righteous Gentile. The government of Israel uses this term to officially honor those non-Jews who risked their lives, freedom, safety, reputation and livelihood to save, protect, shield or assist Jewish people from their pursuers during World War II and at other times.

Sephardi-Sephardim. A name that in its strictly correct use refers only to those Jews of Spanish or Portuguese origin (*Sepharad* means "Spain" in Hebrew). In its popular use, however, it has a far wider meaning, designating all Latin Jews and those from the Mediterranean region.

Talmud. This Hebrew word means "study" or "learning." It is used most commonly to describe that body of teaching that comprises the commentary and discussions of scholars. Composed between A.D. 200 and A.D. 400, it consists of two parts:

The Mishnah, which is the collection of the oral laws or traditions of the elders, as opposed to the written law of God, was compiled and edited by Rabbi Judah Ha-Nasi (A.D. 230). Its object was to preserve the law of God and to apply it to everyday life. From the time of its compilation by Rabbi Judah, in Jewish eyes it has ranked second only to the Old Testament. The word *mishnah* comes from a root meaning "to repeat" and thus "to teach by repetition."

The Gemara is the record of the commentary and discussion on the Mishnah. *Gemara* means "completion" or "tradition." There are two Gemaras, one compiled in Tiberias by Rabbi Johanan in the fourth century A.D. and the other compiled in Babylon toward the end of the fifth century A.D. Thus the Mishnah with the Tiberias Gemara is popularly called "The Jerusalem Talmud," and the Mishnah with the Babylonian Gemara is called "The Babylonian Talmud." The influence of the Talmud upon Jewish life, thought and conduct is inestimable.

Zionism. The movement birthed and organized by Theodor Herzl, who believed the true destiny of the Jewish people could be found only in a national home of their own—in Zion, their ancient covenant home. These "lovers of Zion" urged the Jewish people to flee Europe and return to their ancient homeland for decades before Hitler's storm troopers began to herd millions of European Jews to their destruction.

Recommended Reading

Accattoli, Luigi. *When a Pope Asks Forgiveness: The Mea Culpas of John Paul II.* Boston: Pauline Books & Media, 1998.

Archbold, Norma. *The Mountains of Israel.* Jerusalem: Phoebe's Song Publications, 1993.

Bennett, Ramon. *Saga: Israel and the Demise of Nations.* Jerusalem: Arm of Salvation Press, 1993.

———. *When Day and Night Cease: A Prophetic Study of World Events and How Prophecy Concerning Israel Affects the Nations, the Church and You.* Jerusalem: Arm of Salvation Press, 1992.

Brown, Michael L., and Don Wilkerson. *Our Hands Are Stained with Blood.* Shippensburg, Penn.: Destiny Image Books, 1997.

Chavda, Mahesh and Bonnie. *Watch of the Lord: The Secret Weapon of the Last-Day Church.* Lake Mary, Fla.: Creation House, 1999.

Cho, Paul Yonggi. *Daniel: Insight on the Life and Dreams of the Prophet from Babylon.* Lake Mary, Fla.: Creation House, 1990.

Ekman, Ulf. *The Jews: People of the Future.* Minneapolis: Word of Life Publications, 1993.

Evans, Michael D. *The American Prophecies: Ancient Scriptures Reveal Our Nation's Future.* New York: Time Warner Books, 2004.

Facius, Johannes. *As in the Days of Noah.* Lancaster, England: Sovereign World Ltd., 1997.

———. *Hastening the Coming of the Messiah.* Ventura, Calif.: Renew, 2002.

Finto, Don. *God's Promise and the Future of Israel.* Ventura, Calif.: Regal, 2006.

————. *Your People Shall Be My People.* Ventura, Calif.: Regal, 2001.

Goll, James. *The Lost Art of Intercession: Restoring the Power and Passion of the Watch of the Lord.* Shippensburg, Penn.: Destiny Image, 2007.

————. *Prayers for Israel* CD and audiotape. Kelowna, British Columbia, Canada: Revival Now! Resources, 1999. (May be ordered from Encounters Network at www.encountersnetwork.com.)

————. *The Prophetic Intercessor: Releasing God's Purposes to Change Lives and Influence Nations.* Grand Rapids: Chosen, 2007.

Gottier, Richard F. *Aliyah, God's Last Great Act of Redemption.* Lancaster, England: Sovereign World Ltd., 2002.

Grubb, Norman. *Rees Howells: Intercessor.* Fort Washington, Penn.: Christian Literature Crusade, 1988.

Hamilton, Bernard. *The Crusades.* Phoenix Mill, Gloucestershire, U.K.: Sutton Publishing, Ltd., 1998.

Heflin, Ruth Ward. *Jerusalem, Zion, Israel and the Nations.* Hagerstown, Md.: McDougal Publishing, 1999.

Hess, Tom. *Let My People Go! The Struggle of the Jewish People to Return to Israel.* Washington, D.C.: Progressive Vision, 1988.

————. *The Watchmen: Being Prepared and Preparing the Way for Messiah.* Charlotte, N.C.: MorningStar Publications, 1998.

Intrater, Keith, and Dan Juster. *Israel, the Church and the Last Days.* Shippensburg, Penn.: Destiny Image, 2003.

Josephus. *Josephus: The Jewish War,* ed. G. A. Williamson. New York: Penguin Books, 1970.

Juster, Dan. *Jewish Roots: A Foundation of Biblical Theology.* Shippensburg, Penn.: Destiny Image, 1995.

Kjæ-Hansen, Kai. *Joseph Rabinowitz and the Messianic Movement: The Herzl of Jewish Christianity.* Grand Rapids: Eerdmans; and The Stables, Carberry, Scotland: The Handsel Press Ltd., 1995.

Lambert, Lance. *Battle for Israel.* Eastbourne, England: Kingsway Publications, 1976.

————. *The Uniqueness of Israel.* Eastbourne, England: Kingsway Publications, 1991.

Lightle, Steve. *Exodus II: Let My People Go!* Kingwood, Tex.: Hunter Books, 1983.

————. *Operation Exodus II: Answers You Need to Know About Explosive Future Events.* Tulsa, Okla.: Insight Publishing Group, 1999.

Lindsay, Gordon. *The Miracle of Israel.* Dallas: Christ For The Nations, Inc., 1987.

Lindsey, Hal. *The Late Great Planet Earth.* Grand Rapids: Zondervan, 1970.

Prince, Derek. *The Destiny of Israel and the Church: Restoration and Redemption at the End of the Age.* Milton Keynes, England: Word Ltd., 1992.

———. *The Last Word on the Middle East.* Lincoln, Va.: Chosen, 1982.

———. *Promised Land, God's Word, and the Nation of Israel.* Charlotte, N.C.: Derek Prince Ministries, 2003.

———. *Prophetic Destinies: Who Is Israel? Who Is the Church?* Lake Mary, Fla.: Creation House, 1992.

Prince, Derek, and Lydia Prince. *Appointment in Jerusalem.* New Kensington, Penn.: Whitaker House, 2005.

Ruscoe, Doris M. *The Intercession of Rees Howells.* Fort Washington, Penn.: Christian Literature Crusade, 1988.

Sanchez, Dell F. *The Last Exodus.* San Antonio, Tex.: Jubilee Books, 1998.

Scheller, Gustav, with Jonathan Miles. *Operation Exodus: Prophecy Being Fulfilled.* Tonbridge, England: Sovereign World, 1998.

Sjöberg, Kjell, and Gustav Scheller. *The Prophetic Church.* Chichester, England: New Wine Press, 1992.

Stern, David H. *Complete Jewish Bible: An English Version of the Tanakh (Old Testament) and B'Rit Hadashah (New Testament).* Clarksville, Md.: Jewish New Testament Publications, Inc., 1998.

Ten Boom, Corrie. *The Hiding Place.* Uhlrichsville, Ohio: Barbour & Company, 2000.

Teplinsky, Sandra. *Israel's Anointing: Your Inheritance and End-Time Destiny through Israel.* Grand Rapids: Chosen, 2008.

———. *Out of the Darkness: The Untold Story of Jewish Revival in the Former Soviet Union.* Jacksonville Beach, Fla.: HOIM Publishing, 1998.

———. *Why Care about Israel?* Grand Rapids: Chosen, 2004.

Walvoord, John F. *The Nations, Israel, and the Church in Prophecy.* Grand Rapids: Zondervan, 1988.

Williamson, Clyde, with James Craig. *The Esther Fast Mandate: A Call to End-Time Intercession for the Release, Return, Restoration and Revival of Israel and the Church.* Etobicoke, Ontario: Almond Publications, 1987.

Index

279

James W. Goll is cofounder of Encounters Network, a ministry to the nations. He came to the Lord at an early age and has walked with Him ever since. James has traveled extensively across North Africa, South America, Europe, Asia, the former Soviet Union and Israel teaching and imparting the power of intercession, prophetic ministry and life in the Spirit. After pastoring for thirteen years, James was thrust into a role of equipping leaders and churches in 1987. He is involved as an instructor at the Wagner Leadership Institute and is a member of the Harvest International Ministries apostolic team.

James is the author of numerous books, including *The Lost Art of Intercession, The Prophetic Intercessor, Angelic Encounters, Intercession: The Power and Passion to Shape History, The Beginner's Guide to Hearing God, The Seer* and many others. He also has produced numerous study guides and hundreds of teaching CDs. James is also a contributing writer to *Kairos* magazine and several other periodicals.

In the spirit of revival, James desires to facilitate unity in the Body of Christ by bridge building and networking congregations and ministries in divine cooperation. Praying for Israel is a burden of his heart, as Israel fulfills her role in the consummation of the ages.

James and Michal Ann were married for 32 years before she went home to be with the Lord. They have four grown children: Justin, GraceAnn, Tyler and Rachel. Their home is in the rolling hills of Franklin, Tennessee.